GIANT SPLASH

GIANT SPLASH

Bondsian Blasts, World Series Parades, and
Other Thrilling Moments by the Bay

ANDREW BAGGARLY

TRIUMPH
BOOKS

This book is available in quantity at special discounts for your group or organization. For further information, contact:

Triumph Books LLC
814 North Franklin
Chicago, Illinois 60610
www.triumphbooks.com

Printed in U.S.A.
ISBN: 978-1-62937-031-6
Design by Patricia Frey
Photos courtesy of Getty Images unless otherwise indicated

Contents

Introduction

If you've seen a fair number of Giants games at AT&T Park, here are a few questions for you:

What's the greatest moment you witnessed over the past 15 seasons? When did you react with the most elation, the most passion, feel the most emotionally spent? When did you hug the most total strangers, or yell your way to your worst case of laryngitis? When did the ballpark buzz the loudest and fill your eardrums so close to bursting?

Those were the questions I asked myself as the concept for this book came together. For some major league franchises, there wouldn't be much debate. A no-hitter here, a playoff win there, maybe a four-run comeback in the ninth.

When the Chicago Cubs celebrated the 100th anniversary of baseball at Wrigley Field in 2014, they commissioned a 400-pound cake from a bakery in New Jersey. It cost thousands and required a forklift to move. The media gorged on the photo op. Nobody gorged on the cake.

It was found the next day, unceremoniously thrown in a dumpster—a perfect metaphor for a team that spent 100 years in a beloved ballpark without once bearing witness to a World Series championship.

The San Diego Padres have never thrown a no-hitter in their 45-year history. The Giants have no-hit them three times in the past six years.

In other words, Giants fans have had it pretty good.

It's only when you begin to recount all the history-making, record-breaking, pennant-clinching events at the corner of Third and King that you start to understand what an embarrassment of baseball riches Giants fans have witnessed in San Francisco, especially in the last decade and a half since the team moved to its splendid ballpark on the lip of McCovey Cove.

Since 2000, the little patch of green in China Basin has played host to a perfect game, two no-hitters, an All-Star Game, a trove of milestone homers, a new standard for power in a single season, the coronation of an all-time home run king, and three pennant-grabbing victories—two of them won in delirious, walk-off fashion and a third amid a Biblical downpour.

And, of course, three World Series ring ceremonies.

That's a full and glorious century for any franchise. Giants fans saw all of it in just 15 years. It has to be considered among the most successful, eventful stretches in the history of any major league enterprise. And it did not happen in an inhospitable, wind-whipped concrete cauldron of a ballpark. It happened in a charming, cozy yet frenzied environment that is the envy of baseball, with its brick arcade and Coke bottle and splash hits and sellout crowds that hover so close to the action they nearly cast a shadow over it all.

Their brick-and-steel home on McCovey Cove is such an idyllic wonder, Giants fans would be spoiled if their team were merely competitive every so often. They've been able to cheer so much more than that. It's a cake with layers upon layers of icing, as thick as the crowds that lined all three World Series parade routes.

As a beat reporter covering the Giants since 2004 for the *Oakland Tribune, San Jose Mercury News*, and Comcast SportsNet Bay Area, I'm trained to see the team through an impartial lens. But almost anyone who covers baseball for a living begins his or her relationship with the sport as a fan, and to some degree, that experience informs and directs the coverage. You're writing for fans, after all. You have to connect with them.

The Giants made that so easy. From my seat in the press box, I didn't just connect with fans. I felt them. There were countless nights when the stadium pulsed and reverberated—in a non-seismic way, of course. There were so many grand events to cheer, so many red-letter days, unforgettable feats, and brilliant stars.

You had Barry Bonds splashing his way to the single-season home run record in 2001 along with all those milestone markers on his controversial countdown to Babe Ruth and Hank Aaron. (Nos. 500, 600, 660, 661, 700, 715, and 756 all came at home.) You had Tim Lincecum bursting onto the scene, at once a slacker and an achiever, winning Cy Young Awards with an explosive fastball and gymnastic delivery. You had Jonathan Sanchez throwing one of the most unlikely no-hitters in history to break a 33-year drought, you had the stoic Matt Cain embracing perfection for one night in June, and you had Lincecum, even as the arc of his career had descended steeply downward, throwing his no-hitter when he and his fans could savor it most.

Above all, you had a five-decade vigil of waiting and hoping finally end when a band of misfits charged to a World Series title in 2010 that continues to make no sense years after it happened. Then you had a retooled team, led by The Reverend Hunter Pence, a Kung Fu Panda, and a redemptive Barry Zito, climbing to the top again in 2012. And just when you thought the even-year phenomenon was a trite joke, a 2014 team that limped into October as a wild card and dispatched four playoff opponents as Madison Bumgarner lifted everyone on his broad back to the 27th out of a Game 7 victory in Kansas City.

This book project had gotten off the ground several months before that night at Kauffman Stadium, when the Giants clinched their third World Series title in five seasons and stamped Bruce Bochy as a Hall of Fame manager. The plan was to tell the story of the 15 greatest games in 15 seasons at AT&T Park. When a third parade ended on the steps of City Hall, we solved the problem the only sensible way. The Giants added more chapters to their franchise history. So did we.

In these pages, you'll find the 19 most significant games witnessed at Pacific Bell/SBC/AT&T Park, plus a 20th chapter highlighting the best of the rest. The first part of each chapter provides the setup; the second part delves into the drama. Although the games are presented in chronological order, and some chapters carry into the next one, it might be helpful to think of this book as more a compendium than a continuous narrative. You're encouraged to skip around if you like. Rank them, if you feel so compelled. There are no wrong answers.

Of course, there is one obvious drawback to this book's format: the Giants clinched their three World Series titles in Texas at the Ballpark in Arlington, at Comerica Park in Detroit, and at Kauffman Stadium in Kansas City. Each time, the ultimate celebration happened in road grays, without a single bent blade of grass back home.

Even so, it's staggering to think how many great moments have happened in front of frenzied, orange-splashed crowds in just 15 seasons in China Basin. From the story of the ballpark's construction to No. 756 to Cain's perfection to Sandoval's three-homer opus in Game 1 of the World Series to Marco Scutaro drinking in a downpour to Travis Ishikawa roaring around the bases as a modern-day Bobby Thomson to Bumgarner lassoing one October lineup after another, we present to you the greatest games on the shores of McCovey Cove.

So far, anyway.

Maybe someday, the Giants will clinch a championship at home. Now that would be icing on the cake.

Chapter 1

The First Game

"You'd better bring your glove if you come to this ballpark.
You are going to be right on top of the action."
—Peter Magowan

Tuesday, April 11, 2000
Home opener vs. Los Angeles

In the late 1970s, the San Francisco Giants were as close to irrelevant as any major sports franchise could be.

They struggled to draw 3,000 fans on weeknight games. The fan experience at Candlestick Park, with a frigid wind whipping through the shivering stands, was miserable. By the 1980s, they'd given up trying to market the unmarketable and instead tried to get fans to embrace the awful, hot dog wrapper–blowing experience by handing out a badge of honor—the Croix de Candlestick—and encouraging them to boo an anti-mascot called Crazy Crab.

For most of those years, the story wasn't whether the Giants could contend but where they would unload the moving vans once they left town for good. One year, it was Hackensack, New Jersey. Another year, it was Toronto, with the deal advancing as far as negotiating a payout for breaking the Giants' lease.

Horace Stoneham, the owner who brought the Giants from New York's Polo Grounds in 1958, eventually passed the problem and the team along to Bob Lurie. After several failed ballot initiatives, including two that would've resulted in a move to San Jose, Lurie threw up his hands, too. In 1992, he announced that he had reached an agreement to sell the team to a group of investors from St. Petersburg, Florida, for $115 million.

The Giants were leaving San Francisco. After the final home game in 1992, players scooped infield dirt and pried off pieces of the ballpark, taking whatever tangible memento they could. They were sure they would never set foot in Candlestick again, and as miserable as it could be, a boy always longs for home.

But Dodgers owner Peter O'Malley, sensing the importance of keeping his storied rival on the West Coast, urged Major League Baseball commissioner Fay Vincent to hold out for a local buyer. National League president Bill White, a former Giant who collected the first hit in Candlestick Park history, had a strong preference to see the team stay as well. So despite an agreement in principle with Tampa Bay and threats of a lawsuit, the league allowed a hastily arranged group led by Safeway CEO Peter Magowan to make a last-ditch effort to buy the Giants from Lurie.

Magowan grew up a Giants fan in New York, listened to Bobby Thomson's "Shot Heard 'Round the World" on a transistor radio, and made frequent trips to see his favorite player, Willie Mays, glide across center field at the Polo Grounds. Magowan's family—he is the grandson of Charles Merrill, founder of the Merrill Lynch investment bank that popularized mutual funds to the masses—happened to move to San Francisco around the same time that the Giants went west. But Magowan understood what it meant to uproot a team from its community. He understood the pain that would linger in San Francisco for decades. The day Lurie informed him of the sale to St. Pete, his heart sank.

The next day, he resolved to do something about it.

"I started to scribble down on a piece of paper what would be involved in trying to keep them here," Magowan said. "I said to myself, 'I don't know what can happen, but I'll never forgive myself for not trying.'"

Magowan made a list of San Francisco power players and started dialing phone numbers. Financier Charles Schwab. Real estate magnate Walter Shorenstein. Gap Inc. CEO Donald Fisher. Charles Johnson, the principal at Franklin Templeton, and Johnson's general counsel, Harmon Burns. The Giants' local TV rightsholder at the time, KTVU. He borrowed and scraped and received pledges to the sum of $95 million, and when it became clear that offer wouldn't be enough, he went to the bank and borrowed $5 million more.

Magowan was trying to purchase a team that finished 26 games out of first place the previous season. His group had no plan for a new stadium. They had some idea how they could boost revenue, though. They could upgrade the concessions. They could schedule more day games, when the weather would be better. And they could capture the attention of the marketplace by signing the game's best player—Barry Bonds, a Bay Area native and Mays' godson.

The shocker wasn't that Magowan's group received tentative approval to purchase the team. The real surprise came just two weeks later, when they arrived at baseball's winter meetings in Louisville and announced they had signed Bonds to a record-setting six-year, $43.75 million contract.

Lurie was livid. League owners already had blocked his deal with St. Petersburg, and he'd be receiving a lower price for the Giants as a result (although he did retain a $10 million interest in Magowan's group). Now, if the sale fell through for any reason, Lurie would be saddled with the game's most expensive player.

"You have to have control of the team to sign a ballplayer," Lurie told the *Baltimore Sun* at the time, "and they don't have a team. We do not want Barry Bonds to be a San Francisco Giant at that price."

The Giants already had announced the deal, though, leading to one of the most confusing press conferences in baseball history. Bonds walked into the hotel ballroom with his agent, Dennis Gilbert, and an entourage that included the player's father, Bobby, and the great Willie Mays. They sat on the dais and Bonds prepared to smile as he held up a jersey that represented a family heirloom as well as his new employer. Suddenly, a Major League Baseball official, out of breath, raced into the ballroom and relayed a message to Gilbert. The whole entourage quickly walked out through a kitchen door. If Twitter had existed at the time, it probably would've imploded.

It took 48 hours and some legal maneuverings before a contract could be drawn up that was amenable to all parties and included language that would shield Lurie in case the sale fell through. In the meantime, with Lurie still refusing to be the one to sign, Magowan not yet in charge, and GM Al Rosen having already stepped down, there was nobody left to put pen to paper on the Bonds contract. So Tony Siegle, the club's vice president of administration, shrugged and did it; his signature was as good as anyone's, he figured. In his many decades working for more than a dozen GMs, Siegle is most proud of becoming the answer to an impossible trivia question. He's the guy who signed Bonds' first contract with the Giants.

An odd chapter ended, but baseball in San Francisco did not. Not only did the Giants return to Candlestick Park in 1993, but Bonds, foreshadowing the dramatics to come, hit a home run in his first at-bat in the home opener. At the end of the season, he won the NL MVP award. The Giants had something far better to market than an anti-mascot.

Magowan and chief operating officer Larry Baer still had to solve the Candlestick problem—and unlike Lurie, they would not pin their hopes on public money.

Although the Bonds signing had the immediate impact in the marketplace that Magowan and Baer predicted, with a record-setting 2.6 million fans passing through the turnstiles in 1993, all of their positive momentum evaporated the following year when baseball's labor strife led to the cancellation of the season in August, along with the World Series. (The stoppage came as star third baseman Matt Williams was on pace to hit 60 home runs, threatening Roger Maris' single-season record.)

Attendance plummeted at Candlestick in '95, along with almost every other major league ballpark, and didn't begin to rebound for five years. As a result, the Giants posted millions in operating losses. The inevitable cash calls were too much for some members of the ownership group to bear. They were fine to pitch in and do their civic duty to help keep the team from going to St. Pete. But they didn't sign up for annual soakings.

Magowan had a falling out with Shorenstein. Schwab sold his holdings as well. It was a constant dance for Magowan and Baer to keep the ownership group afloat, operate a team, try to win some actual games—and push forward on a new ballpark, too. Burns, whose personal fortune kept rising as Franklin Templeton's stock soared, often came to the rescue. As other owners bailed out, Burns took up a larger and larger share and would eventually and quietly become the team's chief stakeholder.

In retrospect, it's stunning that Baer and Magowan were able to win support with San Francisco city officials in the aftermath of the most damaging event to hit the game since the 1919 Black Sox scandal. Yet in 1995, the Giants and the city agreed to a proposal to build a 42,000-seat, baseball-only stadium in the rather bleak South of Market area of San Francisco. It would be financed privately through the sale of more than 12,000 charter seats, including luxury boxes, plus corporate naming rights, ballpark signage, and a $170 million loan from Chase Manhattan.

Broadcaster Hank Greenwald suggested to Magowan that the new ballpark could be called the Polo Grounds West, and perhaps present a sponsorship opportunity for fashion designer Ralph Lauren's signature brand. Magowan made a phone call. Lauren thought it was a wonderful idea, and asked if $1 million would suffice. Magowan sheepishly had to tell him: they were looking for 50 times that amount. And they got it, too, from the local Baby Bell.

In March of 1996, San Francisco voters approved a ballot measure and funding proposal by a two-thirds majority. Pacific Bell Park would be squeezed up against the bay into a 13-acre parcel in the area known as China Basin, so named because it was where the China Clippers of the Pacific Mail Steamship line docked in the mid-1800s. China Basin became home to lumber schooners after that, offloading the raw materials that built a growing city. Now the city wanted to redevelop the area, and a new ballpark would put the spurs to it.

Baseball's stadium boom had begun a decade earlier, but the Giants were going against the grain. They relied on public money only as far as securing investments in local transportation and infrastructure. Pacific Bell Park would be the first privately financed Major League Baseball facility to be built since Dodger Stadium almost four decades earlier. The Giants were reestablishing a dangerous precedent for baseball owners, who had grown accustomed to receiving what they wanted for free and threatening to leave town until they got it. Chicago White Sox owner Jerry Reinsdorf, who berated Magowan in a Louisville hotel suite for the Bonds contract back in 1992, criticized the Giants again for taking on debt service and financing $357 million on their own.

But in so many ways, the Giants were ahead of their time. They saw the best of the new stadiums—Baltimore's Oriole Park at Camden Yards among them—and they knew what they did and didn't want. Instead of the double layer of luxury suites that belted many new parks, thus turning the upper deck into true nosebleed territory, Magowan directed for just 65 suites to be built on a single level.

"I think that is what happened in Chicago with Jerry's ballpark," said Magowan, shortly after the groundbreaking at Third and King. "He was really only catering to that corporate office luxury-suite type. He's got 150 suites in there. That's his thing. What he does is to shove everybody in the upper deck another 25 feet higher, because he's got to have two levels of his luxury suites to get up to 150. If you sit in the upper deck in

Comiskey, bring your binoculars, because it's the only way you're going to be able to see the ballgame."

Although the corporate customers always come first, Magowan was interested in a positive fan experience at all price points, and accessibility would be a priority in more ways than one. The Giants didn't have endless space for swaths of parking lots, but they didn't need them. A ferry service would bring fans from Marin County or the East Bay, dropping them off at a promenade just beyond the center-field fence. You could take Caltrain or light rail within blocks of the ballpark. Giants games would become true community events.

Magowan did not have to beg and borrow to sell those 12,000 charter seats. The demand was overwhelming. When the Giants began selling the charter rights in 1996, it didn't take long before they could count more season-ticket holders for 2000—when the new ballpark would open—than they could for 1997.

The Giants had no desire to build a glossier, more expensive version of Candlestick Park. So they consulted with Bruce White, an aeronautical engineering professor at UC Davis, who built a scale model of downtown San Francisco and tested wind patterns to determine just how blustery it would be at China Basin. White had to deliver bad news: the prevailing design, with the skyline view beyond the center-field fence, would have resulted in a ballpark just as windy as Candlestick. But a 90-degree rotation, with a line from home plate to straightaway center field pointing roughly due east, would shield most seats from the wind. The plans were redrawn. Problem solved.

Magowan traveled to Coors Field and toured the Colorado Rockies' new ballpark with Joe Spear, the principal architect for HOK Sport. They talked about sight lines and retro aesthetics. But mostly, Magowan was fixated on how his new park would play. He wanted something unique. He wasn't interested in a cookie-cutter outfield, and besides, the small parcel demanded asymmetry. When the city of San Francisco further insisted on a public walkway between the right-field fence and the bay, shrinking the distance to just 309 feet from home plate to the right-field pole, Spear came up with the idea for a 25-foot brick wall—the arcade—with archways built in so passersby could steal a free look at the action. Some owners would have howled at the idea of giving away their product, even from so far away. But Magowan loved the romantic notion of a modern-day knothole gang. And, of course, there would be the ballpark's official address: 24 Willie Mays Plaza, with 24 palm trees encircling a statue of Magowan's boyhood idol, freezing the Say Hey Kid as he dashed out of the batter's box.

Magowan borrowed from Wrigley Field, too. He liked the way the bullpens were in foul territory, and not hidden behind an outfield fence, so fans could take note of when and which relievers were getting loose. He liked Wrigley's traditional green seats, too, and the way every one of them faced the pitcher's mound. And although the Giants would have the shortest right field in the league, in a nod to the Polo Grounds, the arcade would be designed to bank steeply toward right-center and create a 421-foot crown that would become either a triple's alley or a place where home runs would go to die.

The ballpark's signature feature, however, other than the giant glove and Coke bottle above the left-field bleachers, was the possibility for home runs to splash into a narrow channel of the bay that would become one of the most famous places to paddle a kayak in America. It came to be known as McCovey Cove, as first suggested by *San Jose Mercury News* columnist Mark Purdy and the *Oakland Tribune*'s Leonard Koppett.

As the Giants prepared to open the 2000 season in their splashy and splendid new ballpark, the players still had no idea what to expect. When they took batting practice in the unfinished stadium, the balls rocketed into the stands. Shortstop Rich Aurilia remembered delighting for his own statistics and feeling a twinge of guilt for his pitchers. The prevailing expectation was that Pacific Bell Park would be a bandbox.

The very first game appeared to confirm it.

Kevin Elster sat out the 1999 season. His aspiration was to build and run a bar in Las Vegas, not to restart his baseball career. He dealt with too many injuries and was fed up with too many politics after jumping from the Mets to the Yankees to the Phillies to the Rangers to the Pirates and back to the Rangers over a seven-year span. On Memorial Day weekend in 1995, when the Yankees were playing the Mariners, a Seattle hotel bellhop, not realizing he had the wrong room, knocked on Elster's door.

"Mr. Jeter, your luggage is here."

That's how Elster knew the Yankees had called up their prized prospect and he'd be getting his release papers soon enough.

Elster had an odd career track. A glove-first shortstop when he came up with the Mets in the late 1980s, Elster bolted out of nowhere to hit 24 home runs in 1996 with the Texas Rangers. Then he hit 15 over the next two years combined. Seemingly out of baseball after 1999, he was cajoled into signing with the Dodgers on a minor league contract by Davey Johnson, his onetime manager with the Mets. When Elster made the Dodgers out of spring training, he moved back into his parents' house in Orange County.

At the start of the 2000 season, as the Dodgers began a three-city road trip in Montreal and at New York's Shea Stadium, Elster started four of six games and went 4-for-14 without a home run. When the Dodgers arrived to open up Pacific Bell Park on April 11, Elster was in the lineup at shortstop, batting eighth in front of pitcher Chan Ho Park.

The Giants had opened the season on the road as well. Manager Dusty Baker's team went 86–76 the previous season, good enough for a second-place finish but nowhere near qualifying for the playoffs. They began the 2000 campaign at Florida and Atlanta, losing to future Hall of Famers Greg Maddux and Tom Glavine to finish a 3–4 trip. But they had a day to rest up for the celebratory debut of baseball at Pacific Bell Park, when they would send Kirk Rueter to the mound.

Rueter already had started the first unofficial game at the ballpark 12 days earlier, when the Giants beat the Milwaukee Brewers in an 8–3

Even during the opening ceremonies at Pacific Bell Park, Giants fans sustained the "Beat LA" chant—proving some things would never change. (AP Images)

exhibition victory. The ballpark played even livelier in a second dress rehearsal against the New York Yankees, when Bonds hit the first home run with a first-inning shot off Andy Pettitte. Third baseman Russ Davis also homered twice, but Jorge Posada, Paul O'Neill, and Roberto Kelly went deep for the Yankees in their 11–6 victory.

Then the day finally arrived: the home opener at Pacific Bell Park.

A sellout crowd of 40,930 started chanting "Beat LA" during the opening ceremonies, which included a giant American flag in the outfield and thousands of red, white, and blue balloons. Magowan and Baer rewarded themselves with ceremonial first pitches, which some critics took to be self-aggrandizing. But it was their prerogative, of course. This place was their vision come to life.

When all the revelry had concluded and all the balloons had been released, plate umpire and Bay Area native Ed Montague signaled his readiness to Rueter. To a standing ovation, the first pitch was…a ball. So was the next one. Then Devon White lashed a 2-2 pitch to center field for a single.

Magowan, and a packed house of Giants fans, sat down to consider the business of watching a baseball game in shirtsleeves.

The game was a back-and-forth affair. Bill Mueller singled in the first inning and Bonds scored him with a double down the right-field line. Catcher Doug Mirabelli, as fast as you might expect on the bases, became the first player to find the deepest recesses of right-center while legging out a surprising triple, the first of his career, in the second inning. (To this day, longtime club employees and members of the media still jokingly refer to that distant part of the ballpark as Mirabelli Cove.)

Elster stepped to the plate with one out in the third, and worked the count full before Rueter threw a fastball on the outer edge. Elster extended his arms and drove it past the 404-foot marker in left-center, where a fan in the first row caught it. The Giants would just have to live with it: a Dodger hit the first official home run in Pacific Bell Park history.

Bonds had to settle for being the first Giant to homer in their new home, which he did while taking Park deep to center field for a tiebreaking shot in the bottom of the third. But Elster came up again in the fifth after Todd Hundley had reached on a leadoff single. Rueter threw a fastball to almost the same location on a 2-1 count—belt high and over the plate—and Elster boomed it a dozen rows up in the left-field bleachers. This time, there was nothing ceremonial about it. It was just another Dodger hitting a home run to put his team ahead against their archrivals.

And the fan who retrieved the ball treated it with all the proper scorn. He threw it back onto the field.

The Dodgers led 3–2 and they would not trail again. Shawn Green hit an RBI single off Rueter, who lasted six innings. The Giants got a run back on a wild pitch, but Geronimo Berroa singled off lefty Alan Embree to make it 5–3 in the seventh. Mirabelli homered in the seventh before Elster, who had drawn a two-out walk in the sixth, came to bat again in the eighth. Felix Rodriguez couldn't get Elster to chase a pair of two-strike pitches. Then the right-hander threw a fastball that tailed onto the barrel.

"High fly ball into deep left field, Kevin has hit another one," came Vin Scully's call. "Three home runs for Kevin Elster! Can you believe that story? A guy who had dropped out of baseball, stayed in shape merely to stay in shape, no thought about playing more baseball, and now he has a three–home run game."

Scully described Rodriguez's fastball as "in a B.P. spot, and he just killed it."

"No one ever comes to the ballpark thinking they're going to hit three home runs, least of all me," Elster said. "But it sure feels good to do this on a day like today."

Although J.T. Snow homered in the ninth off Dodgers closer Jeff Shaw, Mirabelli flied out to deep left field and pinch hitter Armando Rios grounded out to seal the Giants' 6–5 loss.

THREE OF A KIND BEATS FULL HOUSE, read the headline in the *Los Angeles Times* the next day.

Snow would go on to hit a much more important home run in the ninth off a closer later that season. For that day, though, the loss could only do so much to dampen a sellout crowd's enthusiasm. They would be able to watch their Giants with a backdrop of the Bay Bridge, moonlight on the water, and no need for players to wrap up a season by scooping infield dirt as a souvenir. The moving vans did come, but they only traveled a handful of miles up Route 101—and landed in the best possible place. The Giants welcomed a new era of baseball.

They had no idea just how eventful, how celebratory, the next 15 years would be.

"People said, 'You'll never be able to keep the team here. You'll never be able to buy it,'" said Magowan, shortly after the groundbreaking. "And once we had, 'You'll never be able to win the election, in San Francisco especially.' We won with a two-thirds vote. Then, 'You'll never get it financed.' And this is all privately done. It's never been done before. 'You guys will not be able to do that.' We got it privately financed. Now they say, 'Nobody will come to the stadium.'

"They're 0-for-3 on their predictions so far, so we'll just have to wait and see what happens with the fourth prediction. But I think people are going to come."

Chapter 2

Lost in a Snowstorm

"You've just hit a huge home run to save the game, the biggest home run of your life—and before you know it, your team lost. It's the strangest feeling."
—J.T. Snow

Thursday, October 5, 2000
NLDS Game 2 vs. New York Mets

Peter Magowan was right again. The fans did come to Pac Bell Park, flocking to see the Giants in record numbers. Every game was a sellout in their debut season, and their final attendance of 3,244,167 was nearly 1.2 million more than they had drawn in their final season at Candlestick Park. The ownership group was deeper in debt than ever, but revenue was pouring in and fan enthusiasm was at an all-time high.

During the Candlestick era, the Giants only averaged better than 30,000 fans per home game once—in 1993, the year before baseball's labor strife resulted in the cancellation of the World Series. They averaged 40,051 in their first season on the shores of McCovey Cove. And for the most part, the sellout crowds went home gloriously happy.

It didn't start out that way, though. A day after Kevin Elster's three home runs sent them to a defeat in the inaugural game at Pac Bell Park, there was actual rain on the Giants' parade. A rare shower forced the suspension of a game the Dodgers led 3–2 in the sixth inning. The Giants ended up losing that game when it was resumed, and were swept in the series. They dropped a pair to the Arizona Diamondbacks, too. And when they returned from their next road trip, they lost a homestand opener to the Montreal Expos.

The Giants were 0–6 in their new home, the one they worked for nearly two decades to plan and finance and build.

"We were just scratching our heads, like, what the heck?" first baseman J.T. Snow recalled.

Snow noticed another difference. Despite the packed stands, the crowds almost seemed quieter than they were at Candlestick. The players would scan the seats and notice plenty of suit coats and ties—something they never saw before. During that first month, Snow remembered turning to Rich Aurilia and Bill Mueller with a lament.

"All of us missed the 10,000 crazies on a Wednesday night against Pittsburgh, getting rowdy," Snow said. "We were playing in front of 40,000 people, but I'm not sure they understood what to do. They didn't know how to act."

The players were noticing other differences as well. Amid that rain-suspended second game, their eyes were opened to how different the park could play at night or when the winds changed. Snow hit two deep drives to right field that died into a glove. Jeff Kent couldn't get his bearings on a pop fly that fell in shallow center field. The grandstands would shelter the fans from the worst of the wind, and you wouldn't see nearly as many swirling hot dog wrappers on the field. But for a baseball aloft, it was a different story. And those archways in the right-field arcade, the ones that allowed for Magowan's romantic knothole gang to get free glimpses of the action, were serving another purpose: ventilation. All the way at home plate, left-handed hitters could feel the breeze coming through the archways. On windier days, hard-hit balls to right field often would get knocked down or pushed toward the huge, Polo Grounds–inspired expanse in right-center. It didn't take long for the Giants, and other teams, to realize that a right fielder would be well served to cheat and play well off the line.

Of course, the Giants adjusted to the park much quicker than their opponents did—and derived an advantage before long. They also had a powerful lineup in which every starting position player, plus backup outfielder Armando Rios, would record double-digit home runs. It would be perhaps their deepest and most productive lineup, top to bottom, in franchise history. Five starting pitchers would finish with double-digit victories, too.

For all the nervousness over their 0–6 start at home, they would not begin 0–7 at 24 Willie Mays Plaza. On April 29, Robb Nen saved a 2–1 victory over Montreal and the Giants took off from there. They posted a 9–3 record on their second homestand in their new park, with Kent providing the biggest thrill May 3 when he hit a three-run home run in the 11th inning off Turk Wendell to beat the New York Mets.

By the All-Star break, the Giants' 4–11 start was a distant memory. They caught fire in the second half and ended the regular season with an average of 5.7 runs per game. Only the Colorado Rockies, who played at souped-up Coors Field, scored more among NL clubs. Kent won the NL MVP award, with Bonds finishing second. (Kent received 22 first-place awards to six for Bonds, but the result likely would be reversed today; Kent had a higher average and more RBIs, but Bonds had a higher on-base percentage, slugging percentage, and offensive WAR.)

With Kent and Bonds finishing 1-2 in the NL MVP voting, it was easy to overlook what Ellis Burks did while batting in the No. 5 spot. Acquired from the Rockies at the July 31 trade deadline in 1998 for outfielder Darryl Hamilton, the 35-year-old hit .344 with 24 home runs and a 1.025 OPS while driving in 96 runs in 120 games. It's hard to imagine those numbers being the third best in any team's lineup. It's even harder to imagine how Burks remained playable so often with chronic, debilitating pain in both knees. Years later, Giants trainers still marveled at how Burks would arrive at the ballpark before noon, receive two hours of treatment, return home for an hour or two, then come back in time for batting practice.

If Bonds was their star and Kent was their MVP, Burks was their soul.

On September 21, with Russ Davis coming off the bench to hit a tiebreaking sacrifice fly in the eighth inning, the Giants beat the Arizona Diamondbacks to clinch their fifth NL West title and sixth trip to the postseason since moving west in 1958. The Giants coasted over the final 10 games and finished at 97–65, the best record in the National League. And despite the 0–6 start, their 55–26 home record matched the wild-card-winning New York Mets for the best among NL clubs.

In the Giants' first year at Pac Bell Park, there would be postseason baseball.

It was Burks, the team's inspirational leader, who got up in front of the group and held a meeting prior to Game 1 of the NL Division Series with the Mets. He had played on four playoff teams with the Red Sox, White Sox, and Rockies, never winning a postseason series. He knew this group represented his best opportunity. He wanted his teammates, especially the young players, to understand that, too.

"I'd been in the league five years but I still considered myself one of those young guys," said left-hander Shawn Estes, a 19-game winner in 1997 who was 15–6 with a 4.26 ERA and would be the club's No. 2 starter against the Mets.

"You might have another opportunity like this, and you might not," Burks told the team. "But even if you do, there are guys in here at the end of their career. So play for those guys."

Estes was inspired. He also felt more pressure than ever.

If Giants ace Livan Hernandez felt any pressure, he didn't show it. As a rookie, the right-hander already had pitched and won Game 1 of the 1997 World Series for the Florida Marlins. He was nearly as good while outpitching Mike Hampton as the Giants took a 5–1 victory in Game 1.

It was Burks who hit the all-important three-run home run in the third inning, but the pivotal play happened just prior to that. Hampton began to walk off the mound, believing he had Bonds struck out on a fastball away. But Hampton didn't get the call, and instead Bonds lashed a tiebreaking triple to right field. Outfielder Derek Bell, in a rush to make a play, turned his ankle and had to come out of the game.

At the time, the Bell injury appeared to be a terrible blow for the Mets. As the series went on, it would turn out to be a twist of fate in their favor.

The Giants and their fans were jubilant after the victory. It was their first postseason win in 11 years, since they clinched the 1989 NL pennant over the Chicago Cubs. It was the start they wanted after losing a wild-card tiebreaker at Wrigley Field in 1998 and getting swept in an NL Division Series in '97.

In 40 seasons at Candlestick Park, the Giants had won just eight home postseason games. Now, in their first season at Pacific Bell Park, they already had one to their credit. And they could take full control of this NL Division Series by winning one more.

But as monumental as that first home playoff victory felt that night, it would not be a game that lingered in memory. The series, and the season, would be forever marked by what happened the following night in Game 2.

Snow didn't need to check the lineup card for Game 2. He knew he wouldn't be in there against Mets left-hander Al Leiter, even though he had started against another southpaw, Hampton, in Game 1.

Snow was much more than a left-handed-hitting platoon first baseman. He played in 155 games in 2000, fewer only than Kent on the team, and his numbers against left-handers (.256 average, .351 on-base percentage, four home runs in 129 at-bats) were near to triumphant for a 32-year-old who had given up switch-hitting the previous year.

As is often the case for switch-hitters, Snow's right-handed swing always represented a battle. Even for naturally right-handed switch-hitters, it's often a struggle to feel sharp when they face only the occasional left-handed pitcher. It's enough of a mental grind to maintain one swing;

it can be overwhelming to try to keep two plates spinning at the same time.

After much deliberation, Snow decided in the spring of 1999 to give up his right-handed swing. He took loads of extra batting practice left on left. Even former MVP and Cy Young Award winner Vida Blue threw to him on the back fields in Scottsdale that spring.

In his first game batting against a left-hander, Snow got a hit.

He didn't get another for a couple weeks.

"It was the right move," Snow said. "But it wasn't going to happen overnight."

There was no guarantee the Giants would wait forever. They planned to platoon Charlie Hayes with Snow, but an injury to Mueller on opening day forced Hayes to move to third base. Snow would get his chance to bat left on left. And besides, he was a four-time-defending Gold Glove winner at first base, and would go on to claim six in a row after winning in 2000. Dusty Baker didn't want to take Snow's defense out of the equation.

Snow had two full seasons to prove he could make it work batting left on left, and he did.

But there was no chance he'd be in the lineup for Game 2 against Leiter, who held left-handed batters to a .118 average during the 2000 season. Baker responded by loading up his lineup with all right-handed hitters, except for Bonds. Kent slid over to substitute for Snow at first base, with Ramon Martinez manning second base.

The Giants had their own left-hander, Estes, on the mound.

"I wasn't a rookie, I'd been in the playoffs in '97, and still, I was a little overwhelmed," Estes said. "I'd been through it, yet it was really tough to control that adrenaline. I obviously felt this was a big game. The Mets were very good at home. Any chance we had to beat them at our place, we had to do it. It was an important game to win."

Mets manager Bobby Valentine made his own lineup changes, moving Edgardo Alfonzo to the unfamiliar No. 2 spot and dropping leadoff hitter Benny Agbayani down to sixth. With Bell's ankle still swollen from chasing after Bonds' triple in Game 1, lightly regarded backup Timo Perez found himself in a starting role.

The game began at 5:07 PM in San Francisco, and the combination of shadows and glare off the center-field scoreboard helped both pitchers early. But Estes, who finished fourth in the NL in walks allowed that season, struggled with both nerves and command as the Mets pieced together a two-run rally in the second inning. Estes fluttered Robin Ventura's jersey with a pitch. Agbayani walked on four consecutive balls. Estes issued another walk to Mike Bordick, loading the bases with one out. Leiter, who did not handle the bat well, probably should have stood with the bat on his shoulder. But he tried to test Kent at first base with a bunt, and was fortunate it only resulted in one out at the plate. It took a hard slide from Ventura into catcher Bobby Estalella to keep the inning alive.

Up stepped Perez, into a moment that wasn't scripted for him. He wasn't just a rookie. He was a September call-up, and had all of nine at-bats against left-handed pitchers in his short major league career—including his strikeout against Estes to start the game, when he took a desperate hack at a curveball.

Estes remembered that swing, and hoped to induce it again. He went back to his curveball on an 0-1 count, and watched in disbelief as Perez stayed through it while lining a two-run single to center field.

Burks led the Giants back in the bottom of the second inning, following Kent's leadoff bloop single with an RBI double that hugged the left-field chalk. But Leiter kept throwing his cutter, the Giants went 0-for-3 while Burks stood on second base, and they moved to the third inning trailing 2–1.

Estes gave up two hits in the third but kept the Mets off the board and finally began to slay the butterflies in his gut. He was getting ahead in the count, and his pitches weren't flat. When Estes went to bat and drew an unexpected four-pitch walk to start the bottom of the third, he was no longer thinking about failing on the big stage. He was thinking about making something happen.

"Dusty had used me as a pinch runner several times over the years, so when I was on the bases, I didn't feel like a pitcher," Estes said. "I felt like I could take an extra base, maybe do something to score."

Mueller hit a chopper to the left side and Estes sprinted to second base, aiming to make it to third if the ball happened to sneak past the shortstop. But Bordick was able to make a backhanded stop, spin, and throw to second base. Estes had it in his mind to take a hard cut and go to third. All of the sudden, he was in the middle of a force play with Alfonzo standing on the base.

"I was too close to slide, so I ended up lunging into the bag at full speed," Estes said. "The front of my foot hit the front of the bag, my foot caught, my knee went over the bag, and I just remember feeling excruciating pain. My whole ankle went numb, and I kind of went into shock."

The Mets added insult to injury. Estes didn't realize it at the time, but umpire Dan Morrison had called him safe. When he hobbled off the bag and Alfonzo tagged him, he was out. Until Estes got to the trainer's room, he hadn't even realized that Alfonzo applied a tag.

"I watched the rest of the game in there with my foot in a bucket," Estes said. "It was the most disappointing feeling I've had in my career, to get hurt like I did."

The Giants called upon Kirk Rueter to rescue them and he responded with 4⅓ shutout innings of relief. The Mets managed just three hits against him, and he erased one of those baserunners with a double play. When Rueter walked off the mound in the eighth, he did so to a standing ovation.

Rueter did everything he could to keep the Giants within striking distance, but they were up against a prime October performance from Leiter, who survived a 10-pitch confrontation with Estalella in the seventh and got Mueller to ground into a double play to end the eighth. Baker's right-handed lineup made no difference against Leiter, who batted for himself in the ninth and would be trusted to protect his own one-run lead. It turned into a 4–1 cushion when Alfonzo hit a two-run home run off Felix Rodriguez that apparently put the game out of reach.

Snow didn't see Alfonzo's shot clear the fence. In the sixth, he had walked down to the indoor batting cage behind the dugout. He was not accustomed to coming off the bench, having just 23 pinch at-bats in his career, but he hoped the Giants might find a way to get Leiter out of the game. In a best-case scenario, the Giants would grab a lead and Snow would enter as a defensive replacement. However he would be used, he wanted to be warm, loose, and ready.

"I'll never forget it was me and Doug Mirabelli in the cage hitting off the machine, and being honest, we were playing home run derby," Snow recalled. "We made up a rule where if you hit it into the net up in the corner, that's a homer. Take five swings, then you've gotta get out and your turn's over. So I'm not kidding you, we were actually down there playing home run derby."

Prior to the game, bench coach Ron Wotus told Snow that he might pinch-hit for Martinez late in the game if the situation presented itself. In the eighth, Wotus walked into the cage and confirmed the plan: Martinez was due up fourth in the ninth, and if the Mets brought in hard-throwing closer Armando Benitez, that would be Snow's assignment.

First the Giants had to get Leiter out of the game. He already had surpassed 120 pitches through eight innings and remained on the mound to face just one more batter: the only left-handed one in the Giants lineup. Bonds came through with a leadoff double, giving the Giants their first runner in scoring position—other than Estes, briefly—since the second inning.

Valentine went to his bullpen, and Benitez, to match up against Kent and Burks.

Benitez was 27 years old, in his physical prime, and right-handers batted just .160 against him that season while he recorded 41 saves. He had a reverse split against left-handers and was even tougher against them, yielding a .134 average and one home run in 119 at-bats.

Benitez also allowed 10 home runs on the season. But with fog beginning to billow below the light standards, the ballpark was playing as big and imposing as ever. Not that anyone paid attention to a stat called win expectancy at the time, but the Mets were 90 percent assured victory.

Neither Kent nor Burks made good contact against Benitez, but Kent did manage to beat out an infield single to bring the tying run to the plate. When Burks popped up the first pitch, though, the Mets announcers considered the major threats weathered. Play-by-play announcer Gary Cohen noted that the Giants didn't have another home run threat like Burks in the batters to follow.

Estes, in the trainer's room, watched the TV broadcast on a 10-second delay and wondered what the mood was like in the Giants dugout.

"I mean, I'm in there thinking it's over," Estes said. "But every team I played for under Dusty, he always made you believe. If we were within a grand slam, we believed. We won a lot of games late, a lot of close ballgames. So I knew there had to be a hopeful feeling in that dugout."

Snow had faced Benitez just twice in his career. In 1999, he also represented the tying run in the ninth. That time, at Shea Stadium, he struck out looking to end the game. Benitez struck him out again in 2000.

Snow had enough warning from Wotus to take a last-second look at video of Benitez before he walked back up the dugout stairs to grab his helmet. He knew the big right-hander fell into a pattern: when he got behind, he always threw fastballs. Snow reminded himself of that fact as he walked to the plate and exhaled. The first two pitches were out of the zone. Snow was able to look dead red, and he aimed for more than the corner of the net.

Benitez tried to bust Snow inside once more with a fastball. And what happened next was unforgettable.

The pitch caught too much of the plate, and just enough of the barrel. Snow turned on it and sent a shot down the right-field line, the ball rising high and deep enough to catch thousands of hearts in throats.

The Giants had the shortest right field in the National League. In this instant, though, the arcade never seemed so far away. Snow took one wandering step out of the batter's box into fair territory, then another, and another, and another, drifting nearly halfway to the mound, his eyes fixed to the sky and left arm hopefully pointing fair. It had been a quarter-century since Carlton Fisk waved his arms and willed his home run fair in the 1975 World Series at Fenway Park. Now, as the ball clanked on the green metal roof atop the right-field arcade, Snow and the Giants had their own Fisk moment.

Six feet to the right and it would've been foul. Three feet shorter and it would've fallen straight down and perhaps in Perez's glove. In no other ballpark in America would it have been a home run. It didn't even reach the first row of the seats.

J.T. Snow tied Game 2 of the 2000 NLDS against the Mets with a dramatic three-run home run in the ninth inning—and gave the Giants their own Carlton Fisk moment.

It skipped off the roof, just missing a fan's cupped hands, and bounced back onto the field as umpires whirled their index fingers to signal a home run. Snow thrust both arms in the air as the crowd went into mad delight.

"I was looking for a fastball up in the zone, just hoping to drive something to the outfield," Snow said. "It was letter high and I don't remember seeing the ball or location or anything. I just remember seeing it up and swinging as hard as I could.

"I remember hitting it right on the barrel, crushing it, and then seeing the replays after the game and thinking, *Gosh, it barely got out*. There was so much wind from right field. I was watching it and just saying, 'please stay fair, stay fair, stay fair…'"

With one swing, the Giants erased a three-run deficit in the ninth, created a new life to take command of the series—and they had their first truly signature moment in Pacific Bell Park history.

If the inaugural game in April was a housewarming, this was their first block party.

In the trainer's room, Estes didn't hear the crowd react. He felt it.

"Those 10 seconds felt like forever," Estes said. "I knew something good happened. Then I'm watching, and, fair or foul? Then the arms go up and the trot. And suddenly, I wasn't feeling any pain."

Snow had never hit a pinch home run in his career. He'd never had so much as a pinch RBI. Now he was pumping his fist around the bases, high-fiving Bonds and putting an arm around Kent at home plate as the noise engulfed them.

"Benitez cannot believe it," shouted Giants commentator Mike Krukow, "and neither do I!"

"In their new home, the Giants have just gotten their greatest gift," KNBR play-by-play announcer Ted Robinson said. "A Pac Bell Park special: a 309-foot fly ball!"

Three teammates, then four, then five, came up to Snow in the dugout with the same joyful message. They jumped up so high when they watched his home run, they smacked their heads on the dugout ceiling.

Snow came out for a curtain call as the crowd thundered. There was simply no way for the Mets to recover from this. The Giants were certain they would win.

Except they did not.

Benitez recorded two outs and Baker went back to Rodriguez in the 10th even though Alfonzo already had tagged him for a two-run home run in the top of the ninth. Closer Robb Nen had warmed up. So had left-hander Alan Embree. But Baker wanted to protect himself if the game lasted deep into extra innings, and as he later explained, he wasn't at a point in the lineup where he felt he could double switch.

Rodriguez recorded two outs with the help of fine defensive plays by Kent, who had moved to second base, and Bonds in left field. But Darryl Hamilton, the former Giant traded for Burks two years earlier, came off the bench and delivered a pinch double. Pitching coach Dave Righetti visited Rodriguez and the decision was made to pitch to Jay Payton, a good fastball hitter who often tried to expand the zone. It wasn't a true pitch-around situation, but there was no reason to throw Payton anything too good.

Rodriguez did, on the first pitch. Payton lined an RBI single up the middle, and the Mets had a 5–4 lead.

Once again, the Giants were down to their final three outs. Rios instilled belief with a pinch single to start the 10th that drove Benitez from the game. The Giants sacrificed Rios to second base. It wouldn't take a home run this time. A bleeder would be enough.

But Rios tried unsuccessfully to advance to third on Mueller's ground ball to the left side. It was a horrific baserunning mistake, and the Giants would not recover from it.

Mets left-hander John Franco finished his career with 424 saves, ranking third on the all-time list at the time he retired, but he had handed over the fireman role to Benitez the previous season. This was his first chance to close out a postseason game. He needed one more out, and with the winning run at the plate, he had to go through Bonds.

Franco fell behind 2-0, got Bonds to chase a high fastball, then located a 3-1 fastball at the hollow of the kneecap for a strike. Bonds shook his head at Gary Cederstrom, as if the plate umpire didn't understand how this script was supposed to finish. Snow already had hit the Giants' most dramatic home run since Brian Johnson's shot against the Dodgers in 1997. The Giants simply could not lose this game.

But after Bonds fouled off a pitch, Franco came back with a sneaky changeup—the pitch that allowed him to thrive for so many seasons after his fastball left him. Cederstrom, after a beat, rang up Bonds, who bent at the waist in protest.

Bonds would end his career with 41 plate appearances against Franco. He never hit a home run against him.

The Mets won 5–4 in 10 innings, they split the first two games in San Francisco, and they traveled east with a chance to end the series if they could win two games at Shea Stadium. That's exactly what they did. The Mets received a monumental home run from Agbayani in the 13th inning in Game 3, then an unlikely one-hitter from Bobby J. Jones in Game 4. They went on to lose to the Yankees in a Subway Series where the enduring images were of an enraged Roger Clemens picking up a shard of Mike Piazza's bat and flinging it at him.

The Giants never recovered after the Game 2 loss. Kent was one of few players that night to stand at his locker and take questions. Yet even in that moment, with just a few minutes to digest the disappointment, he could appreciate what he'd just seen.

"That was a great game, wasn't it?" Kent said, smiling.

"I wouldn't trade that for anything," Baker said. "I wouldn't have traded J.T.'s dramatic three-run homer in the ninth."

It would take Snow much longer to appreciate it.

"I don't remember much," mumbled Snow that night, all jubilance of his home run trot gone from his face. "It was just exciting, the emotions and all the fans here. But I'd trade all that for a win. It doesn't mean a whole lot now."

Years later, it's still difficult for Snow to believe the Giants lost on the night he shined the brightest.

"We were all in disbelief," Snow recalled. "I just sat in front of my locker and it was weird because everybody on the team, I think, came up and said, 'That was awesome, that was so cool,' even though we lost the game.

"I was sitting there thinking, *Man, my whole time with the Giants I played hard, I put up some pretty good numbers, and it was always Barry and Jeff. What if that was my one shining moment?* And I just remember going home that night and having to pack to go to New York, and thinking, *Man, I was always an everyday player in high school, college, minor leagues, the big leagues, and I never hit a pinch home run. Here was my first one. I hit a pinch three-run homer to win that game, and there's no way. How did we lose that game?*"

In so many ways, Game 2 of the 2000 NLDS encapsulated Snow's career as a Giant. His teams always came close, but never close enough. And although the victories were many, the losses felt more permanent. In 2003, when the Giants were eliminated in the NL Division Series at Miami on a play at the plate, it was Snow who thudded into Pudge Rodriguez and couldn't dislodge the ball.

The home run off Benitez, though, along with his consistent effort and professionalism, earned Snow a lasting place in Giants history. In 2008, club officials signed him to a one-day contract, put him on the 40-man roster, started him at first base, and then replaced him prior to the first pitch—all so he could retire as a Giant. It wasn't an honor he requested. It was something the front office felt he deserved. They've never done it for another player, not even for Willie Mays.

And in 2010, when another group of Giants were advancing in October, Snow was along for the ride in uniform as a special assistant. In a critical Game 3 of an NLDS in Atlanta, the Giants' Sergio Romo served up a pinch home run to the Braves' Eric Hinske in the eighth inning that turned the Braves' one-run deficit into a one-run lead. The

Giants came back with two outs in the ninth to win, with first baseman Travis Ishikawa barreling home on a single to score the tying run from second base.

The Giants didn't carry a pinch runner to enter for Ishikawa. They had no pinch runner for Snow that afternoon in Miami. So in the afterglow of that victory in Atlanta, a reporter asked Snow if he had any flashbacks.

He did, but not to Ishikawa's rumble home. He identified most with Hinske.

"I know that feeling," Snow said. "You've just hit a huge home run to save the game, the biggest home run of your life—and before you know it, your team lost. It's the strangest feeling."

No, the Giants didn't win the game the night that Snow took his greatest swing in the big leagues. But they proved it was possible to achieve something amid a loss. Those staid and corporate crowds loosened their ties, yelled themselves hoarse, and never looked back.

"To this day, I still run into people who say they were at that game and it was the loudest they've ever heard the stadium," Snow said. "It's kind of weird to think that was our last game at the stadium in that first year. Our fans figured it out."

Chapter 3

Asking God

"I hear this all the time: 'He's arrogant. He's this...'
I'm not arrogant. I'm good. There's a difference. I'm a
good baseball player. I'm going to have a good year
because Barry Bonds is a good baseball player."
—Barry Bonds

Friday, October 5, 2001
Bonds Bashes Nos. 71 and 72, Passes Big Mac

Barry Bonds didn't lay one brick or plant one blade of grass at Pacific Bell Park, but you could argue he was as responsible as anyone for its creation.

His homecoming in 1993 made for more than a good narrative, more than just the son of Bobby Bonds and godson of Willie Mays returning to the Bay Area. Barry Bonds was the best player in the game by no small margin, and it wasn't long before the Giants constructed a winning team around him.

Although they could boast of other beloved franchise stars in recent decades such as Jack Clark, Jeffrey Leonard, Will Clark, and Kevin Mitchell, nobody did more to make baseball relevant again in San Francisco than Barry Bonds.

Prior to the 1997 season, though, new Giants GM Brian Sabean found himself in a bind. Baseball's labor stoppage continued to depress attendance, and as a result, the onus fell on ownership to soak up operating losses. Sabean was a former scouting director with the New York Yankees who rose through the ranks to oversee a system that produced Derek Jeter, Mariano Rivera, Jorge Posada, and Bernie Williams, among others—the backbone of baseball's last dynasty. He joined the Giants front office in 1993 and was elevated to the GM chair when Bob Quinn stepped down after the '96 season. In baseball circles, everyone knew Sabean could stock a farm system with talent. But he was an unknown in San Francisco. Could he build a roster?

The rookie GM faced an immediate test, and it looked like a no-win scenario. Bonds and Matt Williams were due to make more than 40 percent of the team's payroll in '97 and an expanded budget was out of the question given the financial stress on ownership. There would be no funds to retool a team that went 68–94 the previous season. Either Bonds or Williams would have to go, and no matter what Sabean decided, the fan outrage would be unavoidable.

Sabean made his choice. He traded Williams to the Cleveland Indians for shortstop Jose Vizcaino, right-hander Julian Tavarez, and Jeff Kent, an infielder with a little pop but no real sizzle. The outcry was so loud that Sabean had to go on the Giants' flagship radio station, KNBR, and defend himself with a comment that would be appended to him the rest of his career: "I am not an idiot."

After the Giants surprised to a 90-win season and NL West title in 1997—with Bonds only getting better and Kent driving in 121 runs—nobody was questioning the sanity of the rookie GM.

Bonds provided one of his all-time career highlights, too, performing the pirouette heard 'round the world when he spun out of the batter's box after hitting a critical home run off the Dodgers' Chan Ho Park amid that September pennant race. The Dodgers hated Bonds all the more because of that act, and Giants fans embraced every bit of it. No matter what you thought of him, it was impossible to be a Giants fan without being a Bonds fan.

Prior to the 1999 season, Bonds signed a two-year extension with a club option and arrived in the spring looking like he'd stepped out of a bodybuilding magazine. Effusive stories were written about his off-season workout rituals. Privately, people around the team wondered if the home run chase between Mark McGwire and Sammy Sosa, which captivated the country in the summer of '98, inspired a jealous Bonds to get jacked so he could get in the act. He already was a three-time NL MVP (and should have won four in a row, since his numbers were far superior to the Braves' Terry Pendleton in 1991), an eight-time Gold Glove winner, an eight-time All-Star, a seven-time Silver Slugger, universally acknowledged as the game's best all-around player, and a sure-fire future Hall of Famer as a 34-year-old entering the 1999 season. But nobody seemed to appreciate his greatness any longer.

Amid a shower of nonstop coverage and breaking news bulletins, in 1998, Sosa and McGwire chased and obliterated Roger Maris' 37-year-old single-season record of 61 home runs. Amid that summer-long obsession, a Gold Glove left fielder hitting 37 homers and driving in 122 runs was as noticeable as a common card in a shoe box.

So Bonds arrived in the spring of 1999 looking shredded, and a dozen games into the season, that's exactly what happened. He tore a triceps tendon in his throwing arm that required surgery and sidelined him for nearly two months.

Bonds recovered and hit a career-best 49 home runs in 2000, 25 at home and 24 on the road. He finished second to Kent for the NL MVP Award. When teammates threw public support to Kent's candidacy, Bonds couldn't help but feel disrespected. Even Dusty Baker, a boyhood friend of Bobby Bonds who held Barry on the day he was born, told the media that Kent deserved the award.

Bonds swelled with anger. He always saw himself as more an entertainer than a baseball player, and nobody seemed to notice that he was putting on a better and better show. At an age when most power hitters have to compromise for eroding bat speed, he was getting bigger, stronger, and smarter.

It set up for a dramatic arrival when Bonds reported for spring training in 2001. He would be a free agent again after the season, and his relationship with the Giants was strained at best. When he reported that spring, the burning topic wasn't about home runs or his physique or even his relationship with players or the media.

It was the contract.

The talk got so heated that Bonds surprised everyone by calling into KNBR to clear the air.

"I hear this all the time: 'He's arrogant. He's this…' I'm not arrogant," Bonds said on the air. "I'm good. There's a difference. I'm a good baseball player. I'm going to have a good year because Barry Bonds is a good baseball player."

One unnamed player confided an off-the-record prediction to the *Oakland Tribune*: Bonds would whine about his contract all year, and end up having a terrible season.

There was another reason for Bonds to put pressure on himself as his ninth season as a Giant began. He entered the year needing six home runs to become the 17th player in major league history to join the 500 club. At the time, 14 of the 16 members were in the Hall of Fame, and Eddie Murray would be inducted in his first year of eligibility in 2003.

To hit 500 home runs was to claim a golden ticket to Cooperstown, and to witness a 500th home run was to see a royal coronation. When Bonds reached that milestone, he would be 28 stolen bases away from the 500-homer, 500-steal club, too. He already ranked as the only player in history with 400 homers and 400 steals. He was in the process of redefining exclusive baseball greatness.

Bonds hit a home run on opening day, in 2001, but proceeded to go into a funk. He had a .103 average seven games into the season. At one point, he went hitless in 21 consecutive at-bats. Was it the contract? The pressure over the 500th homer? Would it last all season?

Bonds didn't give anyone much more time to fret. He hit a home run in an April 12 blowout loss at San Diego. Then he hit one each day in a three-game series at Milwaukee. When the Giants opened a homestand

April 17 against the Dodgers, Bonds turned 40,000 ticket stubs into instant souvenirs. He homered for a fifth consecutive game, and his two-run shot in the eighth inning off right-hander Terry Adams did more than erase a one-run deficit and give the Giants a 3–2 victory. It was the 500th of his career.

It was a celebratory scene as fans took in what they understood to be a history-making moment. Bonds crushed a low pitch from Adams and sent it deep into McCovey Cove, where the armada of watercraft made a mad splash for the baseball.

Bonds rounded the bases and jumped down with both feet on home plate, stomping like a kid landing in a hopscotch square. A bat girl, Alexis Busch, was the only one there to greet him. Rich Aurilia, who had tripled ahead of Bonds' homer, stood to the side and gave him a hug. But Kent, in the on-deck circle, didn't offer so much as a high-five. In an awkward scene, the rest of the team stayed in the dugout, and the Dodgers stood and shifted their weight as the game was stopped for more than eight minutes. Bonds embraced his father, other members of his family, and then posed for pictures with Mays and Willie McCovey—all in the eighth inning of a one-run game. Adams later called the delay inexcusable. But in the stands, there was no hurry to move the game along. The fans wanted to marinate in the moment.

"I felt it, big time," Bonds said of the crowd. "I hit it. But it was like we all did it. It was like the whole town did it. It's overwhelming."

The ensuing weeks and months were something beyond overwhelming. Bonds hit his 501st home run the next night, making it six consecutive games with a homer, and he remained in a zone all through the summer.

The first talk of challenging McGwire's three-year-old single-season record of 70 home runs came after a May 19 game at Atlanta. Following a 76-minute rain delay, Bonds doubled and homered. Another thunderstorm caused a delay of more than 90 minutes. When the game resumed, Bonds homered again. Then at almost 1:00 AM, he came to the plate once more and homered a third time. The Giants needed all three shots in a 6–3 victory.

The baseball world already understood Bonds to be an all-time great player. Now he was something beyond that: a video game rendered in flesh.

"Barry just confirmed something we already knew," Atlanta's Chipper Jones said. "You can't throw him anything over the plate. I've never seen anything remotely like it."

Bonds hit two more home runs the next day in Atlanta. He hit a total of six in the series, although the Braves somehow still won two of three. Through 40 games, Bonds had hit 22 homers, and for the first time anyone could remember, the fans at Turner Field gave a standing ovation to a visiting player.

Bonds came into the dugout and sat next to J.T. Snow, an expression of disbelief on his face.

"Even he was amazed," Snow said. "He said, 'I can't believe I'm doing this. I'm in the zone. There's no other way to explain it.' When great players get in the zone, they take off. A normal person can try to stay in it for a few games or a week. For a great player, it can be a month. For Barry, it was all season."

The ranks of reporters began to swell. The interview requests multiplied. The most common question: how was Bonds doing this?

"Ask God," he told the beat reporters on May 21. "There's some things I can't understand right now. The balls that used to line off the wall just go out [of the park]. I can't answer that question. It's like women. Do you understand why they do some things?"

When Bonds hit two more home runs in the next series at Arizona, teammate Shawon Dunston predicted that Big Mac's record was going to fall. Bonds told Dunston he was full of it, and if he did break the record, he'd buy him a Mercedes coupe.

The home runs kept coming—majestic drives to center field, breaking balls snuck over the fence in left, splashdowns in right—and Bonds could barely go a week without passing another hallowed name on the all-time list. He already became the 17th player to join the 500 club. By the end of the season, he shot past 10 of those players: Murray, Mel Ott, Eddie

Mathews, Ernie Banks, Ted Williams, Willie McCovey, Jimmie Foxx, Mickey Mantle, Mike Schmidt, and Reggie Jackson.

But the Giants weren't taking the same trajectory in the standings. Although Bonds had a major league record 39 home runs at the All-Star break, the Giants stood at 46–42 and were 5½ games out of first place. Even July trade acquisitions Andres Galarraga and Jason Schmidt couldn't send the Giants on a hot enough stretch to take control of the NL West.

Bonds had never hit 50 home runs in a season before. He reduced that mark on August 11 at Wrigley Field. Five days later, in an afternoon game at Pacific Bell Park against the Florida Marlins, Bonds hit Nos. 52 and 53 to break the single-season franchise record set by Mays in 1965.

It was another love fest, another curtain call, another series of ovations. And from Mays, in yet another postgame ceremony, there was a challenge: come back and talk when you match 660 career home runs. While everyone else in the Bay Area had McGwire on their minds, Mays was thinking of an even more hallowed pursuit.

"He doesn't realize, this is just one record," Mays said.

By now there seemingly was nothing that Bonds could not do. He was seeing fewer strikes than ever, and even fewer mistakes over the plate. But his swing stayed short and quick, his pitch recognition was uncanny, and he hardly fouled anything back to the screen. He had the vision of Ted Williams, the hand-eye coordination of Tony Gwynn, the power of the Babe, and an almost clairvoyant intelligence at the plate such as the game had never before witnessed. The daily discussion back in San Francisco turned into an obsession. The news of the day narrowed to one thing: whether Bonds had hit another home run.

It would be two more years before a nondescript industrial building in Burlingame a mile south of the airport, Bay Area Laboratories Co-operative, or BALCO, would be raided by federal agents, along with the home of Greg Anderson, Bonds' personal trainer. It would be five years before *San Francisco Chronicle* reporters Lance Williams and Mark Fainaru-Wada would publish *Game of Shadows*, the book that compiled hundreds of documents and interviews to paint a compelling portrait of Bonds as a megalomaniac who used everything from hard-core anabolic steroids to designer drugs in an effort to boost his performance. The Feds, determined to disgrace Bonds, eventually got their man on the smallest of technicalities: an obstruction of justice conviction based on his evasive testimony to a grand jury.

At the time, though, the game's great steroid secret remained mostly out of the daily newspapers and TV reports. For the media, to mention steroids in a major league clubhouse was to invite ostracism. But of course, usage already was widespread and offensive statistics had ballooned out of control. The fact that many pitchers were using only served to further inflate the hitting numbers. Greater velocity plus greater bat speed led to more baseballs over the fence. Jam shots became grand slams.

When the Giants went to New York in late August, where Bonds usually held court and enjoyed smacking around questions like cat toys, a reporter asked him about steroids for the first time.

"People make things up just to have something to do," Bonds said. "If somebody does something good, there has to be a reason why. Why can't he just do it because he's talented? I don't think it's fair."

The single-season home run record was a story again but the country wasn't embracing Bonds the same way it did Sosa and McGwire three summers earlier. Some of that had to do with the Giants being a West Coast team and fewer live news bulletins during waking hours for people on the East Coast. Some of it had to do with the bewildering feeling of putting up parade bleachers again when people were still sweeping up the confetti from McGwire and Sosa. Undoubtedly, a lot of it had to do with Bonds' sour reputation.

In visiting ballparks, though, it became a unique scene. The fans would boo Bonds mercilessly. Then when he would hit a home run, they would cheer and chant his name. And the home runs kept coming.

"Everything around me is unreal," Bonds said. "I can't explain anything."

Bonds had 57 home runs entering September, and anticipation in the Bay Area had become dangerously feverish on some levels. The port authority voted to ban all motorized craft in McCovey Cove, fearing an inevitable accident as kayakers jostled with motorboats for wet souvenirs. On September 6, in the final game of a homestand, Bonds became the fifth player in history to hit 60 homers in a season and rounded the bases with Babe Ruth's visage on the scoreboard. Then on September 9, he launched Nos. 61, 62, and 63 in a game at Coors Field, where Rockies fans implored him to make a curtain call. Whether you liked Bonds or not, the chase was on, and who doesn't want to witness history when they buy a ticket?

The Giants had 18 games remaining and were 1½ games out of first place when they traveled to Houston on September 10. The single-season home run record was a national story again.

The next day, everything changed.

The country was in shock and in mourning, having been attacked on its home soil by a foreign enemy for the first time in two centuries. The Giants did not worry about whether they would begin their series in Houston following the September 11 terrorist attacks. They only worried about how they would get home.

When baseball resumed on September 18, it did its part to serve as a healing distraction. But what about Bonds and the record? For most of the nation, it already seemed like a strange pursuit. For nearly four decades, Babe Ruth held the single-season record of 60. Roger Maris hit No. 61 and held the record for nearly four decades after that. Now after McGwire suspended belief by hitting 70, a total that appeared to be an extreme and unassailable outlier, three years later, it was within someone's reach again?

It's safe to say most of the country was not caught up in Bonds' pursuit. But in San Francisco, fans had already scrambled in the cove to retrieve No. 500. They'd already seen him break Mays' franchise record. They cheered all of the milestones, saved all the ticket stubs, pushed all-in with their sentiment, survived scrapes in the bleachers and on the water to claim souvenir baseballs worth more than a mortgage payment. Bonds had them at his first pirouette.

The only question would be whether, in a pennant race, he would get enough strikes to hit.

Bonds didn't hit a homer in his first two home games after baseball resumed following a one-week period of mourning. But he hit three on the next road trip to San Diego and Los Angeles, then two more in a home series against the Padres to get within one of matching McGwire with seven to play. On September 30, the Padres walked him twice and hit him with a pitch. They only gave him one at-bat, one chance to hit No. 70 in front of the home fans, and it did not happen.

The Giants trailed Arizona by two in the NL West as they traveled back to Houston, the city where they awoke three weeks earlier to scenes of hijackers flying planes into the World Trade Center and Pentagon.

It was clear that Houston manager Larry Dierker wanted no supporting role in a Bonds celebration. The Astros walked Bonds five times and hit him once in the first two games of the series. They walked him with the Giants leading 8–1. By the end of the three-game series, Bonds would see 13 strikes in 14 plate appearances.

Bonds' 10-year-old daughter, Shikari, made a sign for the final game of the series: GIVE OUR DADDY A CHANCE.

In the ninth inning of the series finale, the Astros did. They trailed 9–2 in the ninth inning when a rookie, Wilfredo Rodriguez, jogged from the bullpen to make his second major league appearance. His 1-1 fastball crossed the plate, intersected with Bonds' maple bat, and traveled 454 feet. The crowd of more than 43,000 at Enron Field, mostly there to see history, cheered Bonds and chanted his name. Baker even let Bonds take his position in left field before subbing for him in the bottom of the ninth, just so the road crowd could cheer him some more.

The single-season record belonged to Bonds and McGwire. If Bonds would take it for himself, it would come at home, in the final three games of the regular season against the archrival Dodgers.

It was past 3:00 AM on October 5 when the Giants arrived home from Houston, and Bonds was up early to attend the funeral of a family friend. He arrived at the ballpark on almost no sleep. Somehow, he would have to summon the energy to put on one more show.

The fans expected one they wouldn't forget. Some tickets were selling for as much as 10 times above face value. It was more than a chance to see history. It was a lottery chance to catch it, too.

Bonds had three games to break the single-season home run record. That was no guarantee he'd see a strike, though. And the Giants were playing for more than one man's personal glory. With an 89–70 record, they remained mathematically alive in two playoff races and trailed first-place Arizona by two games.

By the time the Giants and Dodgers reached the middle innings, the Diamondbacks already had wrapped up a victory in Milwaukee. With a Giants loss, Arizona would clinch the division. The Giants would be eliminated from the wild-card race if they lost, too, since the Astros beat the Cardinals to forge a tie at 92–68 atop the NL Central. The Giants needed to win out and get help. The Dodgers wanted nothing more than to knock out their archrivals, and bottle up Bonds in the process.

The night did not start well. Shawn Estes, who struggled against the Dodgers all season, gave up four consecutive singles—including a two-run line drive up the middle from Gary Sheffield—to begin the first inning. Galarraga dropped a pickoff throw at first base for an error. Paul Lo Duca hit a sacrifice fly. When No. 7 batter Jeff Reboulet doubled, Baker had seen enough. He went to long reliever Mark Gardner.

After an intentional walk to Chad Kreuter, pitcher Chan Ho Park blooped an 0-2 pitch for a two-run single and a 5–0 lead, and the energy went out of the stadium. For a team barely clinging to postseason life, the first inning was all splinters and rocky shoals. But it also set up favorable conditions for the Dodgers to pitch to Bonds, especially when he came to bat with nobody on base and two outs in the first inning.

Park's first pitch was a curve low. His second one was over the heart, and Bonds put all his might into it. His drive cut through the air and traveled to the deepest part of the ballpark, 425 feet away and over the 25-foot brick wall, landing in the glove of 49-year-old Jerry Rose, a season-ticket holder who had no right to expect he'd use the glove he brought to the ballpark.

"High drive! Deep into right-center field! To the big part of the ball-park!" Jon Miller boomed in the KNBR booth. "Number 71, and what a

Barry Bonds broke the single-season home run record in a must-win game against the Dodgers, then celebrated the achievement in front of a half-empty stadium after the Giants lost.

shot! Over the 421-foot marker! The deepest part of any ballpark in the National League! Barry Bonds is now the home run king! No. 71, and it was impressive!"

The crowd erupted in mass celebration. This time, the entire Giants team met Bonds at home plate. Dodgers catcher Chad Kreuter stood inches away and watched, all the while holding Bonds' maple bat, because, why not? It was an heirloom just sitting there in the dirt.

"It is amazing when you think about it," said Dodgers announcer Vin Scully, following a much more understated home run call. "Babe Ruth hit 60 home runs in 1927. That lasted till 1961, 34 years, and then Roger Maris. And that record lasted for 37 years until Mark McGwire hit 70, and McGwire's record lasted only three years.

"So despite the fact the Dodgers opened up with a five-run first inning, this crowd is ecstatic. They have come to see, and they have seen it. Home run No. 71."

Major League Baseball commissioner Bud Selig wasn't there to see it, having committed to visit Baltimore for Cal Ripken Jr.'s retirement ceremony and then on to San Diego for Tony Gwynn's final game. Bobby Bonds wasn't there, either, having committed to a charity golf tournament in Connecticut.

But Bonds spoke by phone briefly to his father in the dugout, took the field again for nearly five minutes of curtain calls and hugs, then his demeanor changed. His smile vanished. He dashed back to the dugout, waved his arm as if telling a long-winded speaker to get on with it, and implored everyone to get back to business. The Giants still had a season to save, and eight innings to play.

Eric Davis nearly brought the Giants all the way back with a three-run double in the second inning, but the Dodgers' Marquis Grissom responded with a two-run homer in the third. With the Giants down four runs, Bonds led off the bottom of the third and faced Park once more.

It had become clear that Park wasn't in top form. He stretched between pitches and began throwing from the stretch even with the bases empty. His back had tightened up, and Bonds saw injured prey. He fouled off a pitch, took another below the knees, then picked up the spin of a curveball from the moment it left the pitcher's hand.

Park hung his breaking ball. Bonds launched it toward center field, watching it for a moment like a golfer hoping he used enough club to clear the water hazard that fronts the green. The drive bounced off a fan in the first row as Grissom watched a priceless souvenir clatter back onto the track.

No. 72.

This whole season was about suspending disbelief, wasn't it?

Bonds rounded the bases again. On no sleep, and with massive expectations, he had set the single-season home run record not once but twice by the third inning, and if that wasn't enough drama for one night, the Giants were trying to keep their playoff hopes alive while emptying their bullpen.

The Dodgers' Shawn Green hit a solo homer to make it 9–5, but following an intentional walk to Bonds in the fourth, Kent came through with a three-run double. It was 9–8, and it was just the fourth inning. The game was still young, if not the night.

Gary Sheffield hit a solo homer in the sixth and Aurilia responded with a tying, two-run shot off Giovanni Carrara in the bottom of the inning. The ballpark went insane again. Newspaper reporters furiously wrote and deleted and rewrote their copy, bewildered that they were up against deadline and it was just the sixth inning. And besides…what if Bonds hit another?

He had a chance to put the Giants ahead, but he just barely got under Carrara's pitch and flied out to left field. Then the Dodgers went ahead in the seventh. Reboulet hit a grounder that found a seam, as well as a desperate shortstop trying to make a play. Aurilia's throw sailed into the stands, advancing Reboulet to second base. A ground out moved him to third. With runners at the corners, Grissom hit a chopper to third base where Edwards Guzman, a little-used backup who had entered in a double-switch an inning earlier, fielded it. The ball stuck in his glove and his throw to the plate was wide as Reboulet scored.

By then, the Giants knew a loss would eliminate them from contention. They went down in order in the seventh. Left-hander Jesse Orosco walked Bonds in a scoreless eighth. The Giants were down to their last grains of sand. Galarraga walked to start the ninth and Dante Powell pinch-ran for him, but Calvin Murray popped up a bunt. When Dunston hit a ground ball, the Giants used up their final out. Both the scoreboard and the standings held no more hope.

Bonds leaned against the dugout rail and appeared disconsolate. The record was his. A shot at a World Series ring would have to wait another year.

"On a night of such great joy and great drama, ultimately it's neither. It's complete disappointment for the Giants," Miller said on KNBR. "And for Barry Bonds, on the night he set the home run record, the Giants go down to defeat. And it's been their best night and their worst night, all at the same time. The Giants have been eliminated from any possible postseason contention by the Los Angeles Dodgers."

The game ended seven minutes after midnight. At four hours and 27 minutes, it ranked as the longest nine-inning game in major league history.

The Giants already had a plan set up: if Bonds broke the record, there would be a postgame ceremony. Despite the long game and the awkward circumstances, they went on with it. Barely half the crowd stayed to watch the sequence of speeches, although once again, it was Willie Mays who had the most memorable line of the night.

"I want him to put it where nobody can get it," Mays said of the record.

Two nights later, Bonds reached a higher shelf. He set the record again, connecting off a knuckleball from Dennis Springer for his 73rd and final home run of the season. The ball landed in a mosh pit where fans scrambled for it—and two of them eventually sued each other for the right to keep it.

Over an acrimonious, 15-month legal battle, Alex Popov and Patrick Hayashi paid hundreds of thousands to lawyers only for a California Superior Court judge to play King Solomon and order them to sell the ball and split the proceeds. It sold at auction to comic book creator Todd McFarlane, who paid just $450,000—less than half the ball's pre-auction estimate.

"I knew it wouldn't go for a fraction of what the other one did," McFarlane told ESPN.

He would know. He paid $3.2 million for McGwire's 70th.

The fight over No. 756 was the subject of a 2004 documentary, *Up For Grabs*, provided compelling precedent in the area of property law, and came to symbolize the emptiness of unchecked greed. Hayashi loathed being in the public eye and moved away from the Bay Area. Popov ended up with legal billings that exceeded his settlement, and was sued by his attorney. The home run ball that broke the single-season record became a burden to all involved.

The Giants didn't make the playoffs in 2001, but Dunston did get the Mercedes that Bonds had promised him. And Bonds could afford it, since the Giants signed their 37-year-old slugger to a five-year, $90 million deal in mid-January. So much for that prediction he'd bitch about his contract and have a horrible season. Instead, it turned into the most overwhelming contract drive in baseball history.

There was just one oddity about it. No other team ever acknowledged making Bonds an offer.

Only God knows why.

Chapter 4

A Never-Ending Fight

"Sometimes you have to let sleeping dogs lie."
—Kenny Lofton

Tuesday, October 14, 2002
NLCS Game 5 vs. St. Louis

The Giants received the most overwhelming offensive season from a single player in major league history in 2001, and yet amid 73 home runs from Barry Bonds, they failed to reach postseason play. So GM Brian Sabean attempted to retool for another run.

Across the bay, the Oakland A's were exploiting market inefficiencies, targeting players with lofty on-base percentages and building winning, small-market rosters with a strategy that Michael Lewis would laud in a best-selling book. Meanwhile, Sabean and the Giants operated their own version of "Moneyball." They continued to mine a specific corner of the market: veteran players in their thirties who were catching a second wind.

The Giants traded for third baseman David Bell. They signed outfielder Reggie Sanders as a free agent. And they hoped to squeeze one more season out of 37-year-old catcher Benito Santiago.

Santiago had come to the Giants in the spring of 2001, fewer than two weeks before opening day. Sabean, dissatisfied with a catching tandem of Bobby Estalella and Doug Mirabelli, signed Santiago to a minor league deal with an invitation to camp. Santiago was 36 years old, a year older than Johnny Bench when he retired, and hadn't been the same since he crashed a speeding Ferrari in 1998. Once a rookie sensation who threw out runners from his knees, Santiago had limped through three ineffective seasons with three different teams when the calls stopped coming. It was mutual desperation that brought him and the Giants together.

Santiago surpassed all expectations when he caught 130 games for the Giants in 2001. He proved even better the following season, making the NL All-Star team and providing huge contributions down the stretch.

The time was ending when you could use phrases like "second wind" and "fountain of youth" without rampant and loud suspicion. By the time 2002 came to an end, former NL MVP Ken Caminiti would admit to Tom Verducci of *Sports Illustrated* that he used steroids during his career. Jose Canseco would claim that 85 percent of the league was juiced. And, of course, it wouldn't be long before the FBI would make Bonds the target of the largest, costliest, and most publicized criminal investigation into performance-enhancing drug use among athletes—one that would ensnare Santiago, Estalella, Marvin Benard, and Armando Rios, too.

But the Giants were dealing with a much different controversy in the spring of 2002. It wasn't about steroids. It wasn't even about Bonds, who had a new contract to go with his single-season home run record.

The story was about Jeff Kent. And the story was a lie.

Kent fractured his left wrist on March 1 and told both Giants officials and the media that the mishap occurred when he fell off the tailgate of his truck while washing it. The story was so specific that nobody doubted its credibility. Falling down the stairs was one thing. Who would make up a story about washing a truck?

But the details of Kent's tale began to unravel over the following two weeks. Henry Schulman, the longtime *San Francisco Chronicle* beat reporter, learned from Scottsdale police that the department received two 911 calls about an accident on Hayden Road just two miles north of the Giants' complex on the day Kent injured his wrist. Witnesses to a single-motorcycle accident told police they saw its rider lose control while popping wheelies.

No police report was filed because the motorcycle and rider had left the scene by the time officers arrived. But the facts eventually came out, and the Giants were furious. Kent, when confronted with the evidence, was just as unsuccessful at media spin as he was at bike tricks.

"I think what is sad is that this incident has become bigger than the game," said Kent, when Schulman asked him point-blank if he injured himself when he fell off his motorcycle. "There are so many good things that happen on this field with this team that are good for baseball. I'm not going to comment anymore on the issue. This is becoming bigger and bigger, and if people want to give it wings, go ahead."

Kent insisted he would be ready for opening day. The Giants made him begin the season on the disabled list anyway. For the second consecutive year, the Giants spent the spring in open feud with a star player. And for the second consecutive year, that player was entering his walk year.

For the time being, the Giants knew they had the talent to contend—if only they could keep their clubhouse together. Kent and Bonds were from vastly different backgrounds yet oddly similar in the sense that both came across as loners to teammates. In the middle of their lineup, though, oil and water never mixed so well. Bonds hit a career-best .370 in 2002 to win his first batting title, and Kent's value wasn't to provide lineup protection—pitchers issued 198 walks to Bonds, a major league record—as much as it was to come through with the big hit and make opponents pay.

Although Bonds would never hit 50 home runs in a season again, in most every respect, he was a more productive offensive player than ever in 2002. He finished the season with a .582 on-base percentage, smashing the 61-year-old record of .553 set by Ted Williams.

And his power remained mythic. San Diego Padres manager Bruce Bochy was one of the few skippers who eschewed the intentional walk to Bonds in most circumstances, feeling that the free pass sent the wrong message to his young pitchers. Thanks in part to Bochy, Bonds hit more career home runs against the Padres than any other opponent.

But on June 5, Bochy made sure young right-hander Dennis Tankersley got the message to tread carefully to Bonds with the bases loaded. Instead, the kid threw a first-pitch slider over the plate. Bonds absolutely destroyed it to right field, clearing all 29 rows of the right-field seats and hitting the scoreboard at Qualcomm Stadium. The grand slam was estimated at 482 feet, which was deemed far too conservative by many who witnessed it. Years later, when Bochy became the Giants' manager in 2007, you could still make him whimper at the mention of Dennis Tankersley's name.

The most memorable fireworks in San Diego that season, though, happened on the Giants' next trip to Qualcomm three weeks later.

Bell, the third baseman, fielded a grounder and threw to second base. Kent had expected the throw to go to first base and wasn't on the bag in time. The Giants didn't record an out, the miscommunication bloomed into a four-run inning, and when it ended, Kent snapped at Bell in the dugout.

The argument didn't last long because Bell was due up second the next inning. He shrugged off Kent's bleating, grabbed his helmet, and walked to the on-deck circle—then looked back to the dugout when he heard a commotion. There were Bonds and Kent, in plain view, locked up like two pro wrestlers.

Was Bonds sticking up for a teammate, or had he simply heard enough of Kent's complaining? Maybe some of both? Either way, the Giants lost the game, they were in third place with a 42–33 record, and their two superstars, who never got along particularly well, might as well have been fighting on the set of *The Jerry Springer Show*.

Kent, master of the downplay, shrugged and told reporters that similar altercations happened at least a half-dozen times out of the public eye.

"You expect the competitive adrenaline to be flowing on a good team," Kent said the next day. "Athletes operate on the edge and things like that happen. It's not good and it's not bad. It just happens."

The Giants had the perfect manager to handle a powder keg. Baker always portrayed a cool image as he rolled a toothpick between his teeth. He had newfound perspective on life after a prostate cancer scare in the off-season. One day shortly after receiving his diagnosis, he went duck hunting to clear his head and stopped in a bar where he met a "hippie dude" who wore a hat that identified him as a member of the "I Don't Give a Shit Club." Baker gave the man $3 and received a membership card.

"Right after I joined it, I came back down the mountain and wondered why I did because I really did give a shit," Baker said. "And then I went to Hawaii. I went and prayed on the mountain in the healing center, looked at my son, and said, 'Yeah, I'm going to make it big time.'"

A day after his two stars wrestled in the dugout, Baker acted like he didn't give a…well, you know.

"We've been treading water lately, struggling," Baker said. "Things like that happen all the time. It usually doesn't happen in view of everybody on television. You saw the effect. The cause is our business."

And…

"It's like on the last day of boot camp the sergeant asks if there's anyone who doesn't like someone and they fight it out. That way, you don't carry a grudge into battle."

And…

"You hear about stuff all the time. Sometimes it's better to get it out. I don't like the way it happened, but you're talking about a bunch of dudes with a lot of pride, a lot of everything. I don't know why people expect us to get along all the time."

And…

"One thing's for sure. They've helped each other, and they're more similar than most people realize."

And…

"Usually this happens on good teams. Bad teams always get along."

The Giants knew they were more talented than a third-place team, and perhaps the fight shook something loose. They went home the next day, rallied from a three-run deficit, and beat the Padres on J.T. Snow's single in the 12th inning. It began a stretch in which they won 10 of 15 games, quickening Sabean's resolve on the trade front.

On July 28, with Bonds, Santiago, Benard, Sanders, and center fielder Tsuyoshi Shinjo all out with nagging injuries, Kent hit a two-run homer and Jason Schmidt struck out 10 while combining with two relievers on a four-hitter to beat the Dodgers 3–1 and move the Giants within a game of the NL wild-card lead. After the game, the Giants announced they had acquired veteran outfielder Kenny Lofton from the Chicago White Sox for minor league pitchers Felix Diaz and Ryan Meaux.

To get a six-time All-Star, the Giants gave up two pitchers who would combine to appear in just 18 major league games (all by Diaz). Lofton was a decorated October veteran and he even had the experience of playing in a less than jovial clubhouse during his time in Cleveland. He had the right temperament to be a fit in San Francisco, and although the 35-year-old was past his physical prime—and dealing with a sore hamstring and balky knees—he still represented a threat at the plate.

With Lofton consistently getting on base in the leadoff spot, the Giants were able to apply even more pressure on opponents. The Arizona Diamondbacks appeared to be uncatchable in the NL West, on a pace to win 100 games. But the Giants had one other path to October. On September 9, with Bonds hitting a home run off Odalis Perez measured at 491 feet, the longest in Pacific Bell Park history, the Giants beat the flagging Dodgers 6–5 to draw even with them atop the wild-card standings.

"It's going to be hard for us because I do believe San Francisco has one of the best lineups in baseball," said Perez, already giving a form of concession speech.

The next day, with the Dodgers running out of healthy starting pitchers, they turned to Kevin Brown and hoped their former ace, who hadn't started since May 26, could come back from spinal surgery. Brown's inflamed elbow was an even bigger question mark. They hoped he would have enough left to compete.

He didn't. Lofton singled and scored in the first inning. He doubled and scored in the second inning. The Giants chased Brown after scoring five runs in five innings, and Schmidt was solid again in a 5–2 victory.

The Giants caught fire, but the Dodgers won enough games to stay alive for the wild card entering the final weekend of the season. The Giants would have to fight the whole way.

In their Friday opener against the Astros, Schmidt outpitched Houston's Wade Miller, who hadn't lost in a 16-start stretch that dated to late June. The next day, the Giants clinched. Bonds hit a tiebreaking splash homer in the fifth inning off the Astros' Jeriome Robertson, and backup outfielder Tom Goodwin doubled with the bases loaded to open up a one-run game and send the Giants to a 5–2 victory celebration.

The Giants were ecstatic for several reasons. All through September, the players faced the draining, time zone–hopping prospect of having to make up a rainout in Atlanta from earlier in the season. That became a moot point after they clinched. Adding to their delight, Goodwin was the player who sent their archrivals into a winter chill. The Dodgers had dumped Goodwin in the spring, and were paying nearly all of his $3.5 million salary in 2002. He was collecting their checks and bouncing them from contention all at the same time.

The Giants won 10 of their final 11 games and were back in the playoffs. But they hadn't won a postseason game on the road since 1989, Bonds had never won a postseason series in his life, and, once again, the Atlanta Braves were standing in his way.

The Braves won 101 games on their way to their 11th consecutive division title. They had the lowest rotation ERA in the league, and two future Hall of Famers in Greg Maddux and Tom Glavine. But something about this Giants team was different than the others. Their lineup had an answer for anyone and anything, and as much as you could pitch around Bonds, the Giants didn't need him to beat you.

They smothered Glavine in Game 1 in Atlanta. Snow hit a two-run double in the second inning. Rich Aurilia hit a two-run double in the fourth. Santiago contributed another in the sixth to make it 8–2. Bonds had a single and an intentional walk in five trips, but the Giants still took a relatively easy 8–5 victory.

The Braves came back to win the next two, so the Giants needed to take Game 4 at home to send the series back to Turner Field for a decisive Game 5. The Braves made the fateful decision to start Glavine on short rest, and it backfired. Aurilia hit a three-run home run to drive Glavine to the showers in the third inning and Livan Hernandez came within two outs of a complete game in an 8–3 victory. It was the Giants' first postseason win in an elimination game since Game 6 of the 1962 World Series.

Once again, in Game 5, the Braves turned to a pitcher on short rest. This time it was Kevin Millwood, who mostly cruised in Atlanta's Game 2 victory. Russ Ortiz, who had pitched the Giants to a win in Game 1, would be entrusted to pitch the most important game of his life.

Bonds ruled the day. He singled and scored on Sanders' single in the second inning, then led off the fourth with a home run. The Giants led 3–1 in the ninth, but almost lost a toehold as they were on the verge of finally moving through the division series round. An error and a single put runners at the corners before Robb Nen struck out Gary Sheffield, then got Chipper Jones to hit a grounder that hugged the first-base line. Snow had just taken an extra step toward the chalk and was in position to snag the ball, step on first base, and throw to second in one motion. Aurilia tagged out Julio Franco, and for a full three seconds, Snow was the only one celebrating. Hardly anyone else in Turner Field, or even in the Giants dugout, understood they had just witnessed a game-ending double play.

The victory came on the one-year anniversary of Bonds' 73rd home run.

"I must admit, I'm a little bit shocked," Bonds said. "I've never been past the first round. I don't know how to respond. Should I be happy or just sit here?"

The Giants would advance to play the St. Louis Cardinals for the pennant, and all clubhouse tension aside, they never felt so confident.

They'd already dispatched the team that Sabean called "the beast of the East."

The Giants didn't have home-field advantage but grabbed it quickly enough after winning the first two games at Busch Stadium. They returned home and Bonds provided one of the greatest thrills in the ballpark's history in Game 3, when Chuck Finley, a forkball specialist who made a living throwing in the dirt, tried to bust a fastball inside. The pitch nearly hit Bonds, but his swing was so short and so strong that he whacked it into the cove for a tying, three-run home run in the fifth inning.

Just like Snow's memorable shot against the Mets, in 2000, though, a tying, three-run home run was not enough. The Cardinals' Eli Marrero hit a solo homer off Jay Witasick in the sixth inning and the Giants lost Game 3.

One of two things would happen in Game 4: the Giants would win and take command of the series, or lose and reduce it to a best-of-3 free-for-all. The Cards scratched two runs off Hernandez in the first inning, but Snow got a two-run double to drop in the sixth. The score remained tied in the eighth when Bonds stepped to the plate with two outs and nobody on base. There was no way Cardinals right-hander Rick White would give Bonds anything to hit. St. Louis manager Tony La Russa dropped all pretenses and signaled for an intentional walk.

Santiago was next. His 16 home runs and 73 RBIs were his highest totals in six years, and his presence allowed Baker to flip-flop Kent and Bonds in the lineup during the regular season. When White threw a 3-2 fastball, Santiago swung so hard that his foot slipped and he nearly did a 360-degree spin in the batter's box.

It was the swing that turned the series around. Santiago's two-run home run barely cleared the left-field fence, as the ballpark set what many believed to be a new decibel record.

Nen barely protected the lead in the ninth, as Kerry Robinson reached on a third-strike wild pitch and the Cardinals followed with two singles. Although it wasn't public knowledge at the time, Nen was pitching with major damage in his shoulder. Every pitch squeezed another drop out of his career, and he'd never appear in another big league game after 2002. But he floated a third strike past Albert Pujols, then trusted Santiago to block a slider that struck out J.D. Drew to close out a 4–3 victory that gave the Giants a commanding 3-to-1 lead in the NLCS.

The Giants appeared unstoppable. If you pitched to Bonds, you lost. If you pitched around him, you lost.

"Strategy is judged on whether it works, so it didn't work. Bad strategy," La Russa said after the game. "Bonds is the most dangerous hitter in the game right now and it's tough to walk into [our] clubhouse after giving him a chance to get the hit to beat you. Santiago has been very tough, but it's a little easier to take."

The Giants were one victory away from just their third pennant in more than four decades in San Francisco. And they would have one shot to close it out at home.

As feisty as the Giants could be to each other in their own dugout, they had a way of coming together when encountering an external threat. They prepared to take the field for Game 5, a rematch of the series-opening matchup between Kirk Rueter and Matt Morris—and they hadn't forgotten what happened in Game 1.

Morris, who had a well-earned reputation as a red ass, had served up a home run to Lofton. The Giants' leadoff batter studied the flight of the ball a bit too long and too intently for Morris' liking. The next time up, Lofton received chin music in the form of an inside fastball from reliever Mike Crudale, and barked back at the mound as benches cleared. Baker and La Russa shouted at each other, and nearly had to be separated.

The Cardinals were playing with an emotion that couldn't be measured. They lost iconic Hall of Fame announcer Jack Buck earlier in the season, then endured the tragic and sudden death of pitcher Darryl Kile while on a June road trip in Chicago. Morris was so close to Kile that years later, after he joined the Giants as a free agent, he still couldn't bring himself to talk about his friend's passing.

The Giants knew Morris would be as determined as anyone could be in Game 5 while trying to pitch the series back to St. Louis. But they had their own beloved competitor in Rueter, a left-hander with thinning hair, fringy stuff, a relentlessly sunny disposition, and a knack for keeping hitters off balance. How many ballplayers would be so self-effacing to not only tolerate but embrace a nickname comparing him to Woody from the *Toy Story* movies? Rueter's teammates loved him, especially, because he was apolitical in a clubhouse where the stars could be so polarizing. You didn't have to worry where you stood with Woody. Every side was his good side.

Both pitchers kept the game in check. The Cardinals, who went 3-for-39 with runners in scoring position for the series, collected five singles in the first three innings but were unable to score. Morris didn't allow a base hit until the fifth. But he made a plain enough statement in the fourth, drilling Lofton in the back as plate umpire Tim Welke immediately stepped between them.

Lofton made a show of his slow walk to first base. It was hard to believe that Morris, who had retired the first nine batters, could miss so badly by accident. But the Giants couldn't score Lofton to make the pitcher pay.

They had a chance in the fifth after Santiago drew a leadoff walk and Bell blooped a two-out double to right field. Santiago bumped into Cardinals third baseman Miguel Cairo, and although Baker argued for an obstruction call, umpires determined the contact didn't prevent a run from scoring. Morris got Rueter to ground back to the mound, stranding two runners in scoring position. It was a reminder: in a game like this, any little play, any poor decision, could make the difference.

The Giants made a mistake in the seventh, helping the Cardinals break a scoreless tie. Catcher Mike Matheny hit a leadoff double against Felix Rodriguez that glanced off Lofton's glove in center field, then Morris put down a bunt to the left side of the mound. Rodriguez, perhaps emboldened because the lead runner was a catcher, tried for the out at third base. It was a bad gamble; the Giants didn't record an out, and Fernando Vina followed with a sacrifice fly.

If the Giants hoped to win the pennant and avoid a return trip to St. Louis, they would have to go through Morris. The way he was pitching, that appeared to be a faint hope.

But Lofton found a way to put Morris in the stretch three times. He singled in the sixth inning to snap an 0-for-16 streak that had begun immediately after his homer in Game 1. Then with one out in the eighth, Lofton fought off an 0-2 pitch and singled up the middle. Aurilia followed with a single to left field as the crowd came to life. Morris faced Kent and played a hunch that he'd be cheating on a first-pitch fastball. Morris was certain: one good curveball and Kent would roll it over for a double play. He tried to throw the pitch of his life.

He overthrew it, and Kent made little attempt to get out of the way. Matheny, from behind the plate, implored Kent to bail out as the pitch approached. But Kent was no fool. The Giants would take bases loaded for Bonds, thank you very much.

The Cardinals had walked Bonds 10 times in the series. After Morris hit Kent with a curveball, they had no choice. Morris threw a 95-mph fastball and Bonds hit it just short of the warning track in left field. A Pacific Bell Park crowd that erupted for so many monumental home runs got nearly as loud for a sacrifice fly, as Lofton scored the tying run without a throw.

It stayed tied in the ninth, when La Russa again showed faith in Morris by letting him bat against right-hander Tim Worrell with one out. Morris struck out. The Giants would have the advantage that all home teams enjoy when it's tied in the bottom of the ninth. They would get a chance to end the game with one swing.

Morris recorded two quick outs and the game appeared destined for extra innings. Instead, the next four pitches decided everything.

Bell stepped to the plate. He had never reached a World Series and neither had his father, Buddy, over an 18-year career. His grandfather,

Gus Bell, made it once over his 15 seasons, getting three at-bats in 1961 for a Cincinnati Reds team that barely stood a chance against the Yankees.

Bell knew the Cardinals were going hitter-to-hitter with Morris. He knew Morris didn't want to come out of the game. He anticipated a strike on the first pitch, and he lined it to center field for a single.

Shawon Dunston was next, and like Bell, he had never been to a World Series. Such is the curse of being the No. 1 pick in the country when the Chicago Cubs hold the first selection. Dunston was 39, in the final season of his 18-year career and his second stint with the Giants, and served an important role in the clubhouse. He could talk to almost anyone, including Bonds, without backing down. He did more than any player that season to keep the peace.

Dunston had entered the game on a double-switch in the eighth, and struck out on a curveball—his first at-bat of the NLCS, and just his second in the playoffs. This was the first time in more than two weeks that he had multiple plate appearances in the same game. But Dunston had played with Morris in St. Louis and, like Bell before him, figured Morris would come right after him.

Morris threw a 1-0 fastball and Dunston served it back up the middle. Another hit.

Morris was brilliant all night while pitching with a heavy heart, and La Russa showed him as much faith as any manager could. But he would not let Morris face Lofton one more time. As the pitcher walked back to the dugout, Dunston stood on first base and held out a thumbs-up while shouting encouragement. Morris returned a weary smile.

Like Morris, Cardinals left-hander Steve Kline would end up wearing a Giants uniform before the end of the decade. He would never reach a World Series with them, though. His most memorable contribution to Giants history would happen while wearing a Cardinals uniform.

It was just one pitch.

Amid a cacophony of inflatable thunder sticks, a blizzard of white rally towels, and a deafening noise that Pratt & Whitney couldn't replicate, Kline came set and delivered a slider. Lofton took a slashing swing. The

Kenny Lofton's game-winning hit in Game 5 of the 2002 NLCS sent the Giants to the World Series for the third time since the team moved to the West Coast.

ball streaked into right field, where Drew collected it. There was never a doubt about sending Bell from second base, even though speed was not among his better attributes.

"As soon as I saw it go over [Fernando] Vina's head," Lofton said, "I said, 'We're going to the World Series.' And then I said, 'Come on, David. Go, man. Go.' I was going like, 'Go, go, please go.' It seemed like the ball never got to the outfield after I hit it. And it seemed like David never got to third base. It was like everything stopped. It was crazy, man."

Recalled Bell: "It was like it was all happening in slow motion. I don't know if that's a good thing or not. I mean, I'm not the fastest guy in the world."

Drew needed to make a perfect throw. It was nowhere near the plate. Matheny scrambled in vain to catch it 10 feet up the first-base line, Bell slid across the dish on his stomach, and his teammates were on him immediately. Kline, in an act of duty over sanity, had been backing up the throw home. He felt a wave at his back as the Giants surged past him to embrace Bell, to embrace Lofton, to shove and hug and tackle anyone or anything.

Bonds was the first player out of the dugout, high-kicking straight for Lofton, who couldn't resist a couple of long looks into the Cardinals dugout.

"Sometimes you have to let sleeping dogs lie," Lofton said amid the clubhouse celebration. "They ended up hitting me, but I kept my focus. I said, 'I'm going to get you sooner or later.'"

Bonds was headed to the World Series for the first time in his 17-year career. The Giants would oppose the Anaheim Angels in the first ever matchup of two wild-card teams. Santiago, who was named NLCS MVP for his heroics in Game 4, was bound for his first Fall Classic as well.

"The only thing I told Kenny when he got here was, 'You've been there before. I'm in the water. Just take me to the land,'" said Santiago, after spraying fans with champagne in a victory lap around the warning track. "He became the hero tonight. That's why I'm sitting here as the MVP."

In July, Sabean believed that Lofton still had something left, and he'd be proven right in October and beyond. Lofton would go on to play for seven different teams over the next five seasons, getting back to the playoffs four more times.

Lofton was a Giant for just 46 games, and 17 more in the postseason—less than 3 percent of his 17-year career. But with a swing on a first-pitch slider, he provided one of the most indelible moments in franchise history. The Giants hadn't won the pennant in a walk-off since Bobby Thomson hit the Shot Heard 'Round the World in 1951. This time, a bases-loaded sacrifice fly and a line single to right field got the job done in a 2–1 victory.

For just the third time in the Giants' West Coast history, and in just their third season at Pacific Bell Park, the World Series was coming to San Francisco.

The team that scrapped together stayed together. And in a quiet moment among the October celebrations, Kent dropped his guard and made an admission to longtime beat reporter Nick Peters of the *Sacramento Bee*.

That fight in the San Diego dugout? It really was a big deal.

"When Barry and I scuffled, it was a turning point," Kent said. "It showed the guys on the team, the front office, and the fans how much we really cared. That cleared the air. It showed we were serious about getting something done this season."

Chapter 5

Out of Harm's Way

"Some people think it's cute, but I don't."
—Dusty Baker

Thursday, October 24, 2002
World Series Game 5 vs. Anaheim

You could use so many unflattering words to describe Candlestick Park. But there was an admirable toughness about the place. The fans had to be tough to come out night after night, in their July blankets and overcoats, passing the loyalty test merely by showing up.

And in 1989, when the Giants were minutes away from hosting their first World Series game in 27 years, the stadium had to be tough enough to withstand the most damaging, devastating earthquake to hit the region in almost a century.

Candlestick Park was put to the test. The gray lady shook, and stood.

Years later, Dusty Baker would drive by Candlestick on his way to the Giants' new home on China Basin and allow himself to feel a pang of regret.

"It sure looks raggedy now," Baker said in 2002. "I think about all the guys that played there, and never a championship there. And quite frankly, you don't know how badly I wanted to win our last year at Candlestick Park. That would have meant more to me than even now because this stadium can go on for years and years. But at that time, that meant more to me, trying to win there, than actually it does to win here."

The Giants were in their third season at Candlestick Park when they reached the World Series in 1962. Their third season in Pacific Bell Park proved to be the charm, too, and this much was indisputable: they wouldn't have gotten there without Barry Bonds.

He finally passed his own October test, the one his critics always had marked with red ink.

After the 2000 NL Division Series loss to the Mets, in which Bonds went 3-for-17 with one RBI, he was a three-time NL MVP with a .196 career average in the postseason. He had one home run in 97 playoff at-bats. His teams failed to advance in all five of his postseason series, plus a wild-card tiebreaker loss in 1998 at Wrigley Field.

With the Pirates, where Bonds won two NL MVP awards, his last legacy-shaping act was a dying gasp of a throw that couldn't cut down a lead-footed Sid Bream at the plate as the Atlanta Braves stormed to the pennant in 1992.

In his first nine seasons as a Giant, Bonds won two NL MVP awards and had four more top-five finishes. He received five more Gold Gloves (for a total of eight). Yet the Giants won just one playoff game over that time. Superstars were no guarantee in October. Mays and McCovey never won it all in San Francisco, either.

So in 2000, after two losses at Shea Stadium ousted the Giants in the first round again, the team silently boarded a charter flight home. Bonds sought counsel. He wandered around the plane until he spotted J.T. Snow, and asked to take a seat.

"Barry sat there for more than two hours, and he totally opened up to me," Snow said. "He told me he can't sleep at night, he paces in his hotel room. He didn't know why he was struggling in the postseason, but he felt he had to carry the team.

"It was unbelievable. Here's the best player in the game, talking to me, asking me how I relax, because he'd seen me playing well in the postseason. I remember it being one of the best baseball conversations I've ever had. He's talking to me for two hours, telling me how much pressure he puts on himself and how everybody knows it."

Snow told Bonds what he needed to hear. Maybe it was what Bonds always needed to hear. He didn't need to prove anything to anyone. He didn't need to demonstrate his worth. Everyone already knew how good he was. Everyone, perhaps, except Barry himself, a gnawing fear he papered over with so many superficial boasts.

"It's one of the best memories I have in baseball, that conversation with him," Snow said. "And in 2002, he totally went off."

Bonds hit three home runs in the NLDS against the Braves, his old nemesis, including one in a decisive Game 5 at Turner Field. The Giants finally broke through that first round, and Bonds kept delivering against the Cardinals in the NLCS.

"Once I got past the ghosts," he said, "I just played baseball."

When the Giants clinched the pennant on Kenny Lofton's walk-off single in Game 5, Bonds was the first to hoist him in the air. But following that moment of celebration, as his teammates continued to pose for smiling pictures and spray champagne, Bonds' mood noticeably cooled.

"I think he got really excited," Rich Aurilia noted that night, "and then he caught himself."

Aside from a cup of water his son overturned on him, Bonds stayed dry amid the celebration.

"I'm satisfied with what we've accomplished, but I don't want this to be the end of it," Bonds said. "Thanks for coming, but it's not over yet. We still have a lot to say in the World Series. It's been a great party but it's not over.

"When we win the World Series, I'll celebrate."

Bonds had a sense for what would happen after the season: Jeff Kent, as combative and difficult as he could be, was almost sure to leave as a free agent and the Giants would have the impossible task of replacing him. David Bell and Reggie Sanders would be free agents, too. If the Giants didn't win now, they'd have to do it with Bonds, at the end of his thirties, carrying even more of the load—and probably seeing even fewer pitches to hit.

"I'll never understand that about baseball," said Sanders, who knew he wouldn't be back under any circumstances. "A team wins and they dismantle it. I don't get that. I guess I never will."

Baker was in the final year of his contract, too, and it was common knowledge that he hadn't been on friendly terms with managing partner Peter Magowan since spring training.

"He felt slighted by that statement in the spring, when I said that it was our best team in 10 years," Magowan said. "He felt I was putting pressure on him. That was not my intention. I put it out there because that's what the players told me, and I wanted to reflect it. It shows I believe in them, which I did."

Baker often told players they had to reinvent themselves every few years. He knew, after 10 seasons on the Giants bench, the time was approaching for himself. A cancer scare removed the last trappings of fear that come with accepting a new challenge.

Bonds had a different motivation. He believed that becoming a World Series champion would change the way people thought about him. All politics and spin aside, he knew this was his best, perhaps last chance.

The Giants were facing Anaheim in the first all-wild-card matchup in World Series history. The Angels dragged their own woeful past into the Fall Classic. No one could say "one strike away" in more doleful tones than Angels fans, who had the 1986 AL pennant in their hands before Donnie Moore gave up a home run to Boston's Dave Henderson. Moore committed suicide less than three years later. The Angels were the franchise that endured tragedy with the death of Lyman Bostock, that narrowly avoided casualties when their team bus crashed, that forever played in the 40-mile shadow of the Dodgers. They had ghosts, too.

Against the Giants, though, their main problem was dealing with the specter of Bonds, who was writing an entirely new reputation for himself in October.

Prior to Game 1, Angels pitching coach Bud Black approached Bonds near the batting cage and tried to start some light banter, telling him not to worry, that he would see some strikes in the series.

"He was indifferent," Black said. "You know Barry. He didn't give a… he didn't respond. All I did was infer he wasn't going to get walked 20 times in this series."

No, but the Angels came close. As the two teams split the first four games of the series, the Angels walked Bonds nine times—five of them intentional. He still hit three home runs in eight at-bats, including a shot off Jarrod Washburn in his first World Series plate appearance. Snow and Reggie Sanders also homered to back Jason Schmidt in a 4–3 victory at Edison Field.

A night later, the Angels evened the series in an 11–10 victory, though the game's most memorable moment was a home run from Bonds in the ninth. The Angels had blown a five-run first-inning lead they built off Russ Ortiz, but rallied back from a 9–7 deficit and took the lead on Tim Salmon's two-run shot off Felix Rodriguez in the eighth. The Angels already had walked Bonds three times in the game. But with a two-run lead, two outs, and the bases empty in the ninth, there was no question: headstrong closer Troy Percival had free rein to challenge Bonds.

Percival squinted for a sign that everyone could see: he would rear back and throw as hard as he could. It was power against superhuman power, and for all of Bonds' October misery, this was the kind of confrontation he simply no longer lost. The second pitch was 96 mph and Bonds hit a shot that would have made Dennis Tankersley blush. It soared above the right-field wall and disappeared down a tunnel near the top of the right-field stands. Bonds dropped his bat, walked out of the box, and the Fox broadcast cut to a tight shot on Salmon in the dugout. He was saying, clearly, "That's the farthest ball I've ever seen hit."

More than a decade later, fans still came up to Salmon and mentioned his "farthest ball" comment more often than anything else he did or said in his respected career.

Bonds wasn't giving the media much lip service of any kind. He was as standoffish as ever, leading one reporter to ask Baker if his star was having any fun.

"Yeah, I believe he's having fun," Baker said. "Hard not to have fun when you're hitting balls halfway to the moon."

The home run was monumental but not instrumental. The Angels still won the game and tied the series.

The Giants lost Game 3 at home but came back from a three-run deficit to take a 4–3 victory in Game 4. They managed to come out ahead even though the Angels contained Bonds early in the game, twice issuing intentional walks and then getting Benito Santiago to ground into double plays.

It took some luck in the fifth inning to win Game 4: an infield single from Kirk Rueter, a bunt single from Lofton that weaved fair, then foul, then just fair on the third-base chalk as Troy Glaus picked it up a moment too late, a flared single to right field from Aurilia, then a sacrifice fly. It was an automatic decision to issue a third intentional walk to Bonds with first base open and one out. With one more chance, Santiago came through with a tying single.

The Giants received another break in the eighth when Snow advanced on a passed ball, then scored on David Bell's single to center off hard-throwing rookie Francisco Rodriguez. Robb Nen saved the one-run victory.

The World Series was reduced to a best-of-three, and Bonds already had set single-season playoff records with seven home runs and 23 walks, 11 of them intentional. The Giants had one more game to play at Pacific Bell Park, an unstoppable force in the middle of their lineup, and their best pitcher, Schmidt, taking the mound for Game 5.

Bonds had nothing to prove, and everything to achieve.

"You won't find this at the NBA Finals or the Super Bowl," said Fox Sports World Series pregame host Jeanne Zelasko, introducing a feature story on the Giants' batboys, including adorable three-year-old Darren Baker.

"Going to the office with Daddy, you have to do a little work, but you get the best seat in the house," said Zelasko, as Fox showed footage of little Darren swimming in his uniform, toddling along, forever chasing an oversized helmet as it kept rolling away. "It's the Giants' secret weapon. Let's be honest. The little guy is a good-luck charm. Whenever he goes with Daddy to work, they're 7–0."

That's how it was all season. That's always how it was when Dusty managed. Shawon Dunston's son was a batboy. So was Nikolai Bonds. Little Darren was the youngest and most precocious, and it's true, the Giants hadn't lost whenever he was in the dugout. He had a cold in Anaheim and watched Game 2 from a hotel suite with his mother. When the Giants fell behind 5–0 in the first inning, he begged to go to the ballpark. The team needed him, he pleaded.

"To me it adds life to your workplace," Baker said in the pregame TV piece. "It adds some humor, because they're going to do something or say something to crack you up and keep you loose. At the same time, how many boys get to go to work with your dad? That's one the joys of our occupation."

The romper room dugout was excessive, no doubt. But for Baker, it served a purpose—especially on a team that had its share of prickly personalities and clubhouse friction. (Bonds, when approached by reporters after the stirring comeback win in Game 4, told the group to "go leave me alone and do something else for a living.")

It wasn't the family atmosphere, though, that loosened up the Giants when they took the field for Game 5. They found a better way: three runs in the first inning, three more in the second inning, and a 6–0 lead.

A stubborn Jarrod Washburn once again tried to challenge Bonds and lost while giving up an RBI double in the first inning. When Washburn issued Bonds an intentional walk the next inning, Santiago lined a two-run single.

The Giants led big, but tension would grip the ballpark again. The Angels' relentless lineup kept fouling off pitches until they broke Schmidt in the fifth inning, and it was a two-run game in the sixth when Aurilia lined a two-out single off the glove of Glaus at third base.

Kent stepped to the plate against sidearm right-hander Ben Weber, and he noticed that the Angels didn't have a left-hander getting warm in the bullpen even though Bonds was on deck. Manager Mike Scioscia had no desire to face Bonds with runners on base. As surely as Bonds would get four balls, Kent would see strikes.

Everyone knew this could and likely would be Kent's last home game as a Giant. He could be as hard to embrace as Bonds was. On the field, he was as outwardly emotional as a bat rack. So after Kent connected on a flat slider and sent it soaring into the left-field bleachers, he offered the smallest of fist pumps. It was a tiny display of emotion. For Kent, it was a revelation.

"I think that's the first time I've ever done that," Kent said. "I did show a little something there. It was the last game at Pac Bell Park, in the World Series, and with our bullpen, I finally had the feeling that would be enough [to win]. The guys got a little emotional, and so did I."

Kent entered Game 5 batting just .188 in the series, and his inability to come through with runners on base allowed the Angels to pitch around Bonds the previous two games. If this would be his final home game as a Giant, he wanted to ensure he'd be missed. And when Kent batted again in the seventh inning against Scot Shields, he hit another two-run shot.

"This World Series," said Kent, "is bigger and better than anything the free-agent market can bring."

Courtesy of Kent's two home runs, 10 total bases, and record-tying four runs scored, the game had become a blowout. The ballpark throbbed with energy and the Giants were one more win away from the first World Series title in the club's San Francisco era. The Giants wouldn't need Nen to pitch in the 16–4 victory.

But the Giants needed a save. Snow swooped in and recorded it. And was it ever a precious one.

It happened as the Giants led 8–4 in the seventh, Snow stood on third base, and Bell on second. Lofton ripped a pitch off the right-field arcade for a triple. As Snow looked down to find the plate, he detected movement off to the side. He knew instantly what it was.

The manager's son. His three-and-a-half-year-old son.

"Darren, he does such a great job going out and getting the bats—he's so eager all the time—I knew it was him," Snow said. "I have a four-and-a-half-year-old son of my own at home, and I know how to get a hold of

The Giants moved one game away from winning the World Series in 2002 after claiming Game 5, but everyone was talking about manager Dusty Baker's son, Darren, getting pulled out of harm's way by J.T. Snow. (AP Images)

them when they're running away. I reached down, luckily grabbed him by the collar of the jacket as he was crossing home plate.

"I didn't want him to get hurt. His eyes were huge. I don't think he knew what was going on."

In the dugout, Baker cupped a hand to his face in embarrassment as Snow carried the stunned child down the stairs. Little Darren would have toddled in front of the plate—and into a collision course with Bell, who was chugging home—had Snow not noticed him and interceded.

Darren ran onto the field because Lofton was his favorite player, and he wanted to retrieve his bat. Snow had a little talk with him during the inning, just to make sure the boy wasn't too rattled by the experience. They bumped fists.

After the game, the Darren Baker story received more attention than Kent, or Bonds, or even the fact the Giants had taken a 3–2 edge in the World Series. This was compelling human interest on a national stage, with millions of viewers holding their breath while fearing for the safety of a child. Dusty Baker had some explaining to do—starting with his own wife and also his mother, who had warned him about letting Darren wander onto the field.

"First call I got back in the clubhouse was my mom, to tell me, 'I know you listen to me sometimes. Just listen to me this time,'" Baker said. "She told me to thank J.T. so I thanked him for saving him."

A day later, the questions from the media persisted, and Baker's answers took on a more serious tone.

"It's not going to happen again," Baker said. "I'm not proud of it. I don't like seeing my son all over TV in that light. Some people think it's cute, but I don't. I don't like seeing him in the paper. He told me himself he's tired of being in the paper.

"I'm just hoping they don't come up with some Darren Baker rule that prohibits kids from being in the dugout, being able to do these things."

The league did exactly that after the 2002 season, stipulating that batboys had to be at least 14 years old. (A decade later, when Baker was managing the Cincinnati Reds against the Giants in the 2012 NL Division Series, Darren still wasn't old enough to be the team's batboy.)

When the Giants traveled to Anaheim in search of one more victory, though, there was no question Darren would make the trip.

"He's a good-luck charm right now," Snow said. "We need him as much as we need any of our players."

It turned out the Giants needed more than luck.

The Giants had a five-run lead, the plastic sheets up, and the champagne cold when they stood eight outs away from a clinching victory in Game 6 at Edison Field. The vote already had been taken in the press box and Bonds would be World Series MVP.

But Baker pulled Ortiz in the seventh inning—a failed decision in what was one of his final acts as the team's manager. With the Rally Monkey incessantly jumping on the scoreboard, Scott Spiezio slipped a three-run home run over the fence against Felix Rodriguez. The awakened Angels completed their comeback in the eighth as Glaus hit a two-run double off Nen to take a stunning 6–5 victory.

The Giants, still dazed a day later, never snapped out of it. They sent Livan Hernandez to the mound for Game 7 even though Kirk Rueter was a popular choice in the clubhouse. The Angels took a 4–1 lead after three innings, and that's what the score remained to the Giants' last breath.

Bonds, in his first World Series appearance, hit .471 with a .700 on-base percentage. The Angels walked him 13 times, seven of them intentional. He still hit four home runs and two doubles in 17 at-bats.

But the prize he most wanted was denied. Baker said his heart felt heavy and his stomach felt empty. Kent said, "Everyone here, the fans, the owner, the front office, everybody—they are ticked off and they rightfully should be. We were close. We were as close as you could be."

Bonds barely spoke above a whisper as he stared, as if in a trance, straight over the top of the media crush after the Game 7 loss. This was the last place he wanted to stand. It wasn't good enough. It would never be good enough.

"Doesn't that just show you," he said, "that it takes a team to win it?"

Chapter 6

The Stars Come Out

"It's a four-letter word, and 'oh' is in front of it."
—Ken Griffey Jr.

Tuesday, July 10, 2007
The 78th Major League Baseball All-Star Game

The Giants couldn't have financed their idyllic little ballpark in China Basin without a $50 million naming-rights deal from the local phone company.

But the agreement had its headaches. Thanks to deregulation and consolidation within the telecommunications industry, the stadium signage had to be swapped out a couple times.

Pacific Bell Park became the much less lyrical SBC Park in 2003, when Southwestern Bell out of San Antonio began gobbling up other regional carriers. The park changed names again in 2006, to AT&T Park, when SBC swallowed an even bigger fish and rebranded itself.

No matter what the shingle said, the Giants knew from the moment they put shovels in the ground that they had secured a place near the front of the line for the All-Star Game to return to San Francisco. The Giants hadn't hosted the game since 1984, when intense shadows due to the 5:00 PM start at Candlestick Park led to brutal hitting conditions and a conga line of strikeouts.

But MLB commissioner Bud Selig kept the Giants waiting. He prioritized his former team when he awarded the 2002 game to the Milwaukee Brewers—and it became a debacle, called a draw when both teams ran out of rested pitchers in the 11th inning. Two years later, the game went to Houston. Another two years after that, Pittsburgh played host. Some within the Giants organization began to wonder: was the league snubbing them because they privately financed their ballpark? Did they hope to delay the game in San Francisco long enough for Barry Bonds to slip away into retirement?

Their intense lobbying made an eventual impact, because Selig broke long-standing protocol when he finally awarded the Giants the 2007 midsummer classic. Coming on the heels of the game in Pittsburgh, it marked the first time since 1953 that the venue didn't rotate from one league to the other in consecutive years.

AT&T Park already had played host to three playoff seasons in its first four years, including a World Series. But ever since the 2003 team won 100 regular season games and the Florida Marlins rolled them in the first round, the Giants had fallen back in the standings. The strategy of propping up a Bonds-centric roster with veteran players had taken its toll, especially on the farm system, as the Giants were all too swift to punt compensatory draft picks—on purpose, in some cases—in order to redirect bonus money to the major league payroll.

The Giants narrowly missed the playoffs in 2004, and with Bonds lost to multiple knee surgeries, they plunged to a losing record the following two seasons. Attendance dipped just enough to cause ownership to fret. Managing partner Peter Magowan tried to recapture the marketplace the way he did 14 years earlier, by making a splash on the free-agent market. Prior to the '07 season, the Giants shocked the industry by signing former A's pitcher Barry Zito, a one-time Cy Young Award winner whom many scouts saw as in decline, to a seven-year, $126 million contract.

The Bonds move was a stroke of genius. The Zito move ended up being Magowan's downfall.

The Giants had a new manager in 2007, too, after Felipe Alou's four-year contract came to an end and Bruce Bochy became available following a shake-up in the San Diego Padres' front office. Bonds, now 42 years old and considered the embodiment of baseball's steroids era to most of the country, began the season 21 home runs away from matching Hank Aaron's all-time record. It was a heavy-handed message from Giants management when the media guide cover that season depicted Zito and Bochy, instead.

The Giants were a bad baseball team in 2007. They ended the first half with a 38–48 record, entering the break with a loss after Zito got shelled in St. Louis. They sent just one All-Star to their own game, and that was only after a painfully massive campaign—along with a few rumored shenanigans behind the scenes—pushed Bonds ahead of Alfonso Soriano in the final week of fan balloting to secure a starting spot in the NL outfield.

"I don't think people dislike me—I just don't," said Bonds, after the final tally was announced. "People in San Francisco know me. The fans outside the city only get to see me three days. To judge me on a third party, that's what disappoints me. You're judging me based on a third party when actually I've done nothing wrong to you. I've gone to your stadium and tried to entertain you. I've just tried to play my game the best I can."

It was one of Selig's most awkward moments: he was forced not only to acknowledge a player he considered a personal pariah and a usurper to the game's most revered record held by one of his most cherished friends, but to make him the centerpiece attraction in one of the sport's jewel events.

Bonds entered the break just four home runs away from tying Aaron's record, and Giants officials begged him to participate in the Home Run Derby. This was his ballpark, his venue, and his home. They wanted him to put on a show.

The Giants profited off his talent—oh, did they ever—but they paid a price for it in more ways than one. They put up with his moods and demands. The derby, they felt, was a way for him to give back. He owed it to them.

"I don't think so," said Bonds, who won the derby in 1996 at Philadelphia. "I don't have anything to prove in that."

Instead, Bonds hosted a private All-Star bash at a restaurant in San Francisco on the night of the derby, which Vladimir Guerrero won after nearly hitting the giant glove in left field with a blast measured at 503 feet.

Despite all the power hitters in the field, left-handed hitters—including defending champion Ryan Howard—didn't stand a chance at AT&T Park. Not a single baseball splashed down fair in McCovey Cove, making it a dull night for the armada of watercraft beyond the right-field fence.

The competition was missing the man who owned 34 of the 58 splash homers in the ballpark's eight-year history.

"For him to do what he does every time…" Howard said of Bonds. "You definitely get an appreciation for it."

In a curious move, the Bonds/Aaron home run counter was taken down in right field and replaced with a Major League Baseball advertisement during the derby. A day earlier, the advertisement covered Bonds' name and home run total but left the totals of Aaron, Babe Ruth, and Willie Mays visible on the wall.

Conspiracy theorists saw it as a clear snub of Bonds. Giants executive vice president Larry Baer claimed that the league controlled stadium advertising decisions for peripheral All-Star events, and there was no malicious intent.

Bonds acted like he didn't care about much of anything. When he arrived for the game, he bragged that he had stayed out past 3:00 AM at his party.

"This game isn't going to turn out well," Bonds said. "Really, guys. You'll have to forgive me if I go 0-for-5. I don't care though. My party is more fun."

Bonds was hitting second in the NL lineup, an unusual spot for him. Even though he was the only Giants representative on the team, he told NL manager Tony La Russa that he wasn't interested in playing more than three innings. Hit him high enough in the lineup, get him a second at-bat, and get him out.

At least Bonds had assurances from AL skipper Jim Leyland, his former manager in Pittsburgh, that he would get a pitch over the plate.

"I'm going to answer this question even though it hasn't been asked: I will not intentionally walk Barry Bonds in the All-Star Game," Leyland said.

Bonds responded with two of his favorite traits: boldness and skepticism.

"You throw me three fastballs, you let me know it's coming, I'm going to put it in the cove," Bonds said sharply. "You tell Leyland that. You throw me a changeup and don't tell me, okay then. But if you tell me what's coming, that water's not far enough."

While a Bonds home run in the All-Star Game wouldn't count in his pursuit of Aaron, it certainly would rank as one of the most theatrical in his 15 seasons as a Giant.

"He'll get fastballs from me if I face him," Cleveland Indians pitcher CC Sabathia said. "Hey, man, it's the All-Star Game. Everyone will be coming after Barry. That's what everyone wants to see."

Bonds did not hit a home run in the game. Someone else did, though—and made All-Star history.

When Ichiro Suzuki arrived with the Seattle Mariners in 2001, he was more than the first Japanese-born-and-raised position player in major league history. He was more than a seven-time batting champion with Orix.

He was a fully formed brand. He wore his first name on the back of his uniform—the first major-leaguer permitted to do that since Vida Blue in the 1970s.

He spent the majority of his first spring training fouling off fastballs into the stands above the third-base dugout. Some scouts, perhaps acting on the stereotype that Japanese hitters weren't strong enough to compete in the big leagues, doubted Ichiro could hit 95-mph heat. They didn't understand: he was flicking off those fastballs on purpose. He wanted to get a book on the pitchers he would be facing.

Ichiro's rookie season ranks as perhaps the most accomplished debut by a position player in major league history: 242 hits (the most by anyone since 1930), a batting title (.350 average), a league-best 56 stolen bases, an AL MVP award, and the AL Rookie of the Year honor, of course. The Mariners won a staggering 116 games in the regular season. In an era of muscled-up slugging, the most valuable player in the American League killed opponents with infield hits and blinding speed. And when pitchers tried to bust him inside, he could turn his hips and yank a homer down the line, too.

Ichiro's success was historic beyond the records he set. His impact at the major league level served to challenge long-held perceptions and opened minds of talent evaluators and front office personnel. After Ichiro, an everyday position player could come from anywhere or look like anyone. The runs scored and stolen bases aside, the greatest contribution a player can make to baseball is to expand its horizons, to make it more inclusive. Ichiro was more than a revelation to the game. He was a gift.

Of course, Ichiro also made the All-Star team as a rookie—the first of what would become 10 consecutive appearances. And there, at the midsummer classic, he found a whole new way to surprise his teammates.

Although he used an interpreter for his interviews and mostly kept a reserved profile, Ichiro knew more English than he let on. He'd also let his wry sense of humor slip out here and there, like the time he was asked about playing a makeup game in Cleveland.

"If I ever saw myself saying I'm excited going to Cleveland, I'd punch myself in the face, because I'm lying," he said through a translator.

Once, in a formal TV interview, sitting in plush chairs at the center of a dignified drawing room, Bob Costas asked Ichiro if he had a favorite

American expression. Ichiro laughed, started to answer, laughed some more, then figured, what the hell:

"August…in Kansas City…it's…it's…hotter than two rats ****ing [in a] wool sock."

Costas laughed so hard he almost fell out of his chair.

That was just a crayon swipe. Ichiro's biggest blue streak spilled out once a year, at every All-Star Game, just before the American League players walked out for pregame introductions. Ichiro would appear out of nowhere and charge into the center of the clubhouse, screaming and shouting and stringing together all manner of expletives while disparaging the National League. It was hilarious. It was brilliant. It was "The Aristocrats," turned into a motivational speech. And it couldn't have come from a more unexpected source.

Boston's David Ortiz made sure Ichiro kept the tradition alive year after year. It stayed a well-kept secret until Jeff Passan of Yahoo! Sports got wind of it, and started asking questions. Passan wasn't able to report the particulars of what Ichiro actually said, both because he wrote for a family website and because every player he interviewed couldn't stop laughing at the memory.

Longtime Minnesota Twins first baseman Justin Morneau, a first-time All-Star in 2007, recalled Ichiro's speech from just prior to the game at AT&T Park:

"He was sitting in his locker back there, and David Ortiz said, 'Ichi's got something to say.' And then he pops out and everybody started dying. I had no idea it was coming. It was hilarious.

"It's hard to explain the effect that it has. You know, it's such a tense environment. Everyone's kind of nervous for the game. He doesn't say a lot the whole time he's in there, and all of a sudden the manager gets done with his speech, and he pops off. It's pretty funny."

Ichiro once was asked how he would react if one of his speeches ever got posted online.

"If I were to see that on the Internet," he said, "I'd probably want to go home."

The American Leaguers hardly needed inspiration or a confidence boost heading into the game at AT&T Park. They held a nine-game winning streak in the All-Star Game, not counting the embarrassing tie in Milwaukee.

The ballpark at Third and King never looked so grand, festooned in red, white, and blue bunting as the best players in both leagues tipped their caps and flashed "Hi Mom" messages on their batting gloves during introductions.

Bonds was cheered loudest and longest, 30 seconds solid—the first time he could remember being cheered at an All-Star Game. Even if most of the country couldn't understand it, and even criticized Giants fans for it, this remained his bubble of unconditional love. He was among family here.

"You can't explain it, the feelings you have inside, you just can't," Bonds said. "To be home, on your stage, it's amazing. To be able to wait 22 years and have this opportunity to have an All-Star Game in my hometown, it's a dream."

The Giants took occasion to shine the spotlight on another icon as Willie Mays made the long, slow walk from center field to throw a ceremonial first pitch.

Mays removed pieces of clothing as he went, knowing what they'd fetch at an auction house. He gave his jacket to Bonds, his jersey to Ken Griffey Jr. He didn't care one bit that he was down to his undershirt when a national television audience watched him lob the first pitch home.

Greatness does not adhere to a dress code.

Jake Peavy took the ball for the NL and managed a scoreless first inning after Ichiro chopped a single on the second pitch of the game.

The NL got on the board in the bottom of the inning. Jose Reyes hit a leadoff single against Dan Haren, and then stole second base. Reporters slapped their foreheads in the press box. Leave first base open for Bonds? It's clear Reyes hadn't been watching too many Giants games over the previous seven years.

But Leyland was good to his word. He did not order up an intentional walk.

In pregame batting practice, a day after nobody reached the water in the Home Run Derby, a 42-year-old Bonds lofted the second pitch he saw into McCovey Cove. The crowd cheered and buzzed: could Bonds create a magical moment, as Cal Ripken Jr. did when he homered in his final All-Star Game?

The fans whooped and flashbulbs exploded in a series of twinkles with every pitch thrown to him. Bonds fouled off a 1-1 offering, and then hit a drive to right field as the crowd gasped. But he caught it thin. The line drive still carried almost to the warning track for an out.

For the entirety of the decade, whenever the stage was most brightly lit at AT&T Park for a milestone home run, Bonds had a knack for delivering. But not this time.

Griffey singled home Reyes and the NL still led 1–0 when Bonds batted again in the third against Josh Beckett. Reyes led off the inning with a double, and once again, with first base open, Leyland played it straight.

Bonds had a bit of fun, faking a bunt on the first pitch. He fouled the next offering and then barely missed crushing the 1-1 pitch, hitting a deep out to left field. Bonds wishfully hopped up and down out of the batter's box as the ball was caught on the track, then wearily raised both arms as he jogged back to the dugout and the cheers washed over him.

He told La Russa that he'd get two at-bats and call it quits. Two near misses didn't change his mind.

The Bonds show was over.

The Ichiro show was about to begin.

Chris Young, the 6'10" former basketball player from Princeton, was making the first and only All-Star appearance of his career, and his nerves might have shown in the fifth inning when he took the mound and issued a leadoff walk to Baltimore's Brian Roberts.

Ichiro already was 2-for-2 when he batted with one out. Would he try to bunt for a hit? Maybe slap a single to the left side? Instead, he faced a power pitcher and tried to supply his own. Young threw a first-pitch fastball and Ichiro turned on it, driving the ball over Griffey's head and toward the right-field arcade.

Griffey had played enough games at AT&T Park to know that whenever the ball hit the bricks beyond the sixth archway, it almost always kicked toward center field. He backed off and drifted toward center, like a power forward getting ready to box out for a defensive rebound.

But the ball had other ideas.

The drive glanced off the seventh archway, and under normal circumstances, it would have taken a dead bounce off the chain-link fence. But the league installed additional signage in the form of plastic sheeting that was wrapped tightly around the bottom of the archways. Ichiro's ball hit the signage and instead of deflecting toward center, it kicked hard right.

A phrase flashed through Griffey's mind.

"It's a four-letter word," he said, "and 'oh' is in front of it."

Third-base coach Ron Washington said he never had a doubt about waving Ichiro home with the first inside-the-park home run in All-Star Game history. Ichiro didn't even need to run full speed or slide.

"Noooo, no, no," Washington said. "That was riding a bike over there.... He ended up walking into home plate. There was no doubt. You're looking at a guy who plays as hard as he can and he wasn't going to cheat himself. If you've got any kind of speed, you should be able to make it in there. That wasn't just normal speed. You had exceptional speed right there."

Griffey, upon returning to the NL dugout, made eye contact with Bonds and they shrugged at each other. All those asymmetrical quirks of the ballpark, the ones that Magowan insisted upon during the design stage, created one of the most thrilling moments in All-Star Game history.

Ichiro, with a straight face, joked that he felt the slightest bit of disappointment. He thought the ball had a chance to clear the arcade.

"And when it didn't, I was really bummed," he said, though a Japanese translator.

Maybe he could hit more home runs if he tried?

Known for sending his teammates into fits of laughter, Ichiro Suzuki joked that he was bummed his inside-the-park home run hadn't cleared the arcade.
(USA Today Sports Images)

"Tough question," he said. "If I'm allowed to bat .220, I could probably hit 40. But nobody wants that."

The inside-the-parker gave the AL a 2–1 lead, and a couple of conventional home runs padded it. Tampa Bay's Carl Crawford went deep in the sixth and Cleveland's Victor Martinez hit one out in the eighth.

Trailing 5–2 in the ninth, though, the NL made a two-out charge. Alfonso Soriano, the player who lost his starting outfield spot to Bonds in the last-minute balloting push, hit a two-run home run. Then AL pitchers J.J. Putz and Francisco Rodriguez combined to walk the bases loaded.

The Phillies' Aaron Rowand was next, and La Russa had his own star, Albert Pujols, the major leagues' leading slugger, on the bench. For reasons nobody could understand, La Russa let Rowand hit. One fly out to right field later, the AL pocketed a 5–4 victory—its 10th consecutive triumph in the midsummer classic.

Once again, the Ichiro speech worked. And he was an obvious choice as MVP.

"It's one that I'll never forget," the 33-year-old outfielder said. "The past six years, I never had an All-Star [Game] that I really thought I…was able to give it my all. So, I'm really happy. It was a fun All-Star Game."

Almost before Ichiro set down the trophy, word began to circulate that he and the Seattle Mariners had agreed to a five-year, $90 million contract extension. The player so perfectly tailored for AT&T Park wouldn't be able to consider signing with the Giants after the season.

They would have to find a different offensive centerpiece to replace Bonds.

Chapter 7

Heavy Is
the Crown

*"The record is not tainted at all. At all, period. And
you guys can say whatever you want."*
—Barry Bonds

Friday, August 7, 2007
Bonds hits No. 756

The most impressive home run that Barry Bonds ever hit wasn't
No. 71 or 72 or 73.

It wasn't that gravity-defying shot off Dennis Tankersley in
San Diego or the sub-orbital homer off Troy Percival in the World Series
or even the time he took a 100-mph fastball from Eric Gagne and pulled
it foul into McCovey Cove.

It wasn't the 500th, 600th, or 700th. It wasn't the shot that nudged him
past Willie Mays or Babe Ruth or even Hank Aaron.

The most impressive home run that Barry Bonds ever hit came on
August 30, 2003, in the fourth inning, at Bank One Ballpark in Phoenix.
It came off Randy Johnson.

It came in Bonds' first game back after his father died.

He said it so many times, in response to so many different questions: about his standoffish behavior, his approach at the plate, his place in Giants history, his instincts for the game. About anything, really.

"I'm my daddy's son," he'd say.

Bobby Bonds could be a hard man to know. When he came to the big leagues, a supreme blend of speed and power, they called him the next Willie Mays—the heaviest sequence of words any Giant could bear. Bobby struggled for years with alcoholism, which undermined what might have been a Hall of Fame career. His son was the most supremely talented baseball player of his generation, and yet, praise and approval came out in drips.

He raised his son to be tough. The son was emotionally fragile. The son overcompensated.

Their relationship was complicated, often strained but never estranged. They understood each other too well for that. Bobby Bonds served as the Giants hitting coach for a time, but stepped down after a cancer diagnosis, perhaps caused by years of chain smoking. He fought the disease with both feet in the batter's box. He underwent kidney surgery, lung surgery, open-heart surgery, and brain surgery. Yet the cancer continued its march, taking him at the age of 57.

A week after his father's death, Barry Bonds returned to the Giants lineup, faced the best left-handed pitcher of his generation—and hit a 403-foot home run on the first strike thrown to him in his second at-bat. Around the bases, he pulled his cap low so nobody could see the tears.

"The emotions just went through me," he said. "I felt light-headed and couldn't stop my heart rate from racing. After the home run, I couldn't breathe. That's never happened to me before."

It was Bonds' 40th home run of the season and the 653rd of his career—seven away from matching his godfather, Mays, for third place on the all-time list.

Without his father, and the only swing coach he ever trusted, Bonds kept climbing. His feet never left the batter's box, either.

He already hit Nos. 500 and 600 at home, the latter of those milestones coming off the Pirates' Kip Wells in 2002. On the way to a fourth consecutive NL MVP award in 2004, he hit 660 off Milwaukee's Matt Kinney. He passed Mays with 661 the very next day off Ben Ford. He rounded the bases with 700 glowing on the home scoreboard that September off the Padres' Jake Peavy.

All of those round-number homers came in China Basin, and all were occasions for sellout crowds to save their ticket stubs. This was history, after all. And with their cheers and chants, the fans who packed the ballpark collected mementos, both tangible and emotional, of all his milestone moments.

Say whatever you wanted about Bonds, but in the Bay Area, he was family. You don't get to choose your family. You simply alternate between loving them and putting up with them.

Bonds kept climbing even though the strikes became more and more infrequent. That 10-foot-pole treatment in Houston in the final week of the 2001 season? That was just the beginning. In 2004, a rising level of Bonds groupthink among managers—or an unspoken boycott, take your pick—resulted in a season such that baseball had never seen.

Bonds obliterated major league records with 232 walks and 120 intentional walks. The player who drew the next-most intentional passes that year was Jim Thome, with 26. Before Bonds came along, the single-season major league record was just 45, set in 1969 when Willie McCovey put the fear of God into NL managers.

Yet Bonds still tagged 45 home runs in 2004. Unbelievably, in a span of just four seasons, Bonds had hit his 500th, 600th, and 700th. The trek to the mountaintop is supposed to become more technical, more difficult the closer you get to the summit. Bonds was taking an express elevator.

The higher he climbed, though, the more exposed he became.

By the spring of 2005, Bonds had amassed 703 career home runs and achieving the all-time record appeared to be a matter of when and not if. Also by then, the game's steroid secret had become an open wound, with every day bringing new admissions and revelations of just how widespread and insidious the use of performance-enhancing drugs had become in baseball.

The annual Bonds spring-training arrival in 2005 was bound to go far beyond the usual circus atmosphere. A portion of his grand jury testimony in the BALCO case had been leaked to the *San Francisco Chronicle*, in which he acknowledged using the cream and the clear—substances that prosecutors described as undetectable and highly powerful designer forms of testosterone. Bonds' trainer, Greg Anderson, was indicted by a grand jury and serving time at a federal correctional institution on a contempt charge for refusing to testify.

This was going to be a bit more interesting than asking Bonds about a new contract.

Anyone who knew Bonds understood it would be folly to expect him to come clean or offer some kind of tearfully nebulous apology, as the Yankees' Jason Giambi had done a few days earlier. Instead, Bonds rebuked the media in tones that ranged from fatigued to hostile, charged reporters with outright deception, and compared news reports on the steroid controversy to 1970s TV reruns. It was a contentious, meandering, and utterly fascinating 32-minute prizefight of a news conference.

"What did I do?" said Bonds, when asked if he had a reason to apologize. "I'm just sorry that we're even going through all this rerun stuff. I'm sorry that, you know, this fiction stuff—and maybe some facts, who knows—but…we're all sorry about this. None of us wants to go through this. None of us wants to deal with this stuff. We want to go out and do our job."

Was steroid use a form of cheating?

"I don't know what cheating is," he said. "I don't know if a steroid is going to help you in baseball. I just don't believe it. I don't believe steroids can help you with eye-hand coordination to technically hit a baseball. I just don't believe it and that's just my opinion."

And, in a raised voice: "All you guys lied. All of y'all, in a story or whatever, have lied. Should you have an asterisk behind your name? All of you lied. All of you have said something wrong, all of you have dirt.

All of you. When your closet's clean, then come clean somebody else's. But clean yours first, okay?"

Bonds wanted the media and public to sweep aside the steroid controversy, but that would never happen—certainly not when he refused to show even a glimmer of contrition. How could he, with the Feds trying to take him down and make a high-profile example out of him?

A few days later, though, in a much more private setting at his locker, surrounded by his sycophants and two reporters, Bonds spoke in much softer tones. And he came the closest to admitting that yes, he had used steroids.

"You're talking about something that wasn't even illegal at the time," Bonds said. "All this stuff about supplements, protein shakes, whatever. Man, it's not like this is the Olympics. We don't train four years for, like, a 10-second [event]. We go 162 games. You've got to come back day after day after day. We're entertainers. If I can't go out there and somebody pays $60 for a ticket, and I'm not in the lineup, who's getting cheated? Not me.

"So we all make mistakes. We all do things. We need to turn the page. We need to forget about the past and let us play the game. We're entertainers. Let us entertain."

He scoffed at the notion his head size had grown or his testicles had wasted away. He continued to sidestep the direct question of whether he used steroids, but justified their use by comparing them to prescription lenses.

"You can't see, things look fuzzy, so what do you do? You go get glasses," Bonds said. "Is that cheating? You get glasses so you can see, so you can do your job. What's the difference?

"You want to define cheating in America? When they make a shirt in Korea for $1.50 and sell it here for 500 bucks? And you ask me what cheating means? I'll tell you how I cheat. I cheat because I'm my daddy's son. He taught me the game. He taught me things nobody else knows. So that's how I cheat. I'm my daddy's son."

Except in the space around Bonds' locker, where his legion of paid consorts nodded in agreement to everything he said, the air around baseball was thick with moral castigation. When Bonds missed nearly all of the 2005 season because of an infection in his surgically repaired knee, it only delayed the hand wringing in Bud Selig's office. The commissioner had greater respect for Aaron than anyone in the game. They had been close since their time together in Milwaukee. And the wild-west nature of the steroids era was cutting deeply into Selig's legacy, something that he had taken great pains to cultivate. From Sammy Sosa to Mark McGwire to Bonds, when it came to the single-season home run record, the public already had seen the man behind the curtain. Now Bonds wasn't far from erasing—some would say defiling—the most cherished record in American sport.

Aaron, who always stayed above the controversy, made news when he said he wouldn't be there in person to see Bonds hit No. 756, and wouldn't shake his hand.

"I don't have any thoughts about Barry," Aaron said. "I don't even know how to spell his name."

Neither did marketing executives. A failed ESPN reality series in 2006, *Bonds on Bonds*, caused dissension amid network ranks because it gave editorial oversight to a player it simultaneously was attempting to cover objectively. The only impact the series made was to cause a clubhouse distraction, something the Giants didn't need as they played losing baseball in Bonds' final three seasons in San Francisco.

The headaches weren't worth it. Nobody watched, and the series was canned after 10 episodes.

It was the ultimate mixed message. Nobody cared, supposedly. Yet the march to Aaron remained a huge story. The media kept filling the clubhouse, and the other Giants players tried to create a brighter open house. In the spring of '06, pinch hitter Mark Sweeney organized a "Giants Idol" singing competition and Bonds made the team howl with laughter when he agreed to walk onto the field dressed in drag as judge Paula Abdul.

"I thought he was mildly attractive," left-hander Jack Taschner joked. "I hate to admit it, but I didn't know whether to go for a make-out session or run for the hills."

"No," said shortstop Omar Vizquel, with a laugh. "That's an ugly [woman] right there."

"That's one of the best things I've seen this spring," catcher Mike Matheny said. "He's just one of us, you know? A lot of guys in this room felt very intimidated by him and were maybe a little separated from him, because he's on the superhero level. I played with Mark McGwire and it was the same thing. It's like a fictional character.

"It would be nice to see him, for his own sake, put all that behind him and just play the game that I know he loves and remember how he loved it as a kid. But it's a tall order and I know that's hard for him to do, too."

Bonds tied and passed Babe Ruth in 2006, hitting No. 715 in May at home off Arizona's Byung-Hyun Kim. Only Aaron remained, and although the Giants tried hard to court other free-agent hitters that winter, they were married to the pursuit. The Giants extended Bonds' contract for another year; he would enter 2007 just 21 home runs away from matching the all-time record.

The media attention was searing, and not surprisingly, it wore down his teammates as they continued to plunge deeper and deeper in the standings. First-year manager Bruce Bochy was stoic and patient beyond human reckoning, answering the same questions over and over in his twice-daily sessions. But whether Bonds was a beloved figure or a solitary one, the weight of the chase would've dragged any team down. It was just a warped place and time for a group of competitors who played the game their whole life to win. Suddenly, the win or the loss wasn't the most important result at the end of the day.

It was all Barry, all the time.

Bonds entered the All-Star break needing just four more to tie the record, and got halfway there when he smacked two on July 19 at Wrigley Field. But it came amid a 9–8 loss to the Cubs, and in a cramped clubhouse, Giants right-hander Matt Morris hit a breaking point.

"I don't know what the goal is here anymore," Morris said. "To win games? Or is it…I don't even want to say it.

"It's something we've got to deal with. We're almost waiting to get it over with, we're waiting to deal with it. It's such a dismal time for him to be so close to such an outstanding record. It should be a good time for everybody, but right now it's not. I don't even know if it's a good time for him."

The Giants were in last place, and after the Wrigley game, each of Bonds' last six home runs had come amid losses. Even Sweeney, who tried so hard to befriend Bonds and show off a happy clubhouse to the media the previous year, had turned cold toward the slugger. Bonds reportedly failed an amphetamine test in the off-season and blamed it on something he took from Sweeney's locker. After the story came out, they barely spoke to each other again.

The only people who continued to revel in the pursuit were Giants fans, and everyone was certain the record would fall at home. All his milestones had come in San Francisco, in front of the fans who understood him just a little bit better than the rest of the country.

Just as he did with Ruth, though, Bonds tied Aaron on the road. When he hit No. 755 at San Diego on August 4 to claim a share of baseball's most cherished record, Selig watched from the Petco Park suite level with his hands in his pockets. The home run came off right-hander Clay Hensley, who had served a steroid suspension in the minors two years earlier.

Bonds sat out the series finale at Petco Park. He grabbed a share of the crown there, which was enough. Coronations do not occur on foreign soil. The Giants were coming home.

It didn't matter where Barry Bonds happened to be standing as he wagged his lacquered maple bat. It didn't matter whether he was wearing home whites or road grays. It didn't matter whether the fans were booing or showering him with applause, or what they felt about the all-time home run record. Once he began to inch close to it, the same thing would happen on every pitch.

Flashbulbs. Thousands of them. Twinkles of light from the upper deck and the field seats, turning the stands into a white, crackling Fourth of July sparkler. Top of the first, bottom of the ninth, ball or strike. It didn't matter. Every pitch was a chance to record history. It was one more artifact to prove you were there—even if you had just spent the previous minute booing Bonds as he walked to the plate.

"Yeah but you ain't going to throw the ball back," said Bonds, asked about his reception on the road. "You get a big boo but all the cameras are going in my swing, aren't they? Boo, click-click-click. The fans like baseball, guys. The fans, regardless of what anybody says, they come and they want to see it happen."

What were those cameras recording exactly? What did those moments, those home runs, really mean? Would the images they took be cheapened years later, when the feds finally got a charge to stick to Bonds? Would it matter that, despite a felony conviction in 2011, he could say in the end that the league never punished him for a positive drug test?

Most of the country shunned Bonds. Nearly the entire Bay Area loved him. It was all too easy for the rest of the country to mock San Francisco as parochial and permissive. Who was right? How would these pictures, these snapshots of time, be framed and displayed in greater historical context?

For all the moral outrage, one small point had been obscured. Baseball wasn't golf. It was not a gentleman's game, nor did it ever claim to be. You didn't sign a scorecard or a code of ethics. If a hitter could steal a sign, he did. Pitchers loaded up the baseball when no one was looking. If there was an edge to be taken, you took it. Players of an earlier generation took amphetamines. Players in the steroid era took Winstrol and Deca-Durabolin. Was it their fault that the drugs available to them worked exponentially better, to the point of embarrassment, and warped the game's statistics for more than a decade? They were getting an edge however they could, as ballplayers always had.

Make no mistake, though: steroid use was wrong, it was illegal in most cases, it came with the risk of debilitating long-term health consequences, and worst of all, it created a climate in which some players felt pressured to get on the juice to win or keep their jobs. It was the league and the union's responsibility to protect the welfare of players and maintain a healthy, safe, and competitive environment. Both sides failed. They turned their backs, folded their arms, and counted the money.

Now they were sitting in the mess they created. Selig, who yawned and kept his hands in his pockets while Bonds rounded the bases after hitting No. 755 in San Diego, did not continue with the Giants to AT&T Park in San Francisco. He returned to his office in New York. Aaron wasn't there, either, and continued to give no sign he would acknowledge Bonds when the record fell.

Bonds never hesitated to lash back at his critics. But he refused to utter a bad word about Hammerin' Hank.

"Do you just expect this man to travel around the continent for weeks?" Bonds said. "I just truly believe it's not fair to him. Hank's a great ballplayer. He's the home run king. He will always be the home run king in our hearts and we respect him and we love him. And Hank, if you want to stay home, stay home, brother."

Aaron stayed home, but there wasn't an empty seat in the ballpark on August 7 when the Washington Nationals returned to play the second game of a four-game series. If somehow Bonds didn't homer against them, his old team, the Pittsburgh Pirates, arrived next on the home schedule. The Giants had a chance to set down their bags, stay home for a solid week, and hope to end a historic but often joyless march that had taken its toll on everyone in the clubhouse.

There was no fatigue in the stands, though—and nobody was fool enough to be in a concession or bathroom line when Bonds led off the second inning against 29-year-old left-hander Mike Bacsik.

Bacsik pitched a bit with the Indians, Mets, and Rangers but never stayed on any roster for too long. He went back to the minor leagues for two seasons before resurfacing with the Nationals. He was a former

18th-round pick with fringy stuff and an 86-mph fastball. When he changed out of his uniform after every major league game, there was no guarantee he'd have a locker the next day. Pitching to Bonds sitting on 755 home runs would be the most attention he'd receive in his life, and he knew it.

With the crowd standing and thousands of compact cameras trained, Bacsik gave Bonds a called strike. He gave him another fastball that got fouled back. Bonds received one more pitch to hit, but his line drive down the right-field line wasn't nearly high enough. He doubled.

Bonds came to bat again in the third, and Bacsik started him off with two more fastballs for strikes. Again, Bonds made hard contact to right-center but didn't have the right trajectory. He singled.

Barry Zito started for the Giants that night. He limped through five innings and the score was 4–4 in the bottom of the fifth when Bonds received one more chance against Bacsik with the bases empty. He looked at a strike and fouled off a 2-1 pitch. On a full count, Nationals catcher Brian Schneider called for a fastball and set his glove on the outside corner.

It never reached his mitt. At 8:51 PM, Bonds hit career home run No. 756 to claim sole possession of the most revered record in American sport. Bonds raised both arms in triumph and rounded the bases to a background of fireworks over the bay and an outpouring of adulation. He clapped his hands, eased into his trot, and embraced his 17-year-old son, Nikolai, at home plate.

He needed just 10 plate appearances after tying Aaron to take sole possession of the crown. And then, in the most surprising moment of the night, the Giants played a congratulatory message from Aaron on the video board.

"I would like to offer my congratulations to Barry Bonds on becoming baseball's career home run leader," Aaron said. "It is a great accomplishment which required skill, longevity, and determination.

"Throughout the past century, the home run has held a special place in baseball and I have been privileged to hold this record for 33 of those

Barry Bonds hit his record-breaking 756th career home run on August 7, 2007, surpassing Hank Aaron's mark, which stood for 33 years.

years. I move over now and offer my best wishes to Barry and his family on this historic achievement. My hope today, as it was on that April evening in 1974, is that the achievement of this record will inspire others to chase their own dreams."

Bonds knew what Aaron went through, enduring death threats and racially charged hate mail, before eclipsing Babe Ruth's record of 714 in 1974. It was impossible not to see him on the screen without revering his presence. Bonds watched the video clip with his eyes wide, mouthing the same words over and over: "Wow. Wow. Thank you. Thank you."

"It meant everything, absolutely everything," he said after the game. "I've had the time of my life here. We grew up together. The people in this town grew up together. We're deeper than just me and this uniform."

The celebration halted the game for almost 10 minutes. Bonds received the key to the city, met his family on the field, and took the microphone to thank fans and teammates. His voice broke once.

"My dad..." he said, raising his helmet and looking up.

Bacsik, who rubbed the back of his neck with his hand the moment Bonds raised his arms, pitched the rest of the fifth inning. His major league career would last all of 14 more appearances.

So many pitchers effectively boycotted Bonds by avoiding the strike zone. Nobody wanted to be attached to this record. But Bacsik seemed to delight in becoming the footnote.

"You either have to be a really special player to be remembered in this game, or be part of a special moment," Bacsik said. "I didn't want to give up the home run, but I'm very lucky to be a part of a very special moment in sports history.

"If I didn't give up this home run, nobody would remember me."

Nationals pitcher Tim Redding, who gave up No. 757 to Bonds the next day, would assert later that Bacsik grooved the pitch to Bonds. Bacsik, who worked for a time in sports talk radio following his playing career, responded to the charge from his Twitter account: "I didn't try to give up the home run. I was crappy enough to do it without trying."

The home run landed in the right-center-field seats where a 21-year-old college student, Matt Murphy, secured it on a bounce and then survived an aggressive, skin-scraping scrum until San Francisco police officers could get to him. Murphy wasn't a Giants fan. He was a Mets fan from Queens who happened to have a layover in San Francisco while en route to Australia.

President George W. Bush placed a brief phone call to Bonds. So did Selig—the first time they had spoken in more than two years. Selig also issued a statement in which he referenced the independent investigation that he had commissioned, with former U.S. senator George Mitchell in charge. The Mitchell Report would be released in December of 2007; it castigated the Giants for being complicit while giving Anderson, a convicted steroid dealer, unfettered clubhouse access.

"While the issues which have swirled around this record will continue to work themselves toward resolution, today is a day for congratulations on a truly remarkable achievement," Selig said in the statement.

Bonds, asked about those issues after the game, hardened his voice.

"The record is not tainted at all," he said. "At all, period. And you guys can say whatever you want."

The night Bonds broke the all-time home run record, his trainer and friend, Anderson, sat in a jail cell.

Bonds exited in a double-switch after the fifth inning. The Giants led 6–4 in the eighth before the Nationals rallied against three relievers for four runs. The Giants lost 8–6.

They finished 71–91 that season, and Bonds would hit six more record-breaking home runs. The last one, No. 762, came at Coors Field, with a 43-year-old Bonds hitting a 99-mph fastball from Ubaldo Jimenez that a fan caught while leaning over the left-field fence.

So many observers, even in his own clubhouse, couldn't wait for the home run chase to end. Yet they knew the moment Bonds dropped out of sight, they would never see a more focused, intelligent, controlling force in the batter's box again.

He never stepped out in between pitches, never fiddled with his batting gloves or took a deep breath. He stood there on top of the plate, ready to pounce. The pitcher always begins the action, but Bonds always controlled it—just as his father taught him.

"People don't realize we're watching the best show on earth," said Willie McCovey, shortly after Bonds passed him on the all-time list. "I don't think they appreciate it. I know people around the country don't appreciate it. I don't think we'll ever see anything like this again in our lifetime."

As for the record-setting home run ball? It sold at auction for $750,000 to street fashion mogul Marc Ecko, who decided its fate by launching an online poll that amounted to a publicity campaign for his clothing brand. Fans could vote to shoot the ball into outer space, donate it to the Hall of Fame, or brand it with an asterisk before sending it along to Cooperstown. Almost half of the 10 million votes cast chose the asterisk, which was laser cut into the leather.

Bonds called Ecko "an idiot" and pledged to boycott the Hall of Fame if it accepted and displayed the asterisk-marked ball.

"I don't think you can put an asterisk in the game of baseball and I don't think the Hall of Fame can accept an asterisk in their Hall of Fame," Bonds said in an interview with MSNBC after the season. "You cannot give people the freedom, the right, to alter history. You can't do it. There's no such thing as an asterisk in baseball."

To this day, though, that's how the ball appears in Cooperstown. Hall of Fame president Jeff Idelson, after taking possession of the ball, said he wasn't making a value judgment by choosing to put it on display. It was fulfilling its function as a museum by using an artifact to document the home run record as well as the context in which it was sent.

"For a week in 2007, that's how the public felt," Idelson said. "It doesn't mean that's the way they feel now or will feel in the future.... It also symbolizes for Barry the stigmatism he was under as he went after the all-time home run record.

"Our role is to display it and let the visitors make their own value judgment."

Bonds lobbied to return to the Giants for one more year, but the club was enduring its third consecutive losing season. No matter how young or athletic the Giants tried to get while turning over the lineup, they knew they could not bring back Bonds and pretend to turn the page. As long as he owned a swath of lockers in the corner of the clubhouse, it would still be his team and his room. They needed more than a new direction and a new roster. They needed a new culture.

Managing partner Peter Magowan saw Bonds through to the record. That was where their 15-year relationship would end.

With a week left in the season, Magowan told Bonds that the slugger wouldn't be back in 2008. No team signed him that winter, even for the league minimum. Bonds never did officially announce his retirement, and for years, left open the possibility of suing the league.

In the end, though, there were too many mutual benefits to count between the Giants and Bonds in their 15 years together.

Ask Magowan for his favorite Bonds home run and he does not hesitate: the first one he hit, in his first at-bat wearing a Giants uniform.

Without Bonds, the new ballpark wouldn't have been built. Without that one triumphant homecoming, there wouldn't have been another. No wonder Giants fans remained warm to Bonds until the end. He literally led them out of the cold.

"We had the opportunity to get the best player in the game on the team," said Magowan, his voice trembling. "When we were able to do it, it gave our ownership group instant credibility, that we were here for the long term, that we wanted to win.

"It's always difficult to say good-bye. It was an emotional time for me. A lot of good things have happened, some unfortunate and sad things have happened, but there comes a time when you have to move in a different direction.

"I said this to him: on behalf of our fans, thanks for all the excitement and the memories and the success that this franchise has had, of which he was so central a part. I do believe he's the greatest player of his generation, one of the greatest of all time."

Chapter 8

Making It Count

"I let everybody clear out, had a little cry. It was wonderful."
—Dave Righetti

Friday, July 10, 2009
Jonathan Sanchez's no-hitter

It wasn't a fear of flying that made Sigfredo Sanchez uncomfortable as he crossed four time zones in his airplane seat. A more forceful turbulence was rocking his conscience. It was a father's pride.

He had seen his son, Jonathan, pitch in the big leagues just one time, out of the bullpen, against the Mets in New York. That was two years earlier. He had never traveled from Puerto Rico all the way to San Francisco, and he was too stubborn to allow his son to pay for his ticket. Finally, after months of prodding from his other son, Sigfredo Jr., he relented. It was July 2009, and he was going to see a game at AT&T Park for the first time. With any luck, he'd see Jonathan pitch again.

You no longer needed a family connection to get a good seat at the Giants' waterfront ballpark. In 2008, at the outset of the post-Bonds era, the club failed to draw 3 million fans for the first time since moving from Candlestick Park. The Giants were left with a champagne hangover and a bare cupboard. Their farm system was going on its second decade without producing an everyday position player, the result of an ownership strategy to divert funds to the major league payroll in order to prop up a Bonds-centered lineup with veteran free agents.

The club even intentionally punted its first-round draft pick in 2004, just so it could spend the associated signing bonus on the major league roster. Looking back, it was an unconscionably bad decision. But managing partner Peter Magowan was determined to win with Bonds, convinced that because of his star power, the window would never be opened wider to break the team's World Series drought.

With club officials exhausting their last bit of patience to see Bonds through to Hank Aaron's record, and with Bud Selig and the baseball world eager to put all vestiges of the game's steroids era in the past, the Giants moved in a new direction when they arrived in Scottsdale for spring training in 2008.

There would be no contentious news conference when Bonds arrived, no State of Barry, no entourage of paid friends, and no descriptions of the luxury SUV as it pulled into the parking lot.

There was just manager Bruce Bochy, and a roster of remnants.

The Giants did not spend a single day over .500 in 2008. They finished 72–90. It was their fourth consecutive losing season—something they had not weathered since 1974–77, their coldest and bleakest days at Candlestick Park, when they were lucky to draw 3,000 fans for a midweek game.

Changes were coming. They began at the top.

Magowan, on one of the first road trips of the '08 season to Los Angeles, took the rare step of inviting the newspaper beat reporters to a white-linen luncheon in Pasadena. Over club sandwiches, cold salmon, and Sancerre, he talked excitedly about his achievements and wistfully about his regrets. He acknowledged that his legacy would be a complicated matter, but he hoped people would fondly recall him as the man who made AT&T Park possible and gave the Giants a future in San Francisco.

He was asked how much longer he envisioned himself as managing partner. "I don't know," he said. "It's not 100 percent up to me."

The vote had already been taken. A month later, the news leaked out: a consortium of Giants shareholders forced out Magowan as managing partner.

Publicly, new boss Bill Neukom said Magowan wanted to spend more time at his home in wine country and see more of his grandchildren. Privately, it was a coup that had been building for years, and dissatisfaction over Barry Zito's $126 million contract was the final straw.

Neukom was a corporate lawyer with an interesting personal history. He received a providential knock on the door one day while working as an associate at the Seattle firm of K&L Gates. It was his boss, wondering if Neukom could help his son fill out the papers to set up a business license. The boss was Bill Gates Sr. The favor became one of the biggest ground-floor opportunities in American corporate history. The company became Microsoft, Neukom rose to become its chief legal counsel, and by the time he left active service with the company, he was worth hundreds of millions on paper. He developed a reputation as a merciless litigator, a badger with a bow tie, taking on the U.S. government in antitrust litigation. After years as a minor voice on the Giants' executive council, Neukom was ready to bring his unbending manner to the managing partner's chair.

At his introductory news conference following the 2008 season, Neukom clutched a top-secret folder containing his broad vision for the franchise—three pages of jottings he crafted over a couple of long-haul flights. It was his draft of the "Giants Way"—a manifesto outlining a high-achievement corporate culture he planned to distribute to everyone from departmental vice presidents to the lowest-level minor-leaguer. His principles for success were about more than hitting the cutoff man or getting a bunt down. He expected each employee to outwork and outsmart his or her counterparts.

"It's important that people understand their objectives," said Neukom, "and that they know they will be fairly judged in terms of how they perform against those objectives."

This was not the kind of boss that favored GM Brian Sabean and Bochy, who each had one more year left on their contracts. Neukom did not seek to shield their lame-duck status. But credit him for this: he also didn't pursue summary executions. Neukom didn't demand the ego stroke that came with hiring his own handpicked people from day one. He was going to watch, listen, learn, and not assume knowledge he didn't yet possess. It was the wisest move he could make.

"Both Brian and Bruce enthusiastically have endorsed the notion that we've got so much work to do that we're not going to worry about what their status is," Neukom said. "Job One is identifying the talent, teaching the talent, and playing the game in a winning way. There will be plenty of time for us after the '09 season to evaluate how each of us did and decide where we go from there."

For all of Bochy's overachievements in small-market San Diego, Giants fans hadn't embraced him. His even temper and monotone media sessions were perfect for shepherding the team through the drama of Bonds' final year and the all-time home run record. They did nothing for his Q rating with people in the Bay Area, though. And Sabean had something to prove as well: that he could build a contending team without the game's greatest offensive force since Babe Ruth.

The Giants had a new force of nature, though. Amid a losing season in 2008, they saw Tim Lincecum emerge into a sizzling sensation. In his first full season, and for a team that went 72–90, he finished with an 18–5 record, a 2.62 ERA, and a league-most 265 strikeouts. He bulldozed through lineups with a 97-mph fastball, a hammer curve, and something new he added in his rookie season—a split/changeup that he more or less invented in the span of two side sessions. It became the most effective out pitch in the game, and with his fastball screaming out of his blurry, whip-armed delivery, it was impossible for hitters to react.

Lincecum was a runaway choice as the 2008 NL Cy Young Award winner, receiving 23 of 32 first-place votes. He became the first Giant in 41 years to win the award.

You couldn't really call the Giants a pitching organization over their history. This was the franchise of Bonds and Mays and McCovey, of Cepeda and Will Clark. Hall of Famer Gaylord Perry starred for them on the mound in the 1960s, but his two Cy Youngs came as a member of the San Diego Padres and Cleveland Indians. The great Juan Marichal, regrettably eclipsed by Sandy Koufax or Bob Gibson, only received one Cy Young Award vote in his career—a single third-place choice in 1971.

Mike McCormick was the last Giant to win the award, in 1967.

Lincecum's accomplishment was rare and refreshing. Giants fans finally had someone new worth celebrating, and this time, the object of their admiration struck a chord with the rest of the country, too. Lincecum's Cy Young season lifted him to the title of franchise star. The Giants had what they most coveted, and even spent $126 million trying to buy: a star in the post-Bonds era that their fans could adore.

Lincecum's popularity was only enhanced by his personality. He was a slacker from Seattle who ate cereal for dinner, wore ski hats, and didn't appear to take himself too seriously. San Francisco was a perfect fit for him. Even when he missed the All-Star Game in 2008, curiously being hospitalized in New York for dehydration and never making it to Yankee Stadium, the fans didn't seem to care.

He was approachable. He stood 5'10" in his spikes. He wasn't a muscle-bound superhero who existed on a different plane. You could relate to him.

With Lincecum overwhelming opponents every fifth day and right-hander Matt Cain continuing to establish himself as one of the game's better young pitchers, things finally were looking up for the Giants in 2009. After taking consecutive series from the Houston Astros and Florida Marlins, they were assured of a winning record going into the All-Star break. All that remained was a four-game home series against the San Diego Padres.

Lincecum took the mound on July 9 with a chance to lock up an assignment as the NL's starting pitcher for the All-Star Game at Busch Stadium. He did that, and more. Not only did Lincecum extend a streak to 29 consecutive scoreless innings—the third-longest by a Giant in 52 years—as he entered the seventh against the Padres, but he hadn't allowed a hit in the process.

The fans stood with every pitch by the end of the sixth, convinced they were bound to see history. No Giant had thrown a no-hitter since John "The Count" Montefusco in 1976, and that feat came in a near-empty Atlanta Fulton County Stadium at the end of a losing season. Longtime Giants fans could tell you off the top of their heads that Ed Halicki had thrown the last no-hitter by a Giant in San Francisco, in the second game of a doubleheader against the New York Mets on August 24, 1975.

Lincecum was nine outs away from ending a decades-long wait.

Tony Gwynn Jr. dashed it all with a single to left field while leading off the seventh inning. Two batters later, Kevin Kouzmanoff blooped a hit that scored Gwynn from second base. The Giants won 9–3, and stood nine games over .500 for the first time in four and a half years, but Lincecum's scoreless streak was over. And the no-hitter, as magical as it would have felt in the ballpark that night, would have to come another time for Lincecum. Maybe, someday, when the Padres were back in town.

For all the positivity over Lincecum and Cain, who would both enter the All-Star break as double-digit winners, the Giants still trailed the surging Los Angeles Dodgers by seven games in the NL West. And they still had a lineup that, an ebullient young third baseman named Pablo Sandoval aside, was made up mostly of journeymen and 4-A players. They ranked dead last in runs per game among NL clubs.

On top of that, they had just learned that 45-year-old Bay Area native Randy Johnson, whom they signed for $9 million to occupy a place in the rotation and provide a marketable asset on his way to ending a Hall of Fame career, would be unable to take his turn on July 10.

Johnson had jammed his shoulder into the wet grass while fielding a ball on June 4, when he won his 300th game in front of a sparse, rain-soaked crowd at Washington. He hadn't felt right since then, and in a July 5 start against the Astros, he howled in pain while swinging at a curveball from Roy Oswalt.

Johnson was diagnosed with a strained rotator cuff, and although nobody knew it at the time, he had started the 603rd and final game of his Hall of Fame career. He wouldn't pitch again for the Giants until September, when he made the first of five relief appearances.

It was only because of Johnson's injury that the Giants turned back to Sanchez, their erratic, 26-year-old left-hander, who began the season in the rotation but had pitched his way to a demotion a few weeks prior.

In 13 starts, Sanchez was 2–8 with a 5.62 ERA and had issued 46 walks in 64⅔ innings. He completed six innings just twice and retired a total of just two batters past that point. He didn't own a complete game in his career. He was far too inefficient to even consider something like that.

The Giants were trying to showcase Sanchez because other teams kept bringing up his name in trade discussions. But minor league journeyman Ryan Sadowski made the most of a spot start, and even if he had less impressive stuff, he was giving them a better shot to win. They couldn't keep running Sanchez out there, no matter how much potential he had. They hoped he could sort out his issues in relief, and maybe the demotion would get his attention, too.

Once Johnson's shoulder began barking, though, the Giants found themselves short a starter. They had no other choice. In the final Friday night before the All-Star break, one day after Lincecum flirted with a no-hitter, they handed the ball to Sanchez for his first start in nearly three weeks and hoped for the best.

Sigfredo Sanchez's flight happened to touch down in San Francisco on Thursday. He would see his son start a major league game for the first time after all. For that, he considered himself lucky. He had no idea how fortunate his timing would be.

As he always does before a game, Giants pitching coach Dave Righetti sat down with the starting pitcher and catcher to go over the opposing lineup. There had been a late change to the battery, though, when Bengie Molina's wife went into labor and he received permission to go to the hospital. Backup Eli Whiteside, so aptly named with his clump of curly, prematurely gray hair, would catch Sanchez.

Righetti went over the San Diego hitters, knowing that their relative strengths and weaknesses wouldn't mean much if Sanchez couldn't throw the ball over the plate. In the three weeks following the left-hander's demotion to the bullpen, Sanchez had more than just inconsistent mechanics to fix. One day, in a quiet moment, Righetti had asked Sanchez what he wanted to achieve.

"I just want to pitch," Sanchez replied.

"Yeah, but what do you *really* want to do?" Righetti asked him. "There's more to this than just being here and wanting to win. So here's what I'm going to do: I'm going to try to get everything out of you possible. I want you to make $15 million or whatever the heck they pay starters nowadays. Now let's get to work."

Sanchez had pitched for Puerto Rico in the World Baseball Classic that spring and returned to the Giants with a different delivery. He tried to copy Johan Santana's motion and hand position, but the delivery didn't work as well for someone with Sanchez's rangier body type and slinging, three-quarters arm slot.

"He wasn't getting the turn that I wanted in order to give that arm a chance to coil," Righetti said. "He doesn't have that fast, short arm like Johan does. He was trying to copy the right guy, which is why we let him continue to do it. It works for a short guy the way Santana's built. But in Jonathan's case, it didn't quite fit and there was a lot of pushing of the baseball.

"I had to get rid of it somehow, and that's not easy because he believed in it. He was just searching, you know, trying to make it. He was trying to find his niche."

Righetti understood. He was once a wild, live-armed lefty who missed bats, too.

Righetti incorporated a little more torso rotation into Sanchez's delivery, which helped to slow down his body long enough for his arm to catch up. Working from the stretch would continue to present its challenges, especially since Sanchez showed little regard for keeping baserunners close. To start innings, at least, he'd have a chance to find a consistent arm slot from the windup. The game began and Righetti hoped for the best.

The first inning went well enough, as the Padres went down in order while striking out twice. The second inning offered more encouragement. There were three fly outs, including one to deep left field off Adrian Gonzalez's bat. But Sanchez hadn't thrown ball two to a single hitter.

The Giants rocked Padres pitcher Josh Banks in second inning, with Sanchez's sacrifice bunt helping to set up Aaron Rowand's two-run single. They led 4–0, and Righetti hoped Sanchez could sneak through five innings without a major hiccup. Getting a win could put some wind in his sails.

The third inning went fly out, ground out, fly out. The Padres were 0-for-9 the first time through the order, and Sanchez hadn't thrown ball three to a single batter.

Everth Cabrera tried to lead off the fourth with a bunt single and was thrown out as the Padres again went down in order. Sanchez struck out two in the fifth to keep them off the bases yet again. He'd gone deep enough to qualify for the decision.

Sanchez hadn't won a game in almost two months. That streak safely appeared over when Sandoval lofted a three-run home run in the bottom of the fifth. The game was a rout, and if it were Lincecum on the mound, everyone in the ballpark would be aware he hadn't allowed a baserunner. With Sanchez, it barely seemed to register.

The sixth inning: strikeout, pop out, strikeout.

In the seventh, it finally occurred to Whiteside. Whenever he caught, he would look to the dugout when there were runners on base in case Bochy wanted a pitchout or a throw to check the runner. The catcher realized he hadn't looked to the dugout once all game.

"Nobody'd been on base," Whiteside said. "I was just putting down fingers. His pitches were moving. He made it easy for me."

Sanchez made it to the seventh inning, the same juncture where Lincecum took a no-hit bid the previous night. With one out, he faced Tony Gwynn Jr., the same hitter who had made the ballpark groan.

Sanchez struck him out on a splitter in the dirt. He struck out the side. And instantly, the crowd noise increased from a few incredulous murmurs to pure thunder.

Sanchez, the unpredictable pitcher who hadn't completed seven innings all season, the problem child in a rotation of stars, suddenly needed six more outs to accomplish something that no Giant had ever done. This wasn't just a no-hitter in the making. It was a perfect game.

Sandoval had a sore back after hitting his home run, so Bochy shuffled his infielders in the seventh. Kevin Frandsen entered at second base and Juan Uribe moved from second to third. Perhaps mercifully, the Giants went down quickly in the seventh and kept Sanchez from thinking too hard or for too long in the dugout.

Gonzalez, the Padres' best hitter, led off the eighth and for the first time all game, Sanchez fell behind in the count. He threw three consecutive pitches out of the zone.

"I thought to myself, *It's okay if he walks this guy*," Righetti said. "And then I thought, *Oh no, it isn't!* That's why there have been so few perfect games. You get to thinking about every pitch like that. But in Jonny's case, he probably wasn't. And it showed."

Sanchez threw a called strike, and then Gonzalez hit a drive to the warning track in left field. John Bowker was stationed deep enough that catching it was never in doubt.

Retiring Gonzalez was the highest hurdle, and Sanchez had a clear road to perfection. But almost before that thought could settle in, Chase Headley hit a hard two-hopper to third base. It bounced off Uribe's chest and he scrambled in vain to pick up the carom before realizing there was no fixing it. With a pained expression, he flipped the ball back to Sanchez.

The official scorer called it an error, which it most certainly was.

That's the other reason perfect games are so rare. They require perfection from nine men, not just one.

A wild pitch moved Headley to second base and Righetti wondered how Sanchez, now operating from the stretch, would handle both his mechanics and his nerves. But after a visit from Whiteside, Sanchez kept from unraveling. Pinch hitter Craig Stansberry popped up and catcher Eliezer Alfonzo, Sanchez's good friend, struck out.

Three more to go.

Even on those rare occasions when Sanchez would have a breaking pitch working, he seldom threw enough strikes with his fastball to use them. This time, with a little turn of his back to the hitter, everything aligned. His curveball had more snap than ever, and with his split also sharp, he had two off-speed weapons at his disposal.

Luis Rodriguez showed bunt on the first pitch in the ninth and the crowd let him have it. But it was only a ploy to draw Uribe a little closer. He grounded out.

Sanchez's pitches were starting to ride up in the zone a bit, and he pumped a dangerous 2-0 fastball to Edgar Gonzalez, Adrian's brother. Sanchez whipped around when the swing resulted in a drive to deep center field.

"Center field...hit well...hit *very* well," called Duane Kuiper from the broadcast booth. "Rowand on the move...and Rowand makes the catch! Two down in the ninth!"

Rowand's jump was flawless, and one look at the nose he had smashed in Philadelphia told you he feared no boundaries. He ran full speed to the wall in center field, and his back crashed into it as he timed his jump.

"I was going to go up and over and land on the other side if I had to," Rowand said. "I'm just glad the ball landed in my glove."

Sanchez held up one finger. That's usually the signal for the number of outs in the inning. This time, it signified the number that remained.

He got two strikes on Cabrera and hoped to backdoor a curveball. It was a yo-yo out of his hand, and didn't appear to snap all the way back over the plate. But it was close enough for plate umpire Brian Runge, who pumped his arm as the ballpark filled with the sounds of mad disbelief from the crowd of 30,298.

Sanchez had done it. Uribe's error was the only thing separating him from the 18th perfect game in major league history. For the Giants, the no-hitter was monumental enough. A 33-year wait was long enough.

Sanchez struck out 11 in the 8–0 victory. It was the first complete game of his career.

"We had a toast in there and he said, 'I hope I won't go back to the 'pen,'" said Bochy, soaked in beer. "We saw history. He made history."

Giants fans expected that kind of history-making performance from Lincecum or Cain. Instead, they walked through the turnstiles on a Friday night in July expecting so little and seeing so much. It really was true: any random day, you might see someone become immortal. It might even be your son.

Sigfredo Sanchez had to be cajoled into getting on the plane to San Francisco. He hoped at best to see his son throw a relief inning or two, then spend some time with him over the All-Star break. He shared so much more than that.

At one point late in the game, a friend in Puerto Rico called Sigfredo's cell phone to make sure he was watching on television, aware of what his son was doing. "I'm here," he replied, holding out his phone to the crowd noise as proof.

The father and son stayed awake for hours that night, watching replays and highlights. At one point, Sigfredo disappeared and nobody could account for his whereabouts. He went in search of the morning newspaper, both to take a souvenir, and to see the headline in print. Then he could be sure it was real.

When Righetti threw his no-hitter on the Fourth of July for the Yankees in 1983, somebody stole all his equipment amid the celebration. He made sure that didn't happen to Sanchez, deputizing right-hander Merkin Valdez to collect the left-hander's jacket, glove, and final-out ball from the dugout. But the memories, and the experience, were the most valuable takeaways.

No one expected Jonathon Sanchez to pitch his first career no-hitter, but there was no better time than on his father's first visit to AT&T Park.

"These kinds of things bring teams together," Righetti said. "It really bonds them in a way and makes them think something good's going to happen to the ballclub. That's what we talked about. I let everybody clear out, had a little cry. It was wonderful."

The Giants finished 2009 at 88–74, their first winning record in five seasons—enough progress for Neukom to sign Bochy and Sabean to short-term extensions.

With Righetti's guidance, a young and talented pitching staff became the new core of the team. They could not replace Bonds. But they were beginning to open a new window—one that worked so well for them at their pitcher-friendly home.

"Since the day this park opened, you always felt something good was going to happen—and to the pitchers, too, because it's a fair park," Righetti said. "To see it happen is surreal a little bit. You're trying to get through the game and win and all the sudden you're talking about immortality.

"It's a hell of a thing."

Chapter 9

Torture and Rapture

"You just knew. We never make anything easy."
—Bruce Bochy

Sunday, October 3, 2010
Regular season finale vs. San Diego

The beauty of opening day is that every team begins on equal footing. Every fan is permitted to cling to at least a slice of irrational hope. As winter thaws into spring, though, so too does pragmatism. It is so much harder to suspend doubt when you are a dozen games deep in the standings.

On opening day, though, any team can win it all. There's a reason the home opener is almost always a sellout in every ballpark. It might be the only packed house a team has all season. Hope has a way of marketing itself.

So many times on opening day, the Giants took the field with more than hope. They had something more substantial: authentic belief that their team was capable of winning a World Series. They had Barry Bonds. They had Willie Mays. They had Willie McCovey. Maybe they were coming off a 102-win season or a pennant-winning year or felt they had just the right mix of veterans and "you gotta like these" kids forcing their way into the big leagues.

It's true. You can look it up: no franchise has more players in the Hall of Fame than the Giants. Yet in 52 seasons of baseball in San Francisco, the Giants hadn't won a World Series. They hadn't paraded down Market Street since the day in 1958 that a city celebrated their arrival. Five decades of hope, at turns rational and irrational, went unfulfilled.

When the Giants lifted the lid on the 2010 season at Houston, there was little reason to think they were poised to make history. They always had a good feeling whenever they lined up behind Tim Lincecum, the defending two-time NL Cy Young Award winner, who would take the mound against the Astros on opening day. For whatever it was worth, they were coming off a 21–10 exhibition record in Arizona that ranked as the best in the desert—leading to a fleeting and false rumor among the rookies that the reward for winning the Cactus League would be flat-screen TVs for everyone on the roster. ("Yeah, and the coaches get VCRs," joked bench coach Ron Wotus.)

But GM Brian Sabean had failed to upgrade a moribund offense over the winter. His major off-season move was to sign Mark DeRosa, a complementary player coming off wrist surgery, to a two-year, $12 million contract. The Giants also signed Aubrey Huff, an American League DH coming off a poor season who pounced on a $3 million offer because he had no others.

The Giants lineup for the opener at Houston—Aaron Rowand, Edgar Renteria, Pablo Sandoval, Huff, DeRosa, Bengie Molina, John Bowker, and Juan Uribe—was marginally talented, and outside of Sandoval, who was entering his second full season, offered almost no upside.

To make matters worse, second baseman Freddy Sanchez had a setback in his recovery from shoulder surgery and wouldn't debut until mid-May. And DeRosa's wrist would never heal properly. He would play in just 26 games, and his home run on opening day at Houston would be the only one he'd hit in two seasons as a Giant.

Lincecum might have taken over Bonds' place as the Giants' franchise star, but Sabean had yet to show that he could build a winning lineup without the all-time home run king at its center. The offensive problems were so widespread in 2009 that the Giants took the rare step of firing hitting coach Carney Lansford—an out-of-character move for a franchise whose bench coach, pitching coach, and bullpen coach were on their third manager, and not vice versa.

The way appeared clear for a pair of top prospects to make the club in 2010. But 20-year-old Madison Bumgarner was too inconsistent in the spring to beat out journeyman Todd Wellemeyer for the final rotation spot, and the Giants decided against rushing catcher Buster Posey, the fifth-overall pick in the 2008 draft.

Even if Peter Magowan were still running the team, he wouldn't have made any bold pronouncements about this group.

The Giants did enter the year with some momentum, though. They were coming off their first winning season in five years, Lincecum and Matt Cain formed as solid a young 1-2 punch as any in baseball, and Jonathan Sanchez's no-hitter the previous year did more than give the inconsistent left-hander a confidence boost. It gave the entire team a sense of legitimacy. On a given day, they were talented enough to build a stage, stand upon it, and grab the attention of the baseball world.

The Giants were 47–41 at the All-Star break in 2010, which was respectable enough but only placed them fourth in the NL West standings. The San Diego Padres set a surprising pace in the division, and the Giants kept coming up short against them. The Padres beat the Giants seven times in eight games prior to the break, and after many of those losses, it took every last bit of Bruce Bochy's self-discipline to keep from redecorating the visiting manager's office in Petco Park. The Padres had shown Bochy no loyalty after he led teams with meager payrolls to four NL West titles in his 12 seasons in San Diego. Bochy wanted nothing more than to beat the Padres, even if he steadfastly refused to admit as much. And they were frustrating the Giants at every turn.

The most galling defeat came under dark and drizzling skies at Petco Park on April 20. Jonathan Sanchez dominated the Padres, holding them to one hit while striking out 10 in seven innings. But the Giants were just as stymied by Mat Latos, a hulking right-hander with platinum blond hair and a hard fastball that traveled straight downhill. The Giants managed just four hits in his seven innings, none of them coming at opportune times in a 1–0 loss.

It was the 29th time the Giants held an opponent to one hit or fewer in a nine-inning game in their San Francisco era. It was the first time in those 53 seasons that they lost.

"I can't say I've been in a game like this," said Bochy, who remained stoic in front of the press but began spewing blue language as soon as the reporters filed out of his office. "No way we should've lost tonight's game."

A day later, broadcaster Duane Kuiper continued to ruminate on all the unbelievably wasted opportunities in the 1–0 loss—including a leadoff triple from Nate Schierholtz in the eighth inning—and he opened the telecast with a quick recap. Then he stared into the camera and used the only word he could to summarize the situation.

"Giants baseball," he said.

One beat. Two beats.

"Torture."

It was a one-word slogan that struck a chord with fans. For the remainder of the season, Torture signs dotted the ballpark. When the Giants lost, they lost in excruciating fashion. And when they won, it was almost never a comfortable blowout. More likely, it was a one-run margin and closer Brian Wilson flooding the basepaths before slithering his way to the third out.

Through it all, the Giants were doing more than causing their fans to chew fingernails. They were learning how to manage late-inning tension. They were learning how to win.

Along the way, they were making over their roster with bits of string and spare parts. Pat Burrell arrived after the Tampa Bay Rays dumped him with millions left on his contract. He reunited with Huff, his former University of Miami teammate, and they added a loose energy to the clubhouse. Bumgarner dominated at Triple-A Fresno, graduated at the end of June, and held down his place in the rotation the remainder of the season.

Most critically, the Giants called up Posey at the end of May when it became clear that the best hitter in their entire organization wasn't even on their big league roster. (He was hitting .349 for Triple-A Fresno with a .442 on-base percentage, and 21 of his 60 hits had gone for extra bases.)

Posey made his season debut in a home game against the Arizona Diamondbacks and laced three singles, each of which knocked in a run. After the third one, the stoic 23-year-old stood on first base and finally cracked a smile.

"It was great. It was fun. It's humbling," he said. "I have to slow myself down because it can get you going a little bit."

The Giants weren't the same team that began the season with an opening-day lineup that included six of eight players in their thirties, all acquired via free agency or trade—and three of them coming off surgeries. All of a sudden, they had upside everywhere you looked. Freddy Sanchez came back healthy and stabilized second base. Huff had a resurgent season, and would go on to set career highs in runs scored (100) and on-base percentage (.385) while also burning up his lungs on an inside-the-park home run in April. Sabean felt secure enough to make a critical decision at the start of July, trading Molina, the club's established starting catcher, to the Texas Rangers to free up the everyday job for Posey.

The Giants had a much better team as they turned to the second half, and a revitalized farm system played a major role in that improvement. But they still had to get the Padres out of their heads.

"I swear to God, their guys are in the right position every time," Huff said. "It's like they know what's coming. You've gotta credit their scouts, I guess, or something."

Jonathan Sanchez didn't feel like giving the Padres too much credit. He was 0–2 against them in his first three starts, but he didn't let that affect his confidence. This was the team he no-hit the previous season. This was a lineup he knew he could dominate.

Sanchez was battling through his own issues with consistency. On August 8, the Giants needed a solid start from him to earn a four-game split in Atlanta—a place where they almost never captured a series. The Braves roughed him up for four runs in four innings. Sanchez hadn't thrown consecutive quality starts since April.

But he knew his next outing would come against the Padres—the first time the Giants would cross paths with them in almost three months. And so, after that uneven start in Atlanta, Sanchez made a quiet but bold pronouncement to the beat writers.

"We are going to make the playoffs," said Sanchez, his chin raised. "San Diego has been winning series all year…. But we're going to play San Diego now and we're going to beat them three times. If we get to first place, we're not going to look back."

The beat writers gave Sanchez a chance to hedge his statement. English wasn't his first language, after all. Did he really mean what he said? Was he guaranteeing the Giants would sweep the next series with the Padres and win the NL West?

"Yeah, we will," he said.

It was a juicy story, and Sanchez's comments had instant ramifications. Coaches met with him and told him to knock it off. Bochy refused to take up the megaphone and run with it.

"That's between you all and Jonathan," he said, to a thicker than usual assembly of reporters in the dugout when the Giants returned home. "I know some of the guys were giving him a hard time about it."

Not all of them, though.

"I'll be honest, he's not the only one in this clubhouse who thinks that's possible," reliever Sergio Romo said. "He just happens to be more vocal about it."

The Padres had their say, too. They drove up Sanchez's pitch count, sent him from the game in the sixth inning, and smashed his crystal ball in a 3–2 victory. The Padres won two of three in the series. Sanchez's prediction didn't come true. Not yet, at least. But after the game, he did not duck the media.

"I believe in my team, you know?" he said. "I've got confidence. Nothing against them, but I know we keep fighting out there."

The Giants entered the pennant stretch in need of inspiration, though. They took another of those torturous losses to the Colorado Rockies on August 30, when right fielder Cody Ross, who was acquired on a waiver claim a week earlier from the Florida Marlins, got fooled by Carlos Gonzalez's bat-splintering triple and charged in when he should've sprinted back. Ross was reacting to the sound off the bat. It was as literal as a bad break could be, and Ross felt terrible about it when the triple led to a loss.

The Giants trailed the Padres by five games with 30 to play. They had just lost their fourth out of five. And Huff, who was playing in a pennant race for the first time after a decade spent in the doldrums of the AL East, was in a 2-for-17 slump.

He found his inspiration in his underwear drawer. It was a skimpy, bright red thong with rhinestones on the waistband—a gag he bought one day while out shopping with his wife.

It was the Rally Thong.

"Guys, we've got 30 games left," Huff announced. "Here's 20 wins right here."

Huff paraded around his locker in his Rally Thong. Burrell and Huff celebrated big rallies by punching each other in the dugout. Wilson's beard was getting longer, thicker—and curiously darker. Wilson's live interviews became bizarre performance art, including an unforgettable cameo by a shirtless man wandering through the background wearing only a leather mask, briefs, and harness.

His build bore a striking resemblance to Burrell's. Who was he, really?

"Oh, him?" Wilson said to Chris Rose of Fox Sports. "That's The Machine."

Could it be any more obvious? This wasn't the uptight environment that persisted through the Barry Bonds era. This was a clubhouse of acceptance and permissiveness. The Giants' crew of rookies, castoffs, and misfits came together so quickly because there was so little tension in the air.

For all their clubhouse chemistry and dungeon fetishwear, the Giants made a push in the NL West because their rotation caught fire in September. For the second consecutive season, the pitching staff broke the franchise record for strikeouts. The bearded bullpen was close to unhittable the final month. Burrell and Uribe began hitting game-changing home runs in the late innings. Andres Torres, signed as a non-roster invitee, provided energy atop the lineup and an unrelenting optimism in the dugout. The victories piled up, and San Diego's lead continued to recede.

The Padres spent 148 days in first place, but they heard footsteps and their losing streak hit 10 games on September 5. Five days later, the Giants drew even with them in the standings and then surged ahead with a week remaining.

When the Padres arrived at AT&T Park for the final weekend of the season, the Giants were up two with three to play.

The Giants had three chances to clinch.

Team Torture, true to its nature, lost the first two.

"You just knew," Bochy said, with a groan. "We never make anything easy."

The Giants spent all year chasing the Padres in the NL West, employing a roster full of spare parts to supplement a championship-caliber pitching staff. This wasn't a team structured around a superstar. From the outside looking in, the lineup had as much structure as an amoeba.

They weren't a perfect team. They had obvious flaws. But over the grind of a six-month season, they had proven something to themselves: they could overcome them.

It would come down to game No. 162—and because the baseball gods appreciate drama, it was Jonathan Sanchez's turn to pitch.

Bruce Bochy understood every possible scenario heading into the final regular season game of 2010.

If the Giants won, they clinched the NL West. If they lost, a one-game tiebreaker would be held on Monday at San Diego. And because both teams remained alive in the wild-card picture, too, one scenario existed where the Giants would go from a one-game tiebreaker in San Diego to another in Atlanta—a sure way to burn themselves out even if they managed to sneak into the postseason.

There was an even crazier scenario. If the Braves lost and Padres won on the final Sunday, it was possible for the Giants and Padres to clinch playoff spots on the same field—the Giants as the wild-card team and the Padres, who held the tiebreaker, as NL West champs.

Of course, the simplest math was this: beat the Padres and celebrate. So Bochy, after Barry Zito collapsed in Saturday's loss, called the players together and gave them one instruction.

Don't pack a bag. Bring the clothes on your back and nothing else.

It was an unspoken but clear message: we'll win, and we aren't going anywhere.

Years later, Bochy would look back on that decision and make an admission: "If we'd have lost that game, I'm not sure what we would've done. We'd have been scrambling, for sure."

The Giants were guaranteed one thing in the regular season finale: an absolutely raucous, supportive crowd. All those business suits that populated the stands in the early history of Pacific Bell Park were mostly gone, replaced by so many costumes, fake beards, Panda hats, and splashes of black and orange that every night looked like Halloween.

San Francisco was a city of tolerance and acceptance. So was its baseball team. It was a perfect match.

"We can't have outcasts here," Wilson said. "On this club, everybody pulls for each other. When we get a new guy, he's a part of our family and we'll treat him like part of the family."

Latos did not see a family on the other side of the field. He saw a collection of mercenaries and said as much in an interview with CBS Sports, accusing the Giants of "going out and grabbing guys."

As terrific as Latos pitched all season, even breaking a major league record previously held by Greg Maddux and Mike Scott when he held an opponent to two runs or fewer in 15 consecutive starts, he had stalled in September. The Giants broke his record-setting streak on September 12, when Posey tagged him for a home run—the first of what became four consecutive losses for the big right-hander.

Latos might have been fatigued down the stretch, but nobody forgot that he had outdueled Sanchez in a pair of 1–0 victories earlier in the season. On the very same mound at AT&T Park in May, he finished an infield hit away from throwing a perfect game.

Sanchez didn't say anything to reporters this time. To his teammates, though, he guaranteed victory again.

The buildup for the game and the energy in the stands were unlike anything AT&T Park had seen since Bonds was on the cusp of passing Hank Aaron atop the all-time home run list. There was a different vibe in the stands this time, though. The fans didn't just come to witness history. They came to immerse themselves in it.

And then, in the first inning, they felt robbed.

Torres hit an apparent leadoff double, only for umpire Mike Everitt to call it foul. The ball kicked up chalk on the left-field line, and Bochy was ready to storm onto the field and get himself ejected.

"There's no way that's happening now," Bochy said. "It probably cost us a run. You could see chalk flying. I was stunned. But I didn't want to leave the game in the first inning."

The Giants weren't happy with umpire Tim McClelland's strike zone, either. Sanchez pitched around two walks in the second inning. In the third, with Chris Denorfia at second base and two outs, Sanchez didn't get the call on a first-pitch fastball down the middle to Adrian Gonzalez. Pitching coach Dave Righetti shouted in protest from the dugout. The Giants issued an intentional walk, even though it set up a right-handed matchup with Ryan Ludwick. Sanchez got ahead with two strikes, then threw a wicked curveball past Ludwick's swing to escape the inning.

Latos didn't give up a run in the first two innings, but Giants hitters kept returning to the dugout with the same message: he didn't have confidence in his curveball, and his fastball was up in the zone. If they had good at-bats and didn't chase his slider, they would get to him.

Sandoval started the third inning with a drive to left field and it took a running, wall-crashing catch from Scott Hairston to prevent an extra-base hit. The Padres still seemed to be playing the Giants in exactly the right spot at exactly the right time.

But then something happened that nobody—not even Jonathan Sanchez—would be bold enough to predict.

He swung at the first pitch and hit a flare to right-center field. Denorfia was stationed a step shallow and had no chance to cut it off. The ball shot past him and rolled all the way to the deepest part of the outfield. Sanchez had himself a stand-up triple—the first and only triple he'd ever hit in his career.

Torres struck out and slammed his helmet in the dugout. But with two outs, a pair of pennant-race neophytes came through. Freddy Sanchez lined a single up the middle to score Sanchez. Then Huff hit a drive to left-center. Denorfia gave an all-out sprint and made a full-extension dive—one final act of desperation for a team that could sense a season slipping away. The ball sailed wide of Denorfia's glove by five feet for a double. Freddy Sanchez scored easily and the Giants led 2–0.

Now it was up to their pitchers to make the lead stand up, and Jonathan Sanchez, who ended up leading the NL in walks, was running deep counts but keeping the Padres off the board. When Gonzalez singled to start the sixth, Bochy had right-hander Santiago Casilla begin to warm up. When Sanchez walked Ludwick on four pitches, Casilla was in the game.

The crowd gave Sanchez as loud and long an ovation as he received the day he threw a no-hitter. But after handing off the baseball, Sanchez continued to stand near the mound. He waited for Casilla to reach the rubber, and then gave him a message:

"This is our game."

Two pitches later, Casilla induced a ground ball from Yorvit Torrealba. Sandoval fielded it near third base, stepped on the bag, and threw to second for a double play. Hairston followed with another ground ball to shortstop, where Uribe gloved it deep in the hole and threw across his body from the outfield grass to force Torrealba at second base.

Uribe and Sandoval exchanged double overhand high-fives. The inning was over and the book was closed on Sanchez, along with the regular season. He finished with a 1.03 ERA in his final seven starts, and with a season on the line, he refused to give in.

"You know what? This is one of those games that defines your career," Posey said. "For him to come out and have the poise he had…wow. You could tell he had it. I didn't see any nerves. It was more pure focus."

Just as Casilla picked up Sanchez, right-hander Ramon Ramirez did the same in the seventh. Denorfia singled and Casilla fumbled David Eckstein's weak ground ball for an error. With two outs, Miguel Tejada was next and Ramirez battled him for nine pitches, every one of them soaked with tension. The Giants didn't get the call on a 2-2 fastball. The count went full. With the Padres' best hitter, Gonzalez, on deck, Posey made a gutsy call. Ramirez nodded, threw a slider that tailed away from Tejada's swing, and ended both the nine-pitch battle and the inning.

After Javier Lopez and Romo made quick work of the Padres in the eighth, Posey stepped to the plate in the bottom of the inning and capped the greatest rookie season by a Giant in decades. His home run off Luke Gregerson soared over the fence, and for once, the torture eased a bit.

The 2010 NL West champions stopped their own celebration to greet the fans during a victory lap along the track at AT&T Park.

The Giants still had to protect a 3–0 lead for three more outs, but in the dugout, it appeared to be a matter of fate. And Wilson did not tempt it.

He set down the Padres in order, striking out Will Venable on three pitches to clinch the Giants' first trip to the postseason in eight years. Wilson crossed his arms in memory of his late father. Posey threw off his mask and rushed the mound, flailing his arms and screaming.

"That's the first time I've seen some absolute, unadulterated craziness out of the guy," Wilson said. "I thought he was going to punch me and I was totally accepting of it. I was finding a reason not to thank him for punching me, actually, if he did."

The Giants bullpen was unscored upon in its last 24 innings and finished with a 0.90 ERA after September 1. During Bochy's 12 seasons in San Diego, he had Trevor Hoffman as his closer—the dominant right-hander who would go on to become the game's all-time saves leader. But Bochy never had a group of relievers with this much talent and versatility.

Wilson's save was his 48th, matching the franchise record established by late and beloved closer Rod Beck in 1993.

"As far as I'm concerned he still has the record and I'll stand beside him," Wilson said. "I wanted to throw that last pitch and I wanted my teammates to tackle me."

It was the first time since 1971 that the Giants clinched a postseason berth with a victory in their final regular season game. The last time, Juan Marichal pitched a five-hit complete game at old San Diego Stadium. He did not, as Sanchez helpfully pointed out, hit a triple, too.

"I was right," said Sanchez, between point-blank blasts of champagne. "I believed in the team, you know? We're always together. Look at our team. Look at everybody. We have everything we need to win."

Including an immeasurable level of passion and devotion from the stands. As the players continued to tackle one another on the field, Bochy managed to pry away Burrell, who had become his de facto captain, to make a request.

"Lead these guys around the field," Bochy said. "We owe these fans a victory lap."

"Whatever you say, Skip," Burrell replied.

Sandoval led the way and the Giants, wearing freshly printed T-shirts declaring them the division winners, took a lap around the warning track as fans stretched out their hands.

"Some of them weren't letting go," said Lincecum, who would start Game 1 of the NL Division Series—the club's first playoff game in seven years—against the Atlanta Braves.

It was a moment nobody wanted to end. With their clinching victory, the Giants finished the year on a 20–10 run—just as Huff predicted the day the Rally Thong came into being.

The Giants did not need to rush home and pack. They were NL West champions, and the playoffs were coming to them.

Chapter 10

A-Plus Game

*"Their swings were telling me what I needed
to throw. The game will show you."*
—Tim Lincecum

Thursday, October 7, 2010
NLDS Game 1 vs. Atlanta

The Giants might have won the NL West in 2010 with a collection of unwanted free agents, waiver claims, and misfits, but their personnel decisions began bucking convention long before that.

How else to explain their choice in 2006, when they used the 10th overall pick in the draft to take Tim Lincecum, an unconventional pitcher who stood 5'10" in his spikes and threw from an eccentric, poetic, back-turning, blur-armed delivery in which he leapt off the rubber and finished with his balletic right leg in the air?

The Kansas City Royals took Luke Hochevar with the first pick. The Colorado Rockies wanted Greg Reynolds with the second selection. Brad Lincoln went fourth, to the Pittsburgh Pirates, and Brandon Morrow went fifth, to the Seattle Mariners. The Detroit Tigers took lefty Andrew Miller after that.

The Los Angeles Dodgers were the sixth and final team to take a pitcher while Lincecum remained on the board. They were the only ones who wouldn't regret their decision. Clayton Kershaw turned out to be pretty good in his own right.

The great irony of Lincecum falling to the Giants with the 10th overall pick is that the teams selecting ahead of them were scared off by his size and doubted his durability—and a half-decade later, as several of those other pitchers rehabbed from major surgeries, Lincecum kept piling up innings, strikeouts, and awards.

"I get so sick and tired hearing them talk about how he's going to break down," said Chris Lincecum, an inventory clerk at Boeing and onetime junior college pitcher who began recording his son's lessons when Tim was four years old. "I've heard that for years. I'm going to tell you right now: he's not going to break down on the field. All he needs to do is keep core muscles in shape and all his hinges.

"I mean, I hit 88 mph at 52 years old, and his mechanics are much more efficient than mine ever were."

And about those mechanics?

"He loads like Warren Spahn or Bob Feller, has an extension and a dangle and the looseness of Satchel Paige with the finish and follow-through of Bob Gibson," said Chris Lincecum, leaving behind any sense of modesty. "It's pieces of all of them and it's good for anybody because it's very efficient."

Well, not really. The most important truth in pitching mechanics is that they only work when you can repeat them. Very few athletes had the balance, coordination, and flexibility to throw like Lincecum without falling off the mound, let alone executing pitches and hitting spots. There was so much head tilt in his delivery that almost any pitcher would have trouble keeping his eye on the target. That wasn't a problem for Lincecum, a right-hander who was left-eye dominant. He even batted left-handed.

Chris Lincecum developed an incredibly efficient and powerful way to throw, generating every bit of torque from the legs, hips, and back. And his son, pumping a 98-mph fastball from an impossibly slender body and then bouncing back to play long toss the next day, was gifted enough to pull it off.

So gifted, in fact, that even while he dominated hitters on his way to Cy Young Awards in 2008 and '09, he wasn't always putting in the work. His talent always was enough.

There was the time in his rookie season when he missed a team flight to Cincinnati, received a reprimand from Barry Bonds in front of the whole group, then was forced to deliver bags to the players' rooms with no help and just one luggage cart—a task that took him until 4:00 AM to complete.

And, of course, there was the day after the 2009 season when he was driving back home to Seattle up Interstate 5, a patrolman just north of the Columbia River clocked him doing 74 mph in a 60-mph zone and got a whiff of marijuana when Lincecum rolled down the window of his Mercedes.

Lincecum turned over a pipe along with 3.3 grams of pot, and was cited for possession. Although prosecutors recommended a lesser charge, the local judge seized an opportunity to make a high-profile example. Lincecum had to appear in court and Giants owner Bill Neukom made a surprise appearance, as if to convey the serious matter of the charges.

The conference call to announce Lincecum's second consecutive Cy Young Award became a delicate PR situation. It was his first media availability after the pot bust.

"I made a mistake and I regret my actions," Lincecum said. "I certainly have learned a valuable lesson in all of this and I expect to do better in the future."

There wasn't much moralizing happening in the Bay Area, though. If anything, the marijuana stop made Lincecum even more popular. T-shirts emblazoned with a pot leaf and LET TIM SMOKE became a common sight around AT&T Park. Not only was Lincecum the first two-time Cy Young winner in Giants history, but he was a folk hero for a city that once swam in free love.

Even the razzing he took on the road in 2010 had an air of mirth instead of mean-spiritedness. When he pitched at Atlanta in August, the Turner Field organist played "Puff the Magic Dragon" as he walked to the plate. Lincecum wasn't paying close attention, but his teammates were. When they told him about the song, Lincecum didn't get offended. He had a good laugh over it.

For much of 2010, though, Lincecum wasn't in a laughing mood. All those doubters became so much harder to dismiss, and it began in the spring when reporters asked him about an average fastball velocity that had dipped two miles per hour.

"Yeah, I know," he said, finally losing his cool as the questions persisted. "I'm small and I'm going to break down. Same in high school. Same in college. It used to motivate me. Now it's, 'Get over it. Watch the game.'"

Yet Lincecum knew he had to make an adjustment. He began working on a slider that spring, but it wouldn't break in the thin Arizona air and he kept getting knocked out of exhibition games early. So he went back to his fastball-split combination. He'd figure it out. He always did.

When the season began, Lincecum dominated in Houston on opening day but struggled to find himself over several stretches. He tied his career high in walks in a May 15 home start against the Astros. Then he tied it again in his next outing against Arizona, and again in the start after that against Washington.

"It's completely frustrating," he said, after the loss to the Nationals. "You can see it in my face. It's something I really don't want to show. You start thinking too much and get away from who you are or what you were before."

Lincecum didn't allow a single home run at AT&T Park in 2009. He allowed eight in 2010. Opposing baserunners had begun running wild on him, too. When he became the first Giants pitcher to be selected to three consecutive NL All-Star teams since Juan Marichal in the 1960s, he felt guilty. He knew he got there mostly on reputation.

"When you don't think you deserve something, and I'm not saying I don't deserve this, I guess it's not as gratifying," Lincecum said. "I don't know. It feels weird. This has been kind of a humbling year for me. I won't say I was full of myself, but it puts things in perspective."

The toughest adjustment came on July 1, when the Giants traded catcher Bengie Molina to the Texas Rangers. Word of the trade began to spread as the team flight touched down in Denver. That night, Lincecum went to Molina's hotel room to say good-bye to the only big league catcher he knew. The conversation ended up lasting much longer than that.

"We had our heart to heart," Lincecum said. "I've seen a lot of changes in four years. You understand that's part of the game, but it doesn't make it easier. It's obviously tough to see a guy like that go, who's been such a big influence on myself and our pitching staff. I was glad I had the opportunity to work with him at the start of my career."

Molina gave Lincecum a piece of advice: Buster Posey had a tremendous head on his shoulders and would be a great catcher in the big leagues for a long time. But he was still just a rookie. For the time being, Lincecum would have to take control on the mound.

"Timmy will have to be the driver," Molina said. "He'll have to show Buster what he can and cannot do."

Posey had made an immediate impact at the plate, but the transition wasn't always so smooth behind it. Lincecum hit a full-on crisis in August, when he lost all five of his starts, posted a 7.82 ERA, and allowed opponents a .311 batting average. Lincecum began making drastic mechanical changes, even raising his hands over his head for the first time. It didn't work, and he scrapped it after two starts.

"I've become a big thinker. That's just the way I am," Lincecum said. "Your brain never stops working. You start focusing on the wrong things, or the negatives, and they start to manifest and build up on each other.

"I can't keep searching. I've just gotta go out and pitch."

It wasn't only Lincecum who struggled in August. The Giants rotation had three rotten turns in a row, going 14 games without a victory from a starter over one stretch. That was no way to catch the San Diego Padres in the NL West standings, and going back as far as the All-Star break, GM Brian Sabean didn't like what he was seeing.

"I don't think our pitching has been as advertised," Sabean said. "It hasn't been close. We've got to throw more strikes. We've got to pitch more to contact.... When you're going through a spot when you aren't swinging the bat, you've got to have some people putting up zeroes or have one- or two-run games and we haven't had that. It's been disappointing."

In late August, after Giants starters allowed 13 first-inning runs over three consecutive losses, Sabean marched four-fifths of the rotation into manager Bruce Bochy's office—everyone but Matt Cain, who was pitching the next day—and read them the riot act. The Giants weren't built to win 10–9, so there was no sense whining over the meager offense. This team was built to win with pitching. It wasn't enough if those pitchers were merely okay. It was time for them to be accountable, rise to the occasion, and stop making excuses.

When a reporter asked Sabean if throwing to a rookie catcher might be one of those excuses, the GM bristled.

"You know the answer to that?" he said. "The pitching staff needs to take it upon itself. They've been around the block. They're the ones throwing the baseball. They're the ones that can shake a pitch or throw what they want. They know the advance reports. And we've failed in that area to some extent. Maybe that's because Bengie was so good and they trusted him so much and they didn't take it upon themselves. Now they are more and more responsible and they should be."

Lincecum took the message to heart.

"It was just telling us to wake up," Lincecum said. "We know what we can do and it's not about stats anymore. It's not about individuals. It's just pick up the f---ing guy behind you. Pick up the team. Do it for the team.

"We know what we can do. Just realize it."

Lincecum took the mound with a clearer mind and went 5–1 with a 1.94 ERA in September. He finished the year with a 3.43 ERA, nearly a run higher than the previous season. But he still led the NL with 231 strikeouts, joining Randy Johnson (1999–2002) and Warren Spahn (1949–52) as the only NL pitchers since World War II to pace the league in three consecutive years. In Lincecum's final regular season start, when he struck out Arizona's Chris Young to end the seventh inning, the crowd responded by giving him a thunderous standing ovation.

Now he would be starting the Giants' first playoff game in seven years. The Giants had their ace back just in time, and he entered Game 1 against the Atlanta Braves with a newfound sense of purpose.

He always assumed he had done his part for the team. He had the last two Cy Young Awards to prove it. In that meeting in Bochy's office, though, Lincecum understood something for the first time:

He hadn't accomplished anything truly important yet.

If you could trace the franchise's turnaround to two events, they would be the day it drafted Lincecum in '06 and the day it drafted Posey in '08. They were both recipients of the Golden Spikes Award, honoring the country's best amateur ballplayer. Never before had two Golden Spikes winners formed the same battery in the major leagues.

Now they would join forces against the Braves, who won on the final day of the regular season and celebrated their NL wild-card berth after the Giants defeated the Padres.

When it came to franchises built on pitching, the Braves were the gold standard. They no longer had Greg Maddux, Tom Glavine, and John Smoltz. But their Game 1 starter, Derek Lowe, was the NL's pitcher of the month for September after going 5–0 with a 1.17 ERA in his final five starts. Lowe was a veteran of six postseason teams as a starter and reliever. He had made 10 starts in the playoffs. He also had an exceptional history of pitching on short rest.

Lincecum, by contrast, was a postseason rookie. He had a checkered past in big games, too, struggling to control his adrenaline when he started the 2009 All-Star Game in St. Louis. His first career opening-day start, in 2009 against Milwaukee, was just short of a disaster, too.

No matter how Lincecum handled the nerves of his first playoff assignment, the Giants knew they had to get off to a fast start in the best-of-five series. The Braves' 56–25 home record was the best in the majors. Aside from the 2002 NLDS, when Bonds finally broke through after years of postseason misery, the Giants had an awful history when it came to playing big games in Atlanta.

There are a million X-factors in any short series. But this much was clear: if Lincecum did not pitch his best, the Giants could not hope to escape the first round.

"You've done this a thousand times," Lincecum told himself. "We've been in these situations. It's another game and just treat it like that."

That was easier said than done. A sellout crowd packed AT&T Park. And there was nothing subtle about the surprise guest invited to make the "play ball" announcement. It was Bay Area native Robin Williams, flinging an orange rally towel and shouting, "Yes indeed!" into the microphone.

"Good evening, San Francisco!" Williams boomed. "Let's give it up for the 2010 National League Western Division champion San Francisco Giants! Let's go Giants! Let's go Giants! Vaya los Gigantes! Play ball!"

Lincecum took the mound amid the most pressure-packed atmosphere of his life. He'd pitched on the national stage before, but this was different. This was a season on his shoulders.

And one batter into the game, he was in a world of trouble.

Omar Infante led off with a double to left field, instantly silencing a crowd that had waited seven years to see postseason baseball on the shores of McCovey Cove.

Lincecum's fastball was up, and the Braves were laying off his changeup in the dirt. He had enough confidence to throw his slider for strikes, though, and had leaned on the pitch to get him out of his funk in

September. He knew the Braves would be looking for it, and there wasn't anything more hittable than a hanging slider. He had hoped to incorporate it the second or third time through the lineup, but this was no time to give in with something straight down the middle.

He got Jason Heyward to fly out to left, then threw a 3-2 slider to Derrek Lee, who swung through it for the second out. Then after Brian McCann ran the count full, Lincecum threw another slider. McCann waved and missed, Posey blocked it, and the cheering crowd all but lifted Lincecum back to the dugout as he let out a relieved puff of air.

It was the inning that Lincecum needed to settle down and settle in.

By the second inning, the Braves knew they were in trouble. Lincecum had established his diving changeup along with his slider, his fastball jumped anywhere from 90 to 94 mph, and he was taking advantage of their aggressiveness. Lincecum struck out Alex Gonzalez, who nearly spun himself into the ground, then followed by getting Matt Diaz and Brooks Conrad to chase pitches out of the zone. He threw 14 pitches while striking out the side, nine of them for strikes—every single one of them a swing and miss.

In the third, Lincecum needed just seven pitches to set down the Braves on a pop-up, a strikeout, and a ground out.

The Giants threatened against Lowe in the bottom of the third inning, putting runners at the corners after Cody Ross walked and Andres Torres reached on an error by second baseman Brooks Conrad. Although they failed to score, the inning was the first sign of the defensive woes that would haunt the Braves all series. Conrad was playing out of position because Martin Prado had sustained a season-ending muscle tear. Chipper Jones was out of action, too. The Braves had to move Infante from second base to third. Lee was battling a bad back as well. In many ways, the Braves and Giants were mirror images: teams with lineups that had been cobbled together out of necessity but were seasoned enough to grind out one-run victories behind a solid pitching staff.

Getting a run was going to be a challenge for both teams, though. Lincecum issued a leadoff walk to Heyward in the fourth, but needed just eight pitches to carve up the next three batters in the middle of Atlanta's order.

Then came the bottom of the fourth, and controversy.

Posey, who would go on to outpoint Heyward to win the NL Rookie of the Year award, began the inning with a ground single up the middle. Although Posey was an average runner at best, Bochy hoped to stay out of a potential double play. So he started the rookie with a two-strike pitch to Pat Burrell, and the decision absolutely should have blown up in the manager's face.

Burrell swung through the pitch. McCann came up throwing. The ball tailed to the right of second base, but arrived well ahead of Posey as he braced himself with a defensive slide. Conrad gloved the throw and snapped a tag onto Posey's hip.

Posey's foot clipped the front of the bag and he awkwardly landed on his back directly on top of the base. He waited for the out call. Umpire Paul Emmel called him safe.

It was Posey's first stolen base in the major leagues.

"I guess it's a good thing we don't have instant replay right now," Posey would say after the game. "Beautiful slide, wasn't it?"

Major League Baseball would expand replay just four years later. It was no help to the Braves on this night, though, and Atlanta manager Bobby Cox didn't use his postgame forum to lobby for a change.

"Just leave it the way it is, you know?" Cox said. "It's fine the way it is. We'd be arguing and throwing red flags 10 times a night."

The Braves would do more kicking than throwing in the series. After Juan Uribe struck out for the second out, Cox ordered an intentional walk to Pablo Sandoval. The move raised eyebrows, since Sandoval had struck out on three pitches in his first at-bat. But Cox wanted the matchup with Ross, a player he knew well from facing him in the NL East with the Florida Marlins.

By the end of this postseason, nobody would dare choose to pitch to Ross. The Giants acquired him on a waiver claim in August to keep him away from the Padres, and were surprised when the Marlins dumped his contract on them just to save $1 million. As fate would have it, the Padres hadn't even put in a claim on Ross. The Giants ended up with him almost by accident and had to scramble to find a roster space for him, with right-hander Guillermo Mota suddenly and conveniently coming down with a leg ailment called IT band syndrome.

It turned out to be the finest accidental $1 million the Giants ever spent, as Ross became the Giants' hottest hitter in the postseason—their biggest October surprise since Dusty Rhodes came off the bench to win World Series MVP honors in 1954.

At the outset of his blistering postseason run, though, Ross the Boss received some charity.

Lowe threw a 2-0 fastball to Ross that tailed onto his bat somewhere between the handle and barrel, resulting in a ground ball to the left side. Infante, who had just a couple weeks of regular time at third base, lunged to his left and raised his glove at the exact moment the ball scooted under it. The ball was hit so slowly that left fielder Matt Diaz couldn't reach it in time to make a play on Posey, who scored easily from second base.

"We made the right move," Cox said after the game, tersely. "We made an error. He made the pitch and got a ground ball. We kicked it."

Ross was credited with a single, the Giants had a 1–0 lead, and Lincecum continued to thrive with the slimmest margin for error.

He recorded three more outs in the fifth, all on sliders—a fly out to medium center field, a foul tip into Posey's glove, and a hopper to first base. Then came two more strikeouts in a 1-2-3 sixth inning, including a 92-mph fastball up and away that overpowered Heyward.

Lincecum and Posey, for all their early lumps working together, had become a seamless duo, fulfilling every bit of their promise and potential.

"Their swings were telling me what I needed to throw," Lincecum said. "The game will show you.... And I've got Buster back there helping me, so that makes it twice as easy."

Lincecum no longer had his peak velocity in the latter innings, but he continued to throw heat at the letters when the Braves' slow bats showed they couldn't keep up with it. He retired 19 of 20 after Infante's leadoff single.

The Braves finally managed their second hit of the game in the seventh, when McCann took a rip at the first pitch and lined a one-out double. Gonzalez tapped back to the mound for the second out, which advanced McCann to third base with Diaz due up. Suddenly, Lincecum's options narrowed. No matter how much he could trust Posey, a slider or changeup in the dirt had the potential to bounce to the backstop and score the tying run. Diaz would be looking for a first-pitch fastball, and Lincecum had to throw him one.

Lincecum pumped a 92-mph pitch at the top of the strike zone, where even tame heaters can look overpowering. Diaz flied out to center field. Crisis averted.

It was the last time the Braves put Lincecum in the stretch. Their swings were late, tentative, or both. Pinch hitter Eric Hinske struck out on a changeup in the dirt to end the eighth inning.

Although Bochy asked Sergio Romo to start stretching in the eighth, there was no question that Lincecum would remain in the game for the ninth.

"They said to go warm up and I'm thinking, *Why?*" Romo said. "Hey, I was a fan today. I was entertained from the first pitch to the last pitch. I've never seen that before, especially in the magnitude of a game like this.

"Holy cow. He had his A-plus game today."

With the crowd on its feet and the noise deafening, Lincecum jogged to the mound in the ninth—a puddle of still water as a stadium reverberated around him. He got away with a rare mistake when he hung a changeup to Infante, but Uribe recovered to throw for the out after the hard grounder to short bounced off his chest.

Heyward, the Brave who worked Lincecum the hardest all game, could not lay off a 3-2 changeup in the dirt. Lincecum won two Cy Young Awards with that pitch. When he most needed an out, it served him again.

The Braves had one gasp left. Lincecum had plenty more in the tank.

He had shown Lee every pitch in his arsenal over their first three confrontations, and thus, his simplest weapon became his most effective one. Lee saw two sliders and a changeup to fall behind 1-2 and reduce the Braves to their final strike. Lincecum ended the game with a simple 92-mph fastball perfectly placed on the outside edge of the zone. Lee was powerless as he watched it into Posey's mitt.

Plate umpire Dana DeMuth flapped his arm, and Lincecum never broke face as the crowd erupted. He offered an ever-so-slight fist pump

Tim Lincecum was all business in an incredible postseason shutout of the Braves in 2010. After the final out, he only gave a slight fist pump in recognition of his accomplishment.

as he took the ball from Posey, tucked it in his back pocket, and led the Giants through the handshake line. He never smiled for an instant.

Nine innings. Two hits. A walk. Fourteen strikeouts. On the most important night of his baseball life. And a 1–0 victory.

It wasn't just the greatest postseason pitching performance in the franchise's San Francisco era. It was among the most dominant, period.

A day earlier, Philadelphia's Roy Halladay had thrown a no-hitter over the Cincinnati Reds in Game 1 of the other NL Division Series—the first in the postseason since Don Larsen's perfect game in 1956. Halladay accumulated a game score—a statistic that attempted to account for overall dominance—of 94. Lincecum's NLDS start scored even higher, with 96. By that measure, they were the second- and third-most dominant nine-inning starts in postseason baseball history, and they had come on back-to-back nights.

Only Roger Clemens' one-hit, 15-strikeout game for the Yankees at Seattle in the 2000 ALCS ranked higher than Lincecum's emphatic postseason debut.

"It's one of the best pitching performances I've ever been a part of," Ross said. "It's so, so, so much better to be on this side. I know I never felt comfortable facing him. He's capable of doing what he did tonight day in and day out."

Lincecum didn't just break the Giants' postseason record of 10 strikeouts, set by Jack Sanford in Game 5 of the 1962 World Series at Yankee Stadium. He destroyed it. And he did it by generating an astounding 31 swings and misses—the most by six of any major league pitcher in any game all year.

He became just the third pitcher to strike out 14 in a postseason shutout, joining Bob Gibson and Clemens.

"I don't know how many he struck out, but it was more than fingers on my hand," Cox said. "His breaking stuff is always out of the strike zone. Easier said than done. 'Don't swing at it.' It's almost impossible."

For years, the Braves dominated the NL with their pitching staff. Against them, Lincecum performed with Glavine's accuracy, Smoltz's fearlessness, and Maddux's serenity. He managed to keep his emotions utterly in check, and so did his rookie catcher.

"It's just a relaxed feeling, telling each other we've done this before, no big deal, come out and play the game," Lincecum said. "Throwing to Posey has been so great for me. The guy is a student of the game. He just wants to get better, help us get better."

Lincecum had just thrown the greatest postseason game in the Giants' San Francisco era on a night when anything less probably wouldn't have been enough. His team managed just one run, and needed a blown call plus a single under an infielder's glove to manage that much. Lincecum, so miraculously good on the mound, made loaves and fishes out of it.

In the postgame interview room, though, he spoke in unexcited, even tones. He described his workday as if he just spent three hours manning a concession stand.

"Things feel like they're in the right place," he said. "I think I kept my emotions in check, and I was pretty poised out there."

All the way to the 119th and final pitch.

"You know, it was almost like the game wasn't over for me," said Lincecum, asked why he didn't celebrate the last out. "I was in that mentality where if another batter steps to the plate, I want to be ready for it. You could even see I was surprised to get the ball from Buster when he threw it at me. It's been so long since I've thrown a complete game. I forgot all about that."

Leave it to everyone else, then, to gush—including the famous fan who kicked off one of the greatest and most memorable nights at AT&T Park. As Lincecum pushed through the tunnel that led to the clubhouse, there was Robin Williams, offering a handshake and rapid-fire words of congratulations. It was only then that Lincecum began to understand what he'd done.

He pitched with his soul and accomplished something truly important.

He returned to his locker, where a calendar was pinned to the wall. Out of symbolism or forgetfulness, it remained on August.

He turned the page. So did the Giants. They were a pitching organization now, through and through. And they would beat the Braves at their own game while winning three of four—all tense, torturous, one-run affairs—to push through one of the hardest-fought playoff series in franchise history.

Chapter 11

A Lot of Happy

"If you win the game, you're happy. I want to be happy."
—Juan Uribe

Wednesday, October 20, 2010
NLCS Game 4 vs. Philadelphia

Call them whatever you want. The Band of Misfits. Team Torture. Giants manager Bruce Bochy was fond of The Dirty Dozen, a reference to the 1967 film starring Charles Bronson and Lee Marvin about a group of outcasts sent on a suicide mission behind German lines in World War II. Someone gave Bochy the DVD. He carried it around with him throughout the 2010 postseason as a good-luck charm.

In Bochy's Dirty Dozen, Juan Uribe was the original member. He had joined the Giants on a minor league contract in 2009, unable to get a guaranteed deal with anyone even as a backup. There wasn't much infield depth in the Giants system at the time and Uribe had some versatility with the glove, along with a little pop in his bat. He was a starter on the Chicago White Sox's World Series–winning team in 2005, too. That experience couldn't hurt.

Uribe made the Giants out of spring training. He became the first of many non-roster free-agent signings to emerge as impact players, a list that would include Andres Torres and Santiago Casilla in 2010, then

Gregor Blanco and Ryan Vogelsong in subsequent years. As much as the Giants hit the draft jackpot with top-10 picks Tim Lincecum, Buster Posey, and Madison Bumgarner, nothing showed their front office acumen and scouting savvy as much as their ability to see talent in places where other clubs could not.

But nobody in the country wanted to talk about the Giants' assemblage of talent when they advanced to play the mighty Philadelphia Phillies in the 2010 NLCS, and for good reason. The Phillies led the NL with 97 victories. They had won the World Series in 2008, went back to the Fall Classic the following year, and were trying to become the first NL team to win three consecutive pennants since the 1942–44 St. Louis Cardinals.

The Phillies rotation included a trio of aces—Cole Hamels, Roy Oswalt, and Roy "Doc" Halladay, who was coming off the first no-hitter in the postseason since Don Larsen's perfect game in the 1956 World Series. Halladay would become the unanimous choice as the NL Cy Young Award winner, ending Tim Lincecum's two-year reign.

The Phillies scored the second-most runs in the National League, too. Only the Cincinnati Reds scored more, and the Phillies had just held them to a .124 average while sweeping them in the division series.

"You're not wondering, are you good enough to win?" Phillies shortstop Jimmy Rollins said. "With experience, you're not going to panic or worry about the ups and downs. You know guys are going to execute."

On ESPN.com, all 10 panelists took the Phillies to win the NLCS. Only three of them showed the Giants enough respect to predict the series would go seven games.

Nobody understood what awaited the Giants better than Pat Burrell, who spent his entire career with the Phillies before departing as a free agent after the 2008 season. His final act was to hit a double in Game 5 of the World Series, which led to the tiebreaking run in a championship-clinching victory. Phillies ownership thought so much of Burrell that they asked him to ride in the leading car in their World Series parade, then invited him back for the ring ceremony the following year.

Now Burrell stood in their way.

"You don't get to the World Series two years in a row without being good, and they know they're good," Burrell said. "Obviously, we'll probably be the underdog. But for this team to accomplish what it has, I think we're all proud and we'll give it our best shot.… I'm not going to take anything away from what we're doing. We're a hell of a team and we're coming in pretty confident."

If the Giants had listened to the assessment of others, they wouldn't have made it to the NLCS in the first place. Besides, they had reason to see daylight where others did not. They found a way to defeat Halladay when they faced him in April, didn't they? They beat Oswalt in all three meetings before the Houston Astros dealt him to the Phillies at midseason. Hamels was one of the best left-handers in the game and the 2008 World Series MVP, but they roughed him up for five runs in five innings when they saw him in August.

Phillies manager Charlie Manuel wasn't so pleased with the number of interview-room compliments his players were paying to the Giants pitching staff, either.

"We can score on anybody," said Manuel, getting a bit peevish after hearing one too many questions about Lincecum, Bumgarner, Matt Cain, Jonathan Sanchez, and the league's strongest bullpen. "We can score on the Giants."

The Giants had to overcome more than their underdog status between the lines. They had to begin the series at Citizens Bank Park in front of some of the most vocal fans in baseball, and Burrell understood what that meant, too. He received a standing ovation when the Giants came to town in August, his first trip to the stadium as a visiting player. He hit a home run in his first at-bat. The Phillies fans booed him around the bases, and jeered him the rest of the series.

In that environment, Lincecum and Halladay prepared for a Game 1 duel for the ages. One pitcher was coming off a two-hit, 14-strikeout shutout. The other was coming off a no-hitter.

The Philadelphia crowd tried its best to get inside Lincecum's head. Fans filled the ballpark with wolf whistles in a reference to his long hair—a variation of the taunt that Flyers fans always reserved for Penguins star Jaromir Jagr and his famously frizzy locks.

As Game 1 began, the last person in the world who drew the attention of Phillies fans was Cody Ross, the Giants' No. 8 hitter. If not for a blocking claim in August, Ross wouldn't have been on the Giants roster at all. Nobody dreamed he would be their starting right fielder in the postseason, either. But the Giants left Jose Guillen off their playoff roster, citing a neck injury. (It came out later that Guillen was under investigation after his wife received a shipment of performance-enhancing drugs as part of a federal sting operation.)

Over his well-traveled career, Ross had been traded for players you've never heard of: Steve Colyer in one deal, Ben Kozlowski in another swap, and even the dreaded "cash considerations." At one point, Ross was a 25-year-old with 2,559 at-bats over seven minor league seasons and just 44 in the major leagues.

When Bochy told Ross that he'd be the starting right fielder in the playoffs, Ross wept. Then he spent the entire NLCS bringing Phillies fans to tears.

Halladay came out firing just as everyone expected, retiring the first seven Giants and extending his streak to 35 batters faced without allowing a hit in the postseason. There was no reason to expect any breakthrough as Ross, the No. 8 hitter, stepped to the plate.

Ross was just 3-for-16 in his career off Halladay with no walks and two strikeouts. When Halladay threw his perfect game earlier in the season at Florida, Ross was one of the nine in the Marlins lineup. He grounded out twice and popped to short that day.

So when Ross smacked his home run in his first at-bat of the NLCS, it had all the impact of a smooth stone to the forehead. Ross hit another home run when he came to bat again in the fifth, turning on a cutter that Halladay thought he had thrown to an unhittable spot. The Giants stunned the Phillies with a 4–3 victory in the series opener, and in the aftermath, someone took notice: Cody Ross spelled backward was *ssory doc.*

"Nice garbage find for us, huh?" Aubrey Huff said.

The Giants ended up splitting the first two games in Philadelphia—Ross hit another homer in Game 2 that accounted for their only run in a 6–1 loss—but they regained the upper hand at AT&T Park when Cain held the Phillies to two hits over seven innings of a 3–0 victory in Game 3.

The Phillies might have begun the NLCS eyeing Game 4 as their chance to complete a sweep. Instead, they sent their weakest starting pitcher, Joe Blanton, to a hostile mound, desperate to keep from falling into a deep hole.

Game 4 would be the hardest fought of the series—one that tested the Giants like no other in their postseason run.

It's hard to imagine anyone being more dangerous in October than Barry Bonds in 2002, when he hit eight home runs in 45 at-bats and drew 27 walks, 13 of them intentional.

Cody Ross approached it. The Braves and then the Phillies tried to bust him inside. They tried to get him fishing. They changed eye levels, switched up pitch sequences. None of it mattered. Gleefully skipping out of the batter's box, Ross collected five go-ahead RBIs in the Giants' first seven playoff games. Entering Game 4 of the NLCS at AT&T Park, he had driven in 40 percent of the team's runs in the postseason.

Bruce Bochy made one no-brainer adjustment to the lineup, elevating Ross from eighth to sixth. In the hours before Game 4, though, Bochy was forced to make another tweak. Juan Uribe had jammed his wrist on a slide into second base in Game 1, and although he returned in Game 3, he didn't look right while going hitless in three at-bats. Mike Fontenot committed an error when he started at third base in Game 2. So Bochy went back to Pablo Sandoval, who lost his job down the stretch and had been benched for the five previous playoff games.

"We think it's the right thing to give him the night off," Bochy said of Uribe. "I could tell with his swinging. I talked to him today, and he admitted it's still bothering him."

Bochy also reneged on a pledge to start center fielder Andres Torres in Game 4, instead sticking with Aaron Rowand after he had doubled and scored a key run in Game 3. Torres, whose career languished for years while he dealt with an undiagnosed attention deficit hyperactivity disorder, was able to overcome his condition with medication and emerged as a difference-making catalyst for the Giants all season. He amazed the trainers when he returned to the lineup on September 24 just seven days after an emergency appendectomy. But he lost his rhythm at the plate and simply looked overmatched in the playoffs. He was 3-for-26 with 12 strikeouts and just one walk.

Torres would have a part to play in Game 4, though. So would Uribe. The Giants and Phillies were about to stage a back-and-forth classic—one of the wildest and most entertaining playoff games in recent memory.

There were blown leads, huge at-bats, clutch hits, mistakes, moments of redemption, awe, electricity, wonder, genius, belief...and a whole lot of brilliance from a rookie named Buster Posey.

And torture. Of course, there would be that.

The Giants already held a 2–1 lead in the series, but Game 4 was an absolute must-win. It was the only time all series the Phillies would not start Halladay, Oswalt, or Hamels. The only way to pull the upset would be to seize control of the series in Game 4.

The Giants took an immediate lead in the first inning. Freddy Sanchez singled, advanced to third on two wild pitches, and then Posey lunged after one of Blanton's curveballs. The barrel of his bat almost appeared to get fatter as he kept it in the zone. He chopped the pitch back to the box, off the mound, and through the middle as Sanchez raced home.

Entering Game 4, Posey was just 1-for-11 in the series and battling heavy legs. He had never played so much baseball in a summer. But suddenly there he stood as if transported back to early July, a month when he batted .417, had a 21-game hitting streak, and fireworks seemed to accompany his every trip to the plate.

Posey came through again in the third inning, after Huff laced a two-out single. Blanton threw a 1-1 changeup that veered down and in, Posey took a smooth, steeply angled swing, nearly picked the pitch out of the dirt, and did more than merely find a way to put it into play. He barreled it up, sending a drive over the head of left fielder Ben Francisco. Huff, running on the two-out contact, raced home for a 2–0 lead.

"He did all the damage for us, really," Bochy gushed about Posey after the game. "Every at-bat, be delivered for us, and he's quite a talent. We know it. We've seen it for a while."

Posey made an impact with more than his pure hitting skill at the plate. He and Bumgarner were two rookies against a dangerous and disciplined Phillies lineup, and they had to tailor their game plan as they went. Although Bumgarner struck out five of the first nine batters he faced, the Phillies made an adjustment their next time through the order. They shortened up their swings, concentrated on putting the ball in play, and were able to sustain a rally in the fifth.

Francisco and Carlos Ruiz led off with singles, Blanton advanced them with a sacrifice bunt, and Shane Victorino lined a single up the middle. Francisco raced home and Ruiz tried to follow him.

The Phillies were going to test Rowand, their former teammate, knowing his throws sometimes leaned more toward exuberance than accuracy. This time, Rowand threw on a line to the plate, and Posey did the rest. He skillfully picked the short hop just as Ruiz began his slide, and in one motion lowered his shoulder and thudded into the runner for the out. Posey had begun catching just four years earlier at Florida State, and had learned so much about the position in a short period of time. But those hands, as blurry fast as hummingbird wings, couldn't be taught.

"Rowand made a good throw," said Posey, deflecting credit for preventing the tying run from scoring. "I didn't have to move any. It was a really good throw on his part."

The inning wasn't over yet. Bumgarner continued to labor and the Phillies continued to look more and more comfortable at the plate. So after Chase Utley collected their fourth single of the inning, Bochy went to the bullpen and Santiago Casilla. It was the first time all postseason that the Giants didn't receive a quality start. The Giants led 2–1 but their bullpen had to get the majority of the outs, and Bochy knew the way was littered with hazards.

The lead did not persist for long. Casilla's spike curve had established himself as a late-inning reliever, but he threw a flat one and Placido Polanco connected for a double. Victorino and Utley scored, the Phillies led 3–2, and they were threatening to turn the inning into a sledgehammer. Casilla issued an intentional walk to Ryan Howard, then missed badly while hitting Jayson Werth with a pitch to load the bases.

It made no sense to stick with Casilla, especially since Jimmy Rollins was next—and the last time the Giants had that matchup, Rollins hit a damaging, three-run double off him in Game 2. But Bochy did not make a move toward the mound.

Casilla's wild ride took another turn. He got ahead 1-2 and threw a 97-mph fastball that took a crazy bounce off the front of the plate. The ball popped up so high in the air that it sailed over the backstop netting, which allowed all three runners to advance. Polanco scored to make it a 4–2 Phillies lead.

There was nothing Casilla could do but focus on the batter at the plate. He did, blowing a high fastball past Rollins' bat to end the inning and record one of the most important outs of the night.

The Giants trailed by two runs, their bullpen had to muddle through the rest of the game, and the first batter they sent to the plate in the bottom of the fifth had appeared totally overmatched all postseason. It was Torres, who entered in the No. 9 spot with Casilla as part of a double-switch.

Blanton tried to expand the zone on Torres, and as keyed up as he felt at the plate, he managed to compose himself while drawing a significant leadoff walk. So many of the Giants' rallies in the second half of the season began with Torres getting on base, and his speed might have been a factor when Polanco took his eye off Edgar Renteria's potential double-play grounder. The ball deflected off Polanco's chest, he had to settle for the out at first base, and the Giants took advantage of the mistake when Huff singled up the middle. Torres dashed around third, slid between Ruiz's shin guards, and found the plate.

The Giants still trailed 4–3, but they had knocked Blanton to the dugout, the game had become a battle of the bullpens, and they liked the way their relievers matched up with the Phillies. When Casilla retired the side in the sixth, he ensured that Bochy could save his situational arms to match up the way he wanted.

Bochy wanted nothing better than a lead. In the bottom of the sixth, the Giants seized it.

Burrell began the rally by working a walk off right-hander Chad Durbin. In the late innings, Bochy usually would pinch-run for Burrell and replace him in left field. But not when they trailed by a run. It would take a home run to score Burrell. With Ross at the plate, it wasn't such a far-fetched thought.

But when Ross fouled off a running fastball under his chin, his bat became a fatal casualty. It splintered at the handle, and Ross wore a grim expression as he handed it to the bat boy. He would have to do damage with two strikes against him and a fresh piece of lumber.

On the next pitch, Ross ripped a double down the left-field line. Burrell's sore heel throbbed with every sprinting step to third base as Ross slid ahead of the tag.

Sandoval was next, and he dragged so much baggage to the plate. His second full major league season was a major letdown. The "Camp Panda" fitness boot camp the Giants organized for him the previous winter failed to yield lasting results. HI s conditioning became such an issue that he couldn't field a half-dozen grounders without bending over with his hands on his knees in exhaustion. His lateral range at third base decreased, and although he had a highly accurate arm, the wild throws multiplied as his footwork lagged.

When the Giants went to Atlanta in August, Sandoval was thrown out at third base after Lincecum tried to advance him with a sacrifice bunt. Bochy assumed that Sandoval missed a sign or got a late jump. When he looked at the replay, he was shocked. Sandoval hadn't missed the sign. He was just too slow.

Sandoval remained a fan favorite, though, in part because he maintained his sense of fun on the field. He remained the loudest towel-waving cheerleader in the dugout, masterminded every coordinated handshake ritual, chattered words of support in two languages, and led the league in fielding percentage while simultaneously blowing Bazooka bubbles.

More than anything, the Kung Fu Panda was fiercely loyal to his teammates. In a heated game at Dodger Stadium, when Lincecum hit Matt Kemp with a pitch and the batter took two threatening steps toward the mound, Sandoval raced over from first base before Posey could react from behind the plate. The Panda made an imposing guard dog, and there was no way he'd allow Kemp a clear path to his pitcher.

The toughest obstacle for Sandoval in 2010, other than his weight, was the pressure he put on himself after getting off to a slow start. His swings became more and more desperate as he tried to raise his numbers and rescue his average. He hacked away as if trying to get two hits in every at-bat.

Unfortunately for the Giants, he was at his worst when they needed him the most. A terrific clutch hitter in his first full season, Sandoval hit just .208 with runners in scoring position in 2010. He hadn't knocked in multiple runs in a game since August 24. He remained a positive presence in the dugout, but his joy had dulled a bit.

In those five playoff games when Sandoval rode the bench, injured veteran Mark DeRosa often sat next to him. DeRosa's wrist prevented him from playing, but he had been a part of playoff teams before. He knew his most valuable contribution would be to keep younger players like Sandoval as upbeat and confident as possible.

"Remember," DeRosa told him. "If you deliver in the postseason, nobody remembers your batting average."

Whenever the opportunity came, Sandoval just needed to slow the game down, keep his weight back, react to the pitch—and resist trying to get two hits in every at-bat.

In the sixth inning of Game 4, only Sandoval could find a way to do all of the above.

Durbin threw a first-pitch changeup at the bottom of the zone and Sandoval lashed it down the first-base line. The ball landed on the outermost edge of the chalk line in right field, and Sandoval shrieked and pointed when first-base umpire Jeff Nelson called it foul. Bochy came out to request that Nelson confer with right-field umpire Ted Barrett, but the ball landed almost at Barrett's feet. It was so close to him that it shot past in a blur.

There wasn't anything Sandoval could do. After such a long, wasted season, he had come through with the most important hit of his young career.

Now he'd have to do it again.

Durbin's next pitch was in the dirt and Sandoval swung wildly as if trying to extract it from a sand trap. He stepped out of the box, refastened his batting gloves, and took a deep breath. Then he laid off the next curve in the dirt. He fouled off a fastball up and in.

There was one place left to try. Ruiz began to stand out of his crouch as Durbin delivered a high fastball. He threw the pitch exactly where he wanted. It didn't matter. There wasn't a better neck-high-fastball hitter in the league than Sandoval, who split the gap in left-center as Burrell and Ross raced home to give the Giants a 5–4 lead.

After trying all season to get two hits in one at-bat, Sandoval did exactly that. His first double didn't count. The second one did. And so began a legendary postseason career that would include World Series MVP honors in 2012, followed by a .429 average when the Giants returned to the Fall Classic again in 2014.

Sandoval would end his Giants career as a .344 hitter in the postseason. His second playoff hit, a two-run double off Durbin, would rank among his most significant.

Sandoval stutter-stepped into second base, pointed to the sky, maniacally clapped his hands, and looked into the Giants dugout.

"Everything going crazy," he said of the scene. "I just couldn't believe it. I was so excited. When you're a little kid, you dream of going to the World Series. It's one of the best moments of my life."

The Giants did not celebrate for long, though. They failed to take advantage of a bases-loaded chance in the seventh. Posey started the rally with a double—his third hit of the night—and Rollins committed an error that nearly spelled doom. But Sandoval grounded into a double play to end the inning. It was one of those missed opportunities that almost always leads to regret.

Sure enough, the Phillies tied it in the eighth when Howard doubled off Javier Lopez and Werth doubled off Sergio Romo. But just like Casilla earlier in the night, Romo came back from a letdown to record three of the most unsung outs in the game. With no outs and the tying run at second base, Romo got Rollins to pop up before Francisco and Cruz struck out.

Bochy had to be prepared for the prospect of extra innings when he brought in Brian Wilson to face the Phillies in the ninth. The pitcher's spot was due up fourth in the bottom of the inning. So Bochy double-switched and put Uribe, sore wrist and all, at shortstop.

Wilson retired the side, setting up the Giants for a chance to win in the bottom of the inning. And Manuel found himself in a bind. He wanted to save closer Brad Lidge for a save situation, but he knew he couldn't ask his top setup man, Ryan Madson, to pitch a third inning.

Instead, he trusted his Game 2 starter.

Oswalt, who threw fastball after fastball to overwhelm the Giants in Game 2, had sprinted back to the clubhouse to put on his spikes the moment Werth's tying double landed in the grass. It didn't matter that he'd already thrown his side session earlier in the day and had just two days of rest. He campaigned for the ball, insisting to Phillies pitching coach Rich Dubee that he was fresh and ready.

Oswalt was undefeated in 10 postseason appearances. But the Giants already had found a way to beat Halladay and Hamels in the series. They simply weren't intimidated any longer, no matter who stood on that hill.

The Giants attacked Oswalt's fastball. After Freddy Sanchez lined out, Huff found a bit more daylight with a single through the right side. Then came Posey, who already had three hits.

There were many times in Oswalt's career when he could force a rookie to get himself out. He knew this was not one of those times. Posey already picked a curve out of the dirt for one hit and barreled up a changeup for another. He was just a 23-year-old kid, but Oswalt knew he couldn't hope to trick him. He just had to throw it past him.

Posey went for it all on the first pitch, swinging through 94 mph. Oswalt fed him another fastball, then another, then another. Posey appeared to be calibrating its pace as he fouled one back, then lofted another barely five feet foul into the right-field corner as the crowd groaned. The next 0-2 fastball was Oswalt's best, down and away, but Posey spoiled it with a foul into the Phillies bullpen.

Posey tapped his bat into the ground, suspecting it might have broken. He was satisfied that it hadn't. He already had three hits with that bat. He was about to collect his fourth.

Oswalt wasted a pitch and came back with one more fastball. Posey didn't try to get around on it. He let it get deep in the zone and expertly lined it to right field. It took a sliding stop from Werth to cut it off, make Huff stop at third base, and momentarily save the game.

"The guy throws hard. He's got an electric fastball, and good off-speed stuff as well," Posey said. "So the goal was to let the ball travel, try to see it, and I think when I'm going good, that's what I do."

The Giants had one out, runners at the corners, so many ways to win—and because Bochy had double-switched three times in the game, the original member of his Dirty Dozen stepped to the plate. Uribe already had made one contribution in the top of the ninth, ranging to take away an infield hit from Ross Gload. Swinging a bat was a bit trickier, though. He hadn't looked good in batting practice earlier in the day.

Uribe had one good arm. Bochy hoped it would be enough.

The crowd serenaded him with chants of "OOOO-ribe" just as they did for his late cousin, Jose, in the 1980s. Eighteen years later, the Giants had a Uribe at shortstop again.

Jose Uribe always carried himself with a quiet dignity. Juan was a little more boisterous. He'd entertain fans in the left-field corner during batting practice, sing the Canadian national anthem at random times, and douse himself with cologne—his "hit spray"—before going out to take batting practice. More than anyone, the younger Uribe ensured that the Giants clubhouse had no schism between native English and Spanish speakers. His usual opponent at the dominoes table was Wilson. He usually stood up with most of Wilson's money, too.

And Uribe had come through with so many huge hits in the late innings. He finished second on the club with 24 home runs in 2010, 11 of which either tied the game or put the Giants ahead. When the club's offense began to stall in mid-September and the hitters held a meeting under the Wrigley Field bleachers, Uribe responded with a six-RBI inning to put the Giants back on their path to the NL West title.

Whenever he made hard contact, he'd flash both his white gloves, fingers spread. If you saw Uribe making his jazz hands, it was usually a good sign.

English wasn't Uribe's forte, but sometimes that made it easier for him to find the essence. One night in Cincinnati, after he hit a 433-foot home run, he said this:

"I never think I'm a good player or a bad player. This is what I'm thinking: *I can play*. And I want to play. Every day I come to the ballpark and I only try to do something to help the team. One day, you can win the game with your glove. One day, you can win a game with a hit.

"Win the game, go to the playoffs, go to the World Series. If you go, nobody thinks you hit .100 or .200. If you win the game, you're happy. I want to be happy.

"Me, I'm not thinking maybe. I think this team will go to the play-offs. I believe in this team. I believe in the guys. My teammates are good players and good people, too."

With the crowd standing and imploring for one more hit, Uribe stood in the box and geared himself up for a fastball. Oswalt unleashed a 95-mph heater into Ruiz's mitt. There was no way Oswalt would throw anything soft to a hitter with a bad wrist, and Uribe failed to catch up to it.

The next pitch was pure chin music, backing Uribe off the plate. Then Oswalt came back inside a second time. His fastball appeared to nick Uribe on the hand, but plate umpire Wally Bell ruled that it hit the knob of the bat. Uribe turned to protest and Bochy ventured onto the field to argue. Uribe should have been standing at first with the bases loaded. Instead, he had a 1-2 count.

Oswalt kept on pounding his fastball inside, and one more glanced off Uribe's bat as he tried to get out of the way. Oswalt had thrown four fastballs in a row to Uribe, just as he did to Posey. He backed Uribe off the plate three consecutive times. There was no way that a hitter could be bold enough to lunge over the plate at an outside pitch, was there?

Oswalt threw a changeup down and away. Uribe lunged at it.

The ball hung in the air for what felt like forever, and the volume from the stands began to build as the fans understood what was about to happen. Francisco caught the fly ball in left field and Huff waited an extra millisecond on third base to be sure. Then he sprinted home, slid across the plate, and popped up with both arms raised in a triumphant pose. The Giants spilled onto the field.

They had wrested a 6–5 victory over the mighty Phillies. Uribe's sacrifice fly delivered their first walk-off win in the postseason since Kenny Lofton delivered the pennant in 2002, and the celebration raged all through the stands.

In one back-and-forth classic, Giants fans saw Sandoval redeem a wasted summer and give birth to a career as a postseason hero. They saw Casilla and Romo give up leads only to keep their composure and

Juan Uribe triggered "a lot of happy" with his walk-off sacrifice fly in Game 4 of the 2010 NLCS.

record huge outs. They saw Posey become baptized as more than a talented rookie but a fully formed superstar, with four brilliant hits and an astounding, run-saving defensive play.

In the postgame interview room, someone asked Posey if he could digest what he'd just done.

"I helped the team win," he said. "I guess that's how I digest it."

But did he understand that it was an epic night in a postseason game?

"Well, thank you."

It might have been the night that the Giants forged their well-deserved reputation as the toughest October team in recent baseball history.

They kept on fighting to extinguish the Phillies and win the pennant. They lost Game 5 and had to return to Citizens Bank Park, but Bochy drew a line in the sand. In a non-elimination Game 6, he used three-fourths of his starting rotation—Lincecum and Bumgarner appeared in relief—to win a pennant-clinching game that featured a bases-clearing incident and more back-and-forth drama. Uribe accounted for the tie-breaking run that night, too, with a home run in the eighth inning.

In the aftermath of Game 4, he once again found the essence.

"I go home now, be with my family," said Uribe. "And be a lot of happy."

Uribe repeated those same four words over and over through waves of interviews: "A lot of happy."

There was no better description after a draining, dramatic, and joyous night at AT&T Park.

Chapter 12

Forever Giant

"Thanks to these gentlemen here, the torture is over!"
—Duane Kuiper

Wednesday, October 27, 2010
Game 1 of the World Series vs. Texas

Joe DiMaggio's father came home with the smell of the Pacific Ocean on his hands. Lefty O'Doul's pub still serves corned beef and cabbage in a dimly lit spot near Union Square, five decades after his death. Willie Mays patrolled center field like a falcon, Willie McCovey swung the bat like a sledgehammer, Juan Marichal fired the ball with balletic balance, and Barry Bonds owned the batter's box with a lethal combination of strength and intelligence.

Between its native sons and its own beloved Giants, San Francisco has a grand baseball tradition. But for more than five decades since moving west, a World Series championship always escaped the foggy peninsula.

Whoever hoisted the trophy first would become part of an everlasting legacy. However it happened, the triumphant moment would be met with wet eyes, a familial embrace, and thoughts of loved ones whose devotion was so strong it could be felt from beyond.

For the better part of a decade at AT&T Park, the Giants believed their championship window would remain open as long as they had Bonds on their roster. They came within a handful of outs of fulfilling hopes in 2002. But that time passed, and following a painful transition, a pitching-centric philosophy emerged that gave the Giants a new direction into October.

"In the past we lived and died with one superstar player," GM Brian Sabean said late in the 2010 season. "There aren't any superstars on this team. There might be a couple rising stars, but our organization is built on pitching."

But it required more than a stout rotation or talent to survive three rounds of postseason play. It required more than desire or dashes of good fortune.

It required a fierceness of spirit.

To win a World Series in a Giants uniform meant pushing through more than three opponents. It meant pushing through five decades of cold summers, too.

It meant overcoming Bobby Richardson snaring McCovey's line drive in 1962, the heartache of Game 6 in Anaheim, and the ground shaking at Candlestick. And the longer hopes went dashed, the more daunting the task appeared.

There was no reason to believe the Giants had that team in 2010. They were in fourth place at the All-Star break. They retooled their entire opening-day lineup over the course of 162 games. They snuck into an NL West title on the final day of the regular season. Nobody took them seriously, least of all themselves—and perhaps that worked to their advantage.

They didn't enter the playoffs burdened by decades of unmet expectations. They simply wanted to win for each other. And on a team of former Pirates and Devil Rays, studded with waiver claims and minor league free agents, nobody epitomized their improbable arc better than Edgar Renteria.

He was a lifetime removed from being that 21-year-old rookie with a face of pure elation when he delivered the hit that clinched the 1997 World Series for the Florida Marlins. The first season of Renteria's two-year, $18.5 million contract with the Giants was a disaster, and his

34-year-old body continued to betray him in 2010. He broke down in so many ways, requiring separate stints on the disabled list due to groin, hamstring, and elbow injuries. During a rare 12-game span on the active roster in June, he scored one run, grounded into four double plays, and the Giants went 2–9 in his starts.

Amid an 0-for-15 streak in July, a reporter gently asked Renteria if he had any thoughts of retiring. As bad as he looked at the plate, it was a valid question. He was stunned by it nonetheless.

"Myself, I am too proud," Renteria said. "I always say if I can't play this game, I'd be home. But I can help this team win."

Renteria had become such an afterthought, though, that the Giants made him wait until rosters expanded on September 1 to activate him from his last DL stint. With the club dueling the Padres down the pennant stretch, Renteria started just one of the final 14 games. He barely made the postseason roster, and only found himself back in the starting lineup in the playoffs because a plump Pablo Sandoval had become a defensive liability.

As the Giants began their push to win the NL West, though, it was Renteria who forged their madcap clubhouse together. After a spate of low-scoring losses in September, hitting coach Hensley Meulens called a meeting of the position players. They met in the cramped batting cage underneath the Wrigley Field bleachers.

Renteria took the floor, telling his teammates that no matter how minor a part he would play down the stretch, he stood behind every one of them. He would trust any of them with his life. He asked them to deliver him to the World Series one more time, to give him one last shot. He began to cry, telling them he was convinced he still had something left to give.

"He broke down and we all broke down with him," Aubrey Huff said. "Since then, I've wanted this more for him than anybody."

This had become the unseen element in the Giants clubhouse. The players came from so many unexpected places, but in that perfect moment, their paths so neatly intersected. Among their company, they weren't a group of bearded, thong-wearing rejects, misfits, and castoffs. They were family.

They wanted to win for selfish reasons, sure. But more than anything, they looked around the room and wanted to win for each other.

"It is a long time ago. Thirteen years ago, you know?" Renteria said of his life-changing, 11th-inning hit from that Game 7 of his youth. "But I feel great. I was always ready for a moment like now. I'm trying to trust in whatever I've got."

Nobody would have envisioned the Giants and Texas Rangers meeting in the 2010 World Series, least of all Bengie Molina. He became the first player since Lonnie Smith in 1985 to play in the Fall Classic against the team that traded him in midseason.

Molina held so many secrets after catching the Giants for so many years, and Lincecum did not look forward to facing his former battery-mate. Molina had stayed in touch during Lincecum's miserable, winless August, sending him motivational text messages. To the pitcher, Molina was a friend and a guide.

"I've said it before and I'm going to say it again, he's been half of the reason why I got here outside of my dad and my family and my other teammates," Lincecum said. "He's meant a lot to me, and he's meant a lot to this team. He's a part of the reason why we're here and obviously part of the reason why they're there, too."

Molina called the Giants his brothers, "but in between the lines, I have to defend my colors and they have to defend theirs."

Molina had defended a different set of colors against the Giants in the 2002 World Series. Back then, he was the starting catcher for an Angels club that, like Texas, emerged from the AL West and upset the leading powers with a lineup of tough outs, smart baserunners, and power threats.

Molina was facing a much different opponent now.

"In 2002, the Giants were very powerful," Molina said. "They had Barry Bonds, Jeff Kent. Now they have young guys who can do the job…. It's hard to say which one is better. But I think these guys are more dangerous because of how they play the game. I know what is inside of them."

To most of the outside world, though, the Giants were underdogs yet again. As hot as Cody Ross had gotten in the postseason, Josh Hamilton had just belted four home runs in six games against the Yankees in the ALCS. Nelson Cruz was bashing everything in sight. Most of all, Texas would send left-hander Cliff Lee to the mound against Lincecum in Game 1.

True, the Giants already had found a way to beat one impenetrable ace in the Phillies' Roy Halladay. But Lee was 7–0 with a 1.26 ERA in eight career playoff starts. Against the Rays and Yankees, two of the best offensive clubs in the game, Lee was 3–0 with a 0.75 ERA, 34 strikeouts, and just one walk.

Lee made a few headlines when he deflected a question about the Giants lineup, instead praising their pitchers—especially Lincecum.

"The way he does it…no one else does it that way. I like that," Lee said. "I like when unorthodox works."

When Game 1 of the World Series returned to San Francisco, the Giants were counting on it.

Once again, Lincecum entered as the smaller, less heralded pitcher in the matchup. It was the role he'd played his entire life. The only difference: this was Game 1 of the World Series.

Against the Atlanta Braves in the NLDS, Lincecum turned in one of the greatest pitching performances of all time. Against the Phillies in the NLCS, he outpitched Halladay to give the Giants an important early edge. But the Rangers represented a tougher matchup for him.

Unlike the Braves, who were brittle and beset by injuries, and the Phillies, whose lineup appeared to age before the Giants' eyes, the AL champions from Arlington posed a multidimensional threat. They entered with 15 stolen bases in 17 attempts over 11 postseason games. If there was a glaring weakness in Lincecum's game, it was his ability to hold runners. He had allowed 27 steals in 30 attempts during the season—a 90 percent success rate that was the worst among all major league pitchers with a minimum of 25 attempts.

The wolf whistles from Phillies fans didn't get inside Lincecum's head. Opposing baserunners could. And in the first inning of his first World Series start, they succeeded.

Elvis Andrus led off with a line-drive single, putting Lincecum immediately into the stretch. His attention was divided as he threw over once, tried to use a slide step, and had trouble controlling his pitches as a consequence. Young drew a walk, Hamilton followed with a dribbler to first base that advanced both runners, and the Rangers tallied a run when Vladimir Guerrero's comebacker deflected off Lincecum's left leg for an infield single.

The Rangers had a 1–0 lead, one out, and runners at the corners.

Maybe it was the throbbing pain in his left shin. Maybe it was the boiling cauldron the Rangers instantly created. Maybe it was the frenzied environment of his first World Series start, or maybe it was all of the above. Whatever the reason, Lincecum lost track of everything when he leapt off the mound and plucked Cruz's chopper out of the air. He froze Young in between third base and home but instead of throwing to Juan Uribe, who was begging for the ball, Lincecum merely jogged Young back to third.

The ballpark buzzed with confusion, and when Lincecum looked back to second base, he frowned. He immediately knew.

He screwed this one up, big time.

"A brain fart," he said, admitting he thought the bases were loaded. "It's a first for a lot of us and different atmosphere…and I got outside of myself there."

It was Dave Righetti's job to bring him back. The longtime pitching coach jogged out and told Lincecum what he needed to hear: erase what just happened and focus forward, because this next pitch might be the most important one you'll make.

Ian Kinsler batted with the bases loaded. Buster Posey called for a first-pitch slider, and Lincecum caught too much of the plate with it. But the Giants caught a break, Kinsler's hard grounder down the line was hit right to Uribe, and he stepped on the bag before throwing across for a double play.

Lincecum escaped the cauldron, but the Rangers immersed him in more hot water in the second inning. This time, Lincecum would have to overcome more than his own brain fart. The entire team nearly came unhinged behind him in the second inning.

The Rangers' rally began when Molina punched a single, and with one out, Lee squared to bunt. If anyone should have smelled subterfuge, it was the Giants. They knew Molina was too slow to advance on a sacrifice. It's the reason Bochy always hit him higher than eighth in the lineup.

Instead, they fell for the trap, and they fell hard. Their infielders charged as Lee pulled back his bat and took a slashing swing. It was the old butcher boy play, one of Bochy's favorite gambits, and the Rangers executed it to perfection. Not only did Lee's line drive easily shoot past the infielders, but the outfielders were playing so shallow that it split the gap in left-center for a double.

With runners at second and third, Texas manager Ron Washington and his coaches decided to press their luck. Andrus followed with a fly ball to center field that was deep enough to score most runners, but not Molina. The Rangers sent him anyway, along with a message: if the Giants wanted to beat them, they'd have to execute.

Even a decent throw would have arrived in time to cut down Molina at the plate. But Andres Torres bundled all his adrenaline into a heave that sailed a third of the way up the first-base line. Molina scored easily, Lee saw an opportunity to take third base, and it took a diving effort from Uribe to keep Posey's throw from skipping into left field.

All season long, the Rangers used claw and deer horn hand signals to celebrate their daring on the bases. When Molina returned to a jubilant Texas dugout, they welcomed him with moose antlers.

Lincecum managed to strand Lee, and although it was just a 2–0 deficit after two innings, the Giants simply didn't appear to have their heads in the game. It was clear, too: Lincecum's stuff, especially the slider that carried him to a September resurgence and beyond, was not nearly as crisp.

But Lee wasn't, either.

A 2–0 deficit should have been insurmountable against Lee, but his cutter lacked its usual buzzsaw movement and accuracy. The Giants' plan was to stay on his fastball, which was so much tougher to do when he poured in his overhand curve for strikes. One time through the lineup, it was apparent that Lee didn't have a good feel for his curve.

He still had plenty of guile and the ability to change speeds, though. And he had his reputation. The Giants were so bewildered to find themselves in 2-0 and 3-1 counts that they helped him out by over-swinging.

Freddy Sanchez, a playoff neophyte who had spent almost his entire career on go-nowhere teams in Pittsburgh, should have been among the Giants' most overanxious hitters against Lee. It was fair to wonder if Sanchez would have the nerve and toughness to handle the postseason.

In the Atlanta series, Sanchez was just 2-for-16 while battling two sore shoulders. But his two-out hit in the ninth inning off fireballing closer Craig Kimbrel, followed by another from Huff, a fellow veteran playing in his first postseason, led to the tying run in a Game 3 comeback victory that marked the turning point of that NL Division Series. The Giants advanced past Atlanta, barely, and Sanchez had a chance to shake off the nerves of playing October baseball for the first time.

By Game 1 of the World Series, Sanchez didn't look scared. He looked more like a batting champion.

"At the beginning of the postseason, I was feeling real anxious and not relaxed at the plate, and as the postseason went on, I started to get more comfortable," Sanchez said. "I started to find my swing a little bit."

Sanchez had his swing against Lee all night. He hit a broken-bat double in the first inning, but it was wasted when he got caught between second and third, unsure whether Posey's blooper to right field would fall.

Kinsler made a sensational catch with his back to the infield, then threw across his body to second base. Sanchez slipped, fell, and was doubled off.

Sanchez stepped to the plate with another chance in the third after Young misplayed Renteria's hard grounder at third base for an error. The Giants gave away an out when Lincecum popped up a sacrifice attempt, but Lee, so precise while walking just one batter all postseason, missed with an inside pitch and hit Torres.

Sanchez scolded himself after chasing a high fastball for a second strike, but Lee's fearsome cutter did not have its familiar put-away bite. He left it over the middle and Sanchez lashed it down the left-field line for a double to drive in the Giants' first run. With the crowd fully awakened, Posey followed with a line-drive single up the middle that scored Torres to tie it. The ball cleared the shortstop's glove by a good six feet, but Sanchez was understandably skittish about getting doubled off second base again. He hesitated before continuing to third, and was held there.

Lee struck out Pat Burrell and Ross to end the inning and strand Sanchez at third base. The Giants failed to take the lead, but it was 2–2 and they could sense that the Rangers' ace was wobbling. Sanchez already landed two jabs. His biggest was yet to come.

With one out in the fifth, Torres doubled on a cutter over the middle and the Giants' hottest hitter stepped to the plate again. Lee had gotten Sanchez to chase a high fastball in their first confrontation. He went back to the high heat and Sanchez reacted, muscling the pitch all the way to the base of the left-field wall to give the Giants a 3–2 lead.

It was Sanchez's third double of the game and he used every part of the ballpark, from the right-field chalk to the left-field line to the gap in left-center. He became the first player in World Series history to double in each of his first three career at-bats in the Fall Classic.

He didn't just settle in at the plate. He settled into the record books.

"It's crazy to have my name up there," said Sanchez, after being informed of his unprecedented feat. "It's something special for just a little guy like me to be able to do it."

Freddy Sanchez found confidence at the World Series, hitting three doubles in his first three at-bats and landing himself in the record books.

Against Lee, he said, "You never think you're going to have success against a pitcher like that."

The Giants cracked yet another opponent's ace. They drove Lee from the game in the fifth after consecutive singles from Ross and Huff gave them a 5–2 lead, but the rally wouldn't have continued without the seven-pitch walk to Burrell that preceded the pair of RBI hits. It was just the second walk Lee issued all postseason.

"I was trying to make adjustments," Lee said. "I was up. I was down. I was in. I was out. Nothing was working. My fastball and cutter, I wasn't really able to command either one consistently.... I made some good pitches, too. But for the most part, I was erratic. I couldn't get consistent locating pitches."

There was an undercurrent of disbelief amid the cheers. Giants fans had watched their team advance to the World Series with seven tense playoff victories, six of them decided by one run. A 5–2 lead against Lee was almost too much to fathom.

The Giants weren't done, though, and Uribe sent the stands into delirium.

Darren O'Day replaced Lee on the mound and Uribe crushed a hanging slider, admiring its trajectory as it landed in the left-field bleachers for a three-run home run. The Giants led 8–2, and Uribe's shot capped their first six-run inning in a World Series game since 1937.

All of a sudden, the national storyline wasn't about Cliff Lee, the second coming of Sandy Koufax. It was about the Giants' scorned and stubborn lineup, finding a way to topple yet another of the league's best pitchers.

"You know, we've got some pretty good players too," Burrell said. "We may not have all the accolades, but some guys know how to hit over here."

All season long, the Giants knew they couldn't afford to make mistakes because they seldom outhit them. In Game 1 of the World Series, that's precisely what they did. Sanchez collected his fourth hit of the game amid a three-run eighth inning that included two errors by Guerrero, a designated hitter exposed by AT&T Park's tricky right field.

The Rangers trailed by seven runs in the ninth but Bochy had to use a trio of relievers to subdue a late rally. When Kinsler popped out against Wilson, the Giants emerged with an 11–7 victory.

For a team conditioned to win tight, one-run games, the outpouring of runs was like Christmas morning in October.

"We don't have the most talented lineup," Ross said. "We don't have superstars. But we play with a lot of heart. We like the fact nobody really gives us a chance. We feed off that. We're not scared, that's for sure.

"Everyone in here had confidence that we'd win today."

By scoring 11 runs?

"Oh, no, no, no," Ross said. "Not like this. I was thinking 2–1, something like that."

The Giants had scored four runs in a game exactly once in the previous four weeks.

"Tonight you just saw one of those nights where, every two or three weeks, we actually score more than three runs," Huff said. "It just happened to be in Game 1 of the World Series."

It happened again the next night. The Giants took a 9–0 victory in Game 2, breaking open a tight contest with a seven-run eighth inning as the Rangers ran out of relievers who could throw a strike. Matt Cain, for the third time in his stalwart postseason, did not surrender an earned run. He was as unflappable as ever, and so was 21-year-old rookie Madison Bumgarner when the series shifted to the Ballpark in Arlington.

On Halloween night in Texas, Bumgarner took the ball in Game 4, shut down the Rangers' potent lineup for eight innings, and although nobody knew it at the time, began to fashion a World Series career that would rank among the most legendary in the history of the sport.

"I didn't expect this in my wildest dreams, but I'm definitely glad to be here and have this opportunity," said Bumgarner, after pitching the Giants to a 4–0 victory and a 3–1 series lead. "This might be the only opportunity I get. Hopefully there's a lot more, but you never know."

His 23-year-old rookie batterymate, Posey, became the youngest catcher to hit a home run in the World Series since Johnny Bench was a 22-year-old in 1970. In Game 5, Huff even put down the first sacrifice bunt of his career, one night after he hit a home run in the ballpark where the Texas native once walked through the turnstiles as a fan. And Lincecum, counseled by Righetti to "let the adrenaline take you, because you'll need it," put forth a dominant performance in the clinching Game 5 victory.

The final act was the greatest, of course, and it belonged to Renteria. The Giants' broken-down shortstop had something left, after all. A marginal player down the stretch, Renteria became the most unlikely

World Series MVP in history. His three-run home run off Lee in the seventh inning of Game 5 sent the Giants to a 3–1 victory, and when Wilson struck out Cruz for the final out, it touched off a celebration that stretched across all of Northern California and washed down through generations of Giants fans.

The Giants might have won all three of their playoff series on the road in 2010, including the World Series–clinching victory that eluded so many great players in orange and black. But their homecoming, and that long-awaited parade, were overwhelming enough for everyone.

"We felt your presence against San Diego. We felt your presence in Atlanta. We felt it in Philly, and we certainly felt it in Texas," said Bochy, steeped in sunshine and orange ticker tape on the steps of City Hall. "You guys were out in full force and you made it an incredible ride. Believe me, this trophy belongs to you, San Francisco, as much as it belongs to any of us."

As Duane Kuiper put it: "Thanks to these gentlemen here, the torture is over!"

Huff made a different kind of statement, wrestling the Rally Thong out of his jeans and holding it aloft to the crowd. But while most of the speeches glowed over what the Giants accomplished, only one was focused forward.

"Let's enjoy this today, tomorrow, maybe a week or a month," said Posey, slapping the podium with his hand. "Then let's get back to work and make another run at it."

With Posey emerging as their franchise star, winning the NL MVP award in 2012, the Giants did make another run at it—and climbed to the top again. Then in 2014, they made it three titles in five seasons, stamping themselves as the nearest thing to a dynasty the NL had seen since the Big Red Machine of the 1970s.

It had to start somewhere, though. One group of players had to be bold, brash, and talented enough to break through five decades of disappointment, to step in the box against an intimidating opponent like Cliff Lee and allow desire to trump fear.

The 2010 Giants were that team. They won for a city, for generations of fans—and for each other.

They trailed by two runs in Game 1 of the World Series. They rallied against Lee. They did not trail again in the series, and they finally hoisted that glittering trophy.

There was just one problem. They still had to believe they really did it.

"It hasn't really settled in," said Lincecum, after returning from the parade to pack up his locker. "On the field, you're waving your hands in the air, saying 'Can you believe it?' That's what you're asking everybody. That's what you're asking yourself.

"I'm still waiting for those tears. We'll see when it happens."

Chapter 13

Perfection

"It definitely wasn't just me. Everybody did a lot of work and it just turned out...it turned out perfect."
—Matt Cain

Wednesday, June 13, 2012
Matt Cain throws the first perfect game in Giants history

Over six decades of his baseball life as a pioneering player, coach, manager, and talent evaluator, Felipe Alou came to see every promising minor league prospect through the same lens.

"We know about the player," he'd say, when a top prospect joined the big league roster. "We are about to know the man."

Some rookies had skills that would translate against major league competition and some did not. You could hazard a fair enough guess at that. But would the player with fringe skills find a way to keep his head above water, maybe even exceed expectations? Would the gifted player satisfy by becoming a nice roster piece, or something much more? The ones who became transcendent stars, Alou came to understand, had something heavier in their chests.

So when the Giants called up Matt Cain toward the end of a miserable 2005 season, Alou, in his third of four campaigns as the Giants manager, was eager to evaluate more than the right-hander's diamond drill bit of a fastball. He gazed at the 20-year-old kid from Tennessee on the mound and hoped to see a glimmer of something more precious.

Cain's debut on August 29, 2005, was the Giants' most highly antic-ipated home game that summer. Cain led the Pacific Coast League in strikeouts despite being one of the youngest players on the circuit. He was the youngest Giant to start a big league game in 21 years. One of his new teammates, 42-year-old reliever Jeff Fassero, had begun his professional career before Cain was born.

Cain faced the Colorado Rockies in his debut and no, he didn't throw a no-hitter or strike out 20 or make the blind see. Instead, he sweated and survived through five innings in a 2–1 loss. He emerged without a victory, but with a healthy respect for major league hitters—even when they wear purple pinstripes.

Especially one named Todd Helton.

Cain's last batter in the fifth inning became a test of character. He kept throwing fastballs. Helton, one of the most dangerous hitters in the National League, kept fouling them off. So many young pitchers, after watching their best heaters get spoiled, would gravitate to a curveball or a chase pitch. If you can't beat 'em, fool 'em.

Cain did no such thing. He stood on the mound and kept flinging fastballs. And on the 14th pitch of the at-bat, Helton lofted one to left field for an out. It was an exhaustive, epic battle between a former batting champion and a 20-year-old kid, and the fans understood the spark of magic they had witnessed.

The crowd gave Cain a standing ovation as he walked back to the dugout, and he took off his hat. He wasn't acknowledging the cheers. He had to wipe the sweat from his brow.

"Matt just needs to realize…Todd's pretty good," said his catcher, Mike Matheny. "He's done that to a lot of pitchers. But in that situation, I think everybody in the stands, on the field, and in the dugout had a lot of respect for how he kept coming after him."

Alou saw what he needed to see. Matt Cain turned into a man that day. And in the years to follow, even while Tim Lincecum pulled down

Sports Illustrated covers and Cy Young Awards, Cain was the rotation's ballast below decks.

"You know you can count on him," pitching coach Dave Righetti said. "In this game, that's what we're all about."

It was fitting that Cain took a one-run loss in his debut. He had to take so many more of those while pitching for an organization that couldn't figure out how to build a high-functioning offense in the post-Bonds era. So many times, Cain lost 2–1 to Greg Maddux or Jake Peavy or someone with a much more pedestrian name.

But those frustrating defeats served a purpose. After his second full season, Cain returned home and asked himself a question. It wasn't to bemoan, "Why don't the Giants sign more hitters?" Instead, it was this: "What do I need to do to win those 2–1 or 1–0 games?"

There was only one way: to grow as a pitcher. Cain tightened up his curveball, learned to throw a reliable changeup, understood how to shape his slider. More than anything, he came to realize the value in changing speeds with his fastball. Instead of trying to throw it through the catcher's mitt at 96 mph, he could be even more effective by subtracting here, adding there. You didn't need to make the hitter look bad. You didn't need to strike him out. Most of the time, especially at spacious AT&T Park, you just needed to keep the ball off the barrel. The goal wasn't to feed your ego. It was to get the out. And then get 26 more, ideally.

To watch him pitch to an isolated hitter, or even a full inning, you might not think Cain was something special. He didn't get hitters to screw themselves into the ground, as Lincecum did with his diving changeup. He simply found ways to keep them off balance while throwing his fastballs to spots, not areas. He could be wild out of the strike zone, but seldom missed in a place where hitters could make him pay. He learned the difference between nibbling and recognizing there were times when he best not poke the cage.

In 2010, Cain made three postseason starts—one in each round. Over 21⅓ innings, he did not give up an earned run. In Game 2 of the World Series against the Texas Rangers, leading 2–0 in the eighth inning, Cain issued a one-out walk, induced a fly out, and then trotted off the mound to the loudest ovation of his life.

He didn't tip his cap.

"Can't do it with a runner on base," he said. "Just didn't seem right."

You begin to understand why there wasn't a player more admired in the Giants clubhouse. Even when Cain pitched the game of his life, he made no assumptions and felt no sense of entitlement. The goal wasn't to have a good start. The goal was to win, and it was only the eighth inning.

Bruce Bochy admired Cain the same way that Alou did. He was a twentysomething with an old soul, and he already ranked as the longest-tenured player on the roster. Lincecum had the rock-star popularity and Buster Posey was the unquestioned heir to the face of the franchise. But Cain formed the essence.

If there was one thing he loved almost as much as competing on the mound, it was taking rips from the tee box. Cain became a regular in the Pebble Beach Pro-Am every February, impressing the tour pros with his 300-yard drives.

The U.S. Open returned to Pebble Beach in the summer of 2012, and pro golfer Dustin Johnson came to AT&T Park as part of a publicity appearance. Just prior to batting practice, the PGA set up a mat on home plate and staged a long-drive competition into McCovey Cove. They invited a couple of Giants players to participate.

Cain perked up. You might as well tell a seven-year-old he can skip straight to dessert. There's no way he would miss this.

There was just one problem. He was starting that night against the Houston Astros. And pitchers always sequester themselves the day they pitch. No stretching, minimal interaction with others, no interviews with the media. But Cain couldn't help it. He asked GM Brian Sabean if it would be all right to take one swing.

"Only if I don't watch," Sabean said.

Cain gripped the new driver, waggled it once, and perfectly struck a little power fade over the right-field arcade. For once, a good shot into the drink.

Now Cain would try to keep the Houston Astros from reaching the water. He'd end his night having accomplished a whole lot more than that.

Teammates always pegged Cain to throw a no-hitter at some point in his career.

Entering the 2012 season, he had taken six attempts as deep as the seventh inning. He wasn't always overpowering, but he had a tendency to get a greater share of his outs in the air—and that led to fewer bleeders or bad-luck hits. On days when he had three pitches working, Cain could be near to unhittable.

For all the reasons that Jonathan Sanchez's no-hitter in 2009 came as a shock, the biggest one was this: it wasn't Cain or Lincecum that broke the 33-year franchise drought.

Cain was off to another good start in 2012. He was 7–2 with a 2.41 ERA through his first 12 outings, and had a career-best six-start winning streak in tow when he took the mound for that midweek night game against the Astros on June 13.

Buster Posey usually downplays a pitcher's stuff in the bullpen, but he noticed that Cain had especially good late movement on his cut fastball. He knew Cain liked to establish that pitch the first time through the order, and although the Astros did not have many hitters with sharp teeth, they were perfectly capable of breaking the skin.

First inning: 11 pitches.

Cain threw four fastballs to strike out Jordan Schafer. He went fastball-curve-fastball to strike out Jose Altuve. Jed Lowrie hit a foul pop.

Second inning: 12 pitches.

It wasn't a big deal at the time, but Cain went to a three-ball count against Brett Wallace—a player with the build of a slo-pitch softball player who was perfectly content to work a walk. Cain came back with a 3-1 fastball that Wallace fouled off. Posey called for a changeup, a pitch that Cain hadn't thrown for a strike either of the first two times he tried. Wallace swung through it.

Third inning: 17 pitches.

Cain began to find a groove with his changeup and slider. Houston catcher Chris Snyder and pitcher J.A. Happ took called third strikes on fastballs that snapped back across the zone. Umpire Ted Barrett was giving him the black, as pitchers call it.

Cain had gone through the lineup once. Even at this early juncture, he could sense he had it within himself to no-hit the Astros.

Fourth inning: 22 pitches.

Cain threw 10 of those pitches to Schafer in a grueling confrontation that included five two-strike fouls, including one that came within "a millimeter," as first baseman Brandon Belt saw it, of being a double down the line. Replays were inconclusive but umpire Mike Muchlinski had the only opinion that mattered. It was a foul ball and Cain, suddenly operating with a four-run lead after two-run homers by Belt and Melky Cabrera, had no reason to back down. He threw another fastball and Schafer, who saw eight strikes out of 10 pitches, swung through it.

Fifth inning: 14 pitches.

The Astros put just one ball in play, a ground out to second baseman Ryan Theriot. Cain struck out two, and his fastball just kept getting better and better. Unlike Sanchez's no-hit bid, which snuck up on everyone, the ballpark tingled with excitement and the crowd roared as Cain walked off the mound.

Sixth inning: 10 pitches.

Cain had thrown 76 pitches in five innings, mostly thanks to Schafer, and he needed an economy frame. He got it in the sixth—along with some meteorological, perhaps divine, intervention. With one out, Snyder ripped Cain's first pitch to left field. The right-hander almost didn't whip around to watch. A fly-ball pitcher knows when he's just given up a home run, and the ball had been carrying well when Belt and Cabrera went deep earlier in the game. Gregor Blanco even hit an apparent pop-up that carried into the right-field arcade. The Giants hit six home runs in their first 32 home games. They already had three on the night. Cain was sure of it: Snyder had just hit one into the bleachers.

But the winds shifted in the middle innings, a cool breeze began to blow over the left-field stands, and the ballpark turned into a wind tunnel by the sixth. As Cabrera raced after Snyder's ball, center fielder Angel Pagan watched the play unfold.

"I had the best view," Pagan said. "The ball wasn't going out. It *was* out. It was 10 rows deep, then it cut back. It cut like a banana."

It still required a direct route, above-average speed, and a little leap near the wall for Cabrera to make the catch. It wasn't the kind of play that makes the highlight reel in a run-of-the-mill 5–3 victory. But it was a catch many major league left fielders probably don't make.

The next time Pagan went to bat, he mentioned the flight of the ball to Snyder.

"Yeah, buddy," Snyder told him. "I got the whole thing."

Cain survived one more close call in the sixth, when he struck out Brian Bixler on a curveball in the dirt. Posey blocked it and threw to first base to keep it a no-reach game.

This was more than a no-hit bid. It was a perfect game through six innings, and that meant it required perfection from all nine Giants. Just one third strike in the dirt, one hard two-hopper off a third baseman's chest, would break the spell.

As precious and memorable as a no-hitter was, a perfect game was something else entirely. There had been just 21 of them in major league history, and never one thrown by a Giant in 130 years of franchise lore. Not Christy Mathewson nor Carl Hubbell nor Juan Marichal. Not even Tim Lincecum.

Cain took the mound in the seventh inning oblivious to that fact—which was probably a good thing.

Seventh inning: 17 pitches.

For the first time since the second inning, and just the second time in the game, Cain went to a three-ball count. This time, the sight of ball three to Schafer caused thousands to bite their nails and pray.

Cain threw a 3-2 fastball that cut directly onto Schafer's barrel. The drive rocketed to the deepest part of right-center field, the place where you could hit it and run for days.

"And this is hit out into the alleyway," announced Duane Kuiper, his voice charged with alarm.

The flight of the ball offered no hope. The sight of Blanco, racing over from right field, did.

"A long run for Blanco..." Kuiper continued, "and Blanco's gonna dive...and he MAKES THE CATCH!"

Blanco was the right fielder, but the ball wasn't caught in right field. When Blanco skidded on his stomach to a stop on the warning track, he wasn't far from straightaway center. Years earlier, the Giants figured out before anyone else that it made sense to play the right fielder well off the line at AT&T Park. But Blanco's positioning was flat-out ridiculous. He wasn't supposed to be there, and yet there he was, holding aloft the little white prize so that umpires could see it.

"Everybody kept telling me, 'What are you doing, playing there?'" Blanco said. "Coaches told me that with Schafer, play a little more to the gap. I think I played a little [farther] than that.

"Melky caught his ball. I told myself, 'You have to catch this one, too.'"

In the dugout, Bochy turned to bench coach Ron Wotus and asked if he'd ever seen an outfielder make a catch in that part of the field. They were in agreement. Neither had.

Cain had taken several no-hit bids into the seventh. He even threw a one-hitter in the home opener (after which Pirates pitcher James McDonald expressed contrition for his squeaker of a single in the sixth inning). After Blanco's catch, though, all that experience meant nothing.

"There's really nothing like it," Cain said. "You get deep into the game like that, and really even [Blanco's] defining play...he makes it in the beginning of the seventh inning and I've still got to get two more outs and the place is going crazy.

"I was literally having to recheck myself just to be able to see the signs Buster was putting down because there was so much adrenaline, so much stuff going on."

Cain found a way to channel that adrenaline. He struck out the next two batters, but had a precarious full count to Jed Lowrie. With no margin for error, his 101st pitch of the night was a 94-mph fastball—his hardest of the game. When Lowrie fouled it off, Posey had the guts to call for a changeup. Cain didn't hesitate, throwing one that was written in disappearing ink as it fluttered past Lowrie's swing.

"I was as nervous as I've ever been on a baseball field. I'm not gonna lie," Posey said. "It's a different kind of nervousness than the playoffs or the World Series."

Maybe it was a good thing that Cain's spot in the lineup came up in the bottom of the seventh. Any sane pitcher would rest his bat on his shoulder, take three strikes, and go back to the dugout to clear his head for the task that awaited him. Instead, Cain took a rip at the first pitch. And Righetti, watching from in the dugout, understood why. A day earlier, Madison Bumgarner hit a home run.

"And Bum struck out 12, so Cain had to get more than that," Righetti said. "That's what peer pressure does. It does wonderful things."

Cain needed six more outs, he already received the pixie-dust catch from Blanco that always seems to play a role in a magical night, and he walked through jet-engine noise on his way to the dugout. He needed nothing more than to meditate for a moment in his usual seat.

When he got there, it was occupied. Belt had plopped himself in Cain's spot.

"Cainer just stopped and stared at me," said Belt, recalling the moment his eyes grew wide with panic. "Yeah, I guess everything was okay until I sat in his seat."

This was a prime violation of baseball superstition. Belt bolted upright and moved to sit next to Ryan Vogelsong, a pitcher who has more game-day superstitions than a witch doctor. Vogelsong stared daggers into Belt, too, as he shook his head.

Eighth inning: 11 pitches.

Run support wasn't an issue for Cain this time. The Giants had a 10–0 lead through seven innings, but Bochy was managing as if trying to protect a one-run margin in Game 7 of the World Series. He took third baseman Pablo Sandoval out, inserted Brandon Crawford at shortstop, and moved Joaquin Arias to third. An inning before that, he substituted Emmanuel Burriss at second base for Theriot.

The moves paid off immediately. Arias charged a slow roller off the bat of J.D. Martinez, then made an accurate throw on the run to get the out—a play that the heftier Sandoval might not have made.

Next came another dangerous three-ball count after Wallace laid off a pair of two-strike sliders. Cain didn't want to give in, but he sure as hell wasn't going to give up. He came back with his simplest, best pitch—a challenge fastball—and Wallace watched it for a third strike.

It was Cain's 14th strikeout on the night, besting his previous career high of 12 that he set as a 21-year-old fireballer in 2006. The difference now: he wasn't trying for them. They were simply a byproduct of executing pitches.

Chris Johnson followed by hitting a tricky, topspin hopper to short. It was the kind of ball that had eaten up Crawford so many times in April and early May, and he was cold off the bench. But the talented defender backpedaled to make sure he wasn't caught in between hops, then made a clean pickup, transfer, and throw.

Suddenly, Cain was three outs away. This was it. It was real, all of it.

And Bochy had to cover his ass. Cain had thrown 114 pitches through eight innings. One bloop single and Bochy would protect his stalwart right-hander, immediately going to a reliever. But the manager was superstitious, too. He didn't want to send anyone to the bullpen mound, didn't want to put the tiniest doubt in Cain's head that he wouldn't see it through. Bochy knew the loudest messages he sent to players didn't come through speeches.

So he solved the problem the only way he could. He quietly had his long reliever, Shane Loux, start getting loose in the batting cage behind the dugout.

"I'll be honest. We had somebody ready," Bochy said. "You couldn't see him, but he was ready."

Bochy could adhere to superstition. And Cain, bless him, could make life easier on his manager by getting these last three outs on a minimum of pitches.

In the booth, Kuiper let out a deep breath before the ninth inning. He played in a perfect game three decades earlier, behind the Indians' Len Barker on May 15, 1981. He had never broadcast one before. He wasn't sure, but he thought he felt more nervous in the booth than he felt at second base.

Ninth inning: 11 pitches.

Bochy didn't move an inch from where he stood in the dugout. Belt was just hoping not to double over.

"I was going to throw up," he said. "I said that to everybody, but I really was. I was about to throw up in the ninth inning."

Cain walked to the mound, his blank expression hiding not only his nerves but a growing sense of wonder.

"Honestly, right then I was thinking that it felt like the World Series, but it also felt a little louder, a little crazier," he said. "Every strike, they were going nuts for. It was really amazing. I've never had that much excitement in every pitch, every strike, every swing."

Brian Bogusevic lifted a 2-2 fastball to left field. Cabrera raced over to catch it near the line. Snyder lifted a 1-0 fastball. Cabrera barely had to move for it.

Pinch hitter Jason Castro was last. Cain jumped ahead with a 1-2 count. Then he threw one final fastball. It was his 125th pitch. It was 94 mph. It matched his hardest of the night.

Castro, a left-handed hitter, almost slapped it out of Posey's glove while hitting a weak chopper down the third-base line. Arias, desperate to avoid getting caught between hops, approached it indecisively and nearly lost his balance. The ball found his glove, and flat-footed, with his body falling away from first base, he somehow managed to get something on his throw across the diamond. It hit Belt's glove on a line.

It was instant euphoria. It was a red-letter day. It was the 22nd perfect game in baseball history.

Cain watched the ball into Belt's glove, thrust a roundhouse punch, and Posey wrapped his arms around him. The night was one enormous, energetic run-on sentence, and Cain punctuated it.

Matt Cain was the first Giant in 130 years to throw a perfect game, but he didn't do it alone. Though Cain struck out 14, he couldn't have done it without his teammates.

He did it 107 years to the day after Christy Mathewson threw a no-hitter. But Mathewson had never thrown a perfect game. In 130 years, no Giant ever had. And Cain made history on top of history: he matched Sandy Koufax in 1965 as the only pitchers to throw a perfect game with 14 strikeouts.

There are many baseball historians who consider Koufax's 14-strikeout perfect game against the Chicago Cubs as the greatest game ever pitched. On a midweek night in June against the Houston Astros, a sellout crowd at AT&T Park watched Cain throw its equal.

Cain's first reaction, to Bochy: "This is stupid."

Sweetly, blessedly, unforgettably stupid.

Lincecum, who never sits still in the dugout, watched Cain's perfect game unfold from every angle.

"You realize what's at stake and you think about it, and you think, man, you're just hoping it happens," Lincecum said. "And when it does, you don't even know how to talk about it. It's one of the most single difficult things to do, ever, in any kind of sport.

"And the way he controlled the game made it even more special. I mean, 14 punchouts? Koufax? That's pretty good company. Things were in the right place at the right time. I'm just glad I got to witness it."

The celebration was such a sudden rush that Aubrey Huff tripped over the dugout rail and put himself on the disabled list with a knee injury. Lincecum found Cain in the postgame pile and took his turn giving him a hug and congratulations. But he wanted to circle back later, when Cain's head wasn't in a complete whirlwind. He found him later that night.

"When everything calmed down, he was at his locker," Lincecum said. "I walked up to him and just said, 'I'm proud of ya, it's been fun to watch that, and I'm happy for you.'"

Belt might have sat in Cain's seat, but when he caught the final out, he had the presence of mind to tuck the ball in his back pocket for safe-keeping.

"It was just so incredible to be a part of this," Belt said. "We knew it was going to happen eventually. I knew this pitching staff had it in 'em. But it never really registered to me that I could play in a perfect game."

Cain donated his hat and cleats to the Hall of Fame. He kept the final-out ball. The Giants sent another game-used ball to Cooperstown, in addition to the first-base bag, some infield dirt, and one of the 14 K signs that hung on the right-field wall.

How difficult, how elusive, how magically fated is a perfect game? Consider that Cain got 14 of the 27 outs on his own—more than anyone besides Koufax in a perfect game—yet he still needed so much help.

"It definitely wasn't just me," said Cain, flanked in the interview room by Posey and Blanco. "Running down balls, hitting home runs, making plays, it was an all-around effort tonight.

"Everybody did a lot of work and it turned out…it turned out perfect."

So much for getting hurt swinging a golf club. Cain threw 65 fastballs, 23 sliders, 21 changeups, and 16 curveballs. Of his 125 pitches, the most ever required to complete a perfect game, 86 were strikes.

He threw first-pitch strikes to 19 of the 27 batters he faced.

Of his career-high 14 strikeouts, 11 came on fastballs. He went to a three-ball count four times, and only once did umpire Ted Barrett, who also worked the plate for David Cone's perfect game in 1999, have to make the call between ball or strike.

"He's gotta hear the whole crowd," said Cain, who didn't forget to mention Barrett's consistent strike zone as he delivered his Oscar-quality acceptance speech. "That's got to be a lot of stress on him. He did a great job back there. He was consistent with everything, he called a lot of strikes that were on the plate, and he stayed the same way the whole night. He didn't change a bit."

Cain changed, though, from the early days when he was a "bull in a china closet," as Righetti once described him. Cain knew the hitters better, he knew his body and his mechanics better. He knew himself better.

"But the determination is still the same," said Righetti. "The same guy still sits there. You see him on game day, just so calm. He's that way. He always has been."

Two years earlier, when Sanchez became the first Giant in 33 years to throw a no-hitter, Righetti waited until the coaches cleared out and let slip a few tears. He'd thrown a no-hitter himself, with the Yankees. He understood what it meant.

The emotions were similar for Righetti after Cain's perfect night, and yet they were so different. This wasn't just a no-hitter in a 10–0 victory over the Houston Astros. This was perfection. It was immortality.

Nobody can identify with that. You simply stand in awe of it.

Chapter 14

Drinking It In

*"It never rains here in the Bay Area. I spent four years
in Oakland and I don't think it rained once."*
—Marco Scutaro

Monday, October 22, 2012
NLCS Game 7 vs. St. Louis

The pain hit Marco Scutaro in two waves.

The first one surged through him at the moment of impact, as Matt Holliday flung his 245-pound body sideways into first base. The hard, late, and questionably legal slide in the second inning was meant to break up a double play. As Scutaro gritted his teeth, his left leg pinned under Holliday's barrel roll, he feared he had broken more than that.

"I literally felt like he took my leg and…pulled it apart like a [piece of] chicken," Scutaro reflected. "When he hit me, something moved in there."

The second wave hit later that night. Adrenaline masked it for a time, and so did sweet retribution in the form of Scutaro's bases-loaded single that included two RBIs and a third run crossing the plate when Holliday bungled the ball in left field for an error.

But the later it got in Game 2 of the 2012 NLCS, Scutaro's left hip kept getting stiffer and stiffer.

Scutaro always had to manage back and hip discomfort, the result of one leg being slightly shorter than the other. This felt different. Something was seriously wrong. It was pain mixed with a spreading numbness from his knee to his waist. By the fifth inning, Scutaro realized that if a ground ball came right to him, he wouldn't be able to bend down to field it. He had to come out of the game.

The Giants took a 7–1 victory over St. Louis Cardinals that night at AT&T Park, squaring up the NLCS as it shifted to Busch Stadium. But the outlook for Scutaro was not good. He barely was able to board the team flight to St. Louis. At minimum, he had a bad bone bruise. His prospects for returning to the lineup were dim.

The Giants were more than angry. They were aggrieved.

"They got away with an illegal slide there," said manager Bruce Bochy, noting that his little second baseman gave up more than 80 pounds to Holliday. "He didn't really hit dirt until he was past the bag. Marco was behind the bag and got smoked. It's a shame somebody got hurt because of this. That's more of a rolling block...and that's a big guy running."

Even Cardinals manager Mike Matheny offered a half-hearted endorsement, at best.

"As I watched it live, it looked like it was a hard slide," Matheny said. "We teach our guys to go hard. Play the game clean, play it hard, and don't try to hurt anybody. I hated to see that it ended up that way. That's not how we play the game. We do go hard, but within the rules."

Holliday made his remorse known right away. He talked to catcher Buster Posey before his next at-bat, inquiring about Scutaro's welfare and acknowledging that he started his slide too late.

"I don't think there was intent to hurt him," Posey said. "But that doesn't take away from the fact it was a late slide."

Remorse only goes so far when one of your most important players is laid up in the trainer's room. And besides, the Giants were conditioned to be a bit sensitive over this kind of thing. Nobody could forget the searing sight a year earlier in May, when Posey writhed in pain, his left

Marco Scutaro was hobbled by Matt Holliday's questionable slide in Game 2 of the 2012 NLCS, but came back to inspire the Giants on their way to the World Series.
(AP Images)

leg shattered after Florida Marlins pinch runner Scott Cousins wiped him out with a targeted, shoulder-on-shoulder hit at home plate. Along with Posey's ankle, the play effectively destroyed the Giants' chance to defend their title in 2011.

The Giants made it back to October in 2012 in no small part because of Scutaro, who came over from the Colorado Rockies for minor-leaguer Charlie Culberson in a late July trade that hardly appeared to be a blockbuster at the time. Scutaro was 36 years old, a career .270 hitter over 11 seasons with five different clubs, a guy who never hit for much power and put up pedestrian numbers even while playing half his games at lively Coors Field.

But year after year, Scutaro also ranked as one of the hardest players to strike out in the major leagues. He had a short, quick, low-maintenance swing and tremendous bat control. All the time Scutaro played for the A's, Red Sox, and Blue Jays, he was out of his element. Those were slugging teams. His value was in his ability to put the ball in play, hit behind the runner, keep the line moving. That made him a perfect fit for the Giants, who had to find creative ways to score because they hit the fewest home runs in the major leagues. Scutaro was a perfect fit for their ballpark, too.

When the Giants took a shot to the solar plexus on August 15, learning that No. 2 hitter Melky Cabrera would be suspended for the remainder of the season for a violation of the league's performance-enhancing drug policy, it was Scutaro who helped them regain their breath.

Cabrera was leading the major leagues in hits and runs scored on the day he disappeared without addressing his teammates. The whole sordid story eventually came out: he had tested positive for synthetic testosterone in early July; filed an appeal; and a handler who worked for his agents, Sam and Seth Levinson, concocted a phony website in an effort to claim that Cabrera had inadvertently purchased a tainted supplement.

The story unraveled, but not before Cabrera won the All-Star Game MVP award. Commissioner Bud Selig handed over car keys and a trophy to a player he knew had flunked a drug test, and it wouldn't be long before the league figured out the phony web scam and upheld the 50-game suspension.

In cases when a player appeals, though, his team isn't notified until the conclusion of the process. The Giants, deadlocked with the Dodgers atop the NL West standings, received word 90 minutes before the first pitch August 15. Right up until that moment, Cabrera's name was still on their lineup sheet.

The suspension should have crushed their morale. Instead, it brought them together. They held a team meeting, and even though he had only been wearing the uniform for a couple weeks, Scutaro took the floor and spoke his piece. Then something remarkable happened.

The Giants took off. They won 10 of their next 13 games, opened up a 4½-game lead over the Dodgers, and never looked back. And Scutaro, who moved into Cabrera's lineup spot, hit .362 in 61 games following the trade.

His new teammates gave him a nickname: Blockbuster.

It wasn't just Scutaro's bat control and base hits that made an impact. It was his leadership in the clubhouse, too. With his self-effacing sense of humor, he had a way of connecting with pitchers and hitters alike. The team's sizable Venezuelan contingent would gather around his locker and listen to him spin stories. Clubhouse chemistry and leadership roles usually begin to form in spring training. By the end of the regular season, though, two trade-deadline additions, Scutaro and Hunter Pence, had become so ingrained within the clubhouse that they felt comfortable enough to become team spokesmen. And the rest of the group thought enough of them to listen.

The Giants easily won the NL West with a 94–68 record, but were in desperate need of a pep talk after losing the first two games at home to Dusty Baker's Cincinnati Reds in their best-of-five NL Division Series. It would take nothing short of three consecutive wins on the road to advance, and the Reds hadn't been swept in a home series all year.

"It was like we blinked and we were down 0–2," Pence said. "It was, 'Holy cow, this is everything we've worked for and we're already in the biggest hole in the snap of our fingers.'"

In the hours before Game 3, Pence, Scutaro, and left-hander Javier Lopez discussed it in the kitchen adjacent to the visiting clubhouse: the team was way, way too sedate.

"Somebody's got to get up and say something," said Scutaro, "or we're going to lose."

Like Scutaro, Pence was a newcomer after coming over from the Philadelphia Phillies in July. He never really fit in with the clubhouse establishment there, and his spastic style at the plate didn't resonate with Phillies manager Charlie Manuel, an old hitting coach. Everything Pence did on the field looked odd, right down to his bird legs and knee-high socks. But something about San Francisco clicked with him. The front office, the fans, and his teammates didn't stand in judgment of how he looked or how he tried to get a runner home from third base with one out. They only cared if he did it. For the first time in his career, Pence felt like he fit in, like he was part of a brotherhood. And he didn't want it to end.

"So I went up to Buster Posey, because we all know this is his team, and asked if he minded if I said a little something," Pence said. "He told me, 'No, I want it to be you.' But still, I didn't know if I would."

Bochy spoke first. He already had used up his *Days of Thunder* and *Braveheart* speeches earlier in the year. This time, he went to the Old Testament and relayed the story of Gideon, who triumphed in the face of defeat over the Midianites. He recounted the history of teams that came back from a two-game deficit, including his own 1984 Padres squad on which he served as a backup catcher.

"It was a great speech, a positive speech," Pence said. "But it was still a little too quiet in the clubhouse. I wanted to bring everyone into the moment, to think sideways a little. And I wanted them to know how much I loved to play the game with them."

"I can't even remember all that I said. Some of it's been written down, and some of that is true, some of it isn't. I was just lost in the moment, and it was a collection of so many thoughts that other teammates had given to me.

"I said, 'I don't really care about the past. It doesn't matter. I don't care about who's over there or who's done what. That's over. All that matters is what we decide to do right now, and I've made my decision. I'm going to give absolutely everything I have for one more day because I love playing with you guys. I don't care if we have to win 100 in a row. We're going to win today and I'm giving everything I have for you because I love you.'

"It was this beautiful disaster of emotions going on—stress, focus, joy. That's what I like to call it—a beautiful disaster."

The room wasn't sedate any longer. Still, when Bochy exchanged lineup cards with Reds manager Dusty Baker, he said something along the lines of "We're embarrassed. We hope we can give you half a game."

Somehow, the Giants avoided disaster in Game 3. They managed to win a game in which the opposing pitcher, Homer Bailey, struck out 10 and allowed just one hit in his seven innings. But Ryan Vogelsong matched him pitch for pitch, Pence set the tone with a sliding catch near the line in right field and third baseman Scott Rolen, an eight-time Gold Glove winner, made an error that led to the winning run in the 10th inning.

The next day, Pence wasn't about to break with tradition. The Reverend fired up the clubhouse again. The Giants won again. They added a frenzied, high school football–style huddle in the dugout prior to the first pitch, and when they won Game 4, they had to continue that tradition, too. It only expanded from there. Ryan Theriot began spraying the assembly with sunflower seeds.

"It's constantly evolving," Theriot said. "There's different things thrown around every time. Someone is firing gum or seeds. I got hit in the head with a coffee creamer the other day."

The Giants' energy never waned, and they escaped Cincinnati by winning all three elimination games. Posey rocked old foe Mat Latos for a grand slam in Game 5, and Sergio Romo survived an epic confrontation with Jay Bruce in the ninth, when any of the 12 pitches he threw could've resulted in a season-ending home run.

Afterward, as the Giants awaited the identity of their NLCS opponent, Pence went out to dinner with Posey and Jeremy Affeldt.

"We were just so exhausted and drained," Pence said. "We couldn't believe what happened. It was a snap of the fingers and then three games that felt like a yearlong adventure. But it wasn't over."

The Giants already resuscitated themselves once in the postseason. Against the Cardinals, they'd have to do it again. Scutaro, following Holliday's bone-crunching slide in Game 2, somehow made it back onto the field at St. Louis. But the Cardinals won Games 3 and 4 at Busch Stadium to take a 3–1 edge.

Once again, the Giants had to rattle off three consecutive wins with their backs against the wall. Although they already accomplished the same Heartbreak Hill climb in Cincinnati, there was more lactic acid in their legs now. And generals on horseback can only deliver a war speech once.

The Cardinals reported to the ballpark for Game 5 knowing a victory would end the series and prevent a return trip to San Francisco. They came with their bags packed. That was the order from management. It's not the order that Bochy would have given.

"We're packed," Cardinals third baseman David Freese said. "Hopefully, we can unpack."

Thanks to the greatest start of Barry Zito's baseball life, the Giants won 5–0 in Game 5 to force the series back to AT&T Park. Once there, Vogelsong dominated again in Game 6 and Scutaro hit a two-run double in a 6–1 victory.

Scutaro was 8-for-18 since Holliday knocked him to the dirt. In the postgame interview room, he sat side by side with Vogelsong—the 36-year-old contact man and the 35-year-old right-hander, both 27 outs away from their first World Series.

"I think a lot of the nation is finally getting to see the kind of player that Marco is because of this postseason," Vogelsong said. "But the things he's doing are not a surprise to anybody on this club. You know he's going to put a professional at-bat on you. He's going to battle you. And he's one of the best clutch hitters I've ever seen."

It was a fitting sight to see Vogelsong and Scutaro seated next to each other in the postgame news conference. Vogelsong hopped so many continents, accepted so many release papers, worked for every second and third and fourth chance to make something of his career. When the Giants needed him most, he threw a two-seam fastball that conjured visions of Greg Maddux, with a little more power and just as much movement.

Scutaro was traded before he ever reached the big leagues, was claimed off waivers twice in his career, and the Rockies even paid a quarter of the $2 million left on his deal when they dealt him to the Giants in July.

Vogelsong reminded Scutaro that they faced each other in winter ball a decade earlier.

"I was, like, 21 years old, right?" Scutaro said.

"Me too," nodded Vogelsong.

For all the attention that Pence's pregame speeches received, Vogelsong revealed that Scutaro was making just as important an impact with his messages to the group. In fact, immediately after Pence's first "one more day" sermon in Cincinnati, there was a moment of awkward silence. It was Scutaro who pierced it and carried the emotion forward.

"It was, 'Concentrate and win every pitch, win every swing, win every inning,'" Vogelsong said. "I think we just go with that. And it's been working for us."

That short-term focus helped the Giants survive five elimination games against the Reds and Cardinals. They already had become the first band of big league believers to prevail five times with their postseason lives on the line. One more in front of their home crowd and they would claim a pennant.

"Do I believe in clutch?" said Pence, narrowing his intense eyes as if trying to stare down the abstraction. "I don't know. But I believe in adversity. And I believe that's when you find out what you're made of."

The Giants had to stare down one other nagging fact: in 129 years of dancing on diamonds, they had never won a Game 7. They were 0–5 in franchise history, and the disappointments included a roaring red surge in the 2002 World Series at Anaheim, Bobby Richardson gloving Willie McCovey's line drive in the 1962 World Series, and, most applicably given their current foe, Jose Oquendo's three-run knockout shot against Atlee Hammaker in the 1987 NLCS at old Busch Stadium.

The Cardinals would never replace the Dodgers as the Giants' archrival. But they were becoming quite the spirited foe. The bad blood reached back to 1988, one year after Oquendo knocked out the Giants, when there was a benches-clearing, punches-thrown incident between the two teams in St. Louis.

Will Clark set off hostilities with—wouldn't you know it—a hard slide into second base. But he led with his feet, not with a flying sideways body block.

Now a special assistant, Clark was asked if he took umbrage at Holliday's slide.

"Now that's a big word," he said. "Better watch out!"

How about "ticked off"?

"There you go," he said.

Clark recalled that back in 1988, the Cardinals threw at him the next chance they got. The Giants hadn't plunked Holliday after his slide in Game 2. But Matt Cain, who took the mound for Game 7, had more on his mind than retribution. Barely four months after throwing the first perfect game in franchise history, he would try to become the first Giant to punch them through a Game 7 glass ceiling that had created so many bad memories over the years.

"There's ways to get even," Clark said.

Said Cain: "If one gets away, it gets away."

For all the Giants' postseason experience, Theriot was the only soul on the roster who had played in a Game 7. He gained that experience the previous year, in a St. Louis uniform. The Giants weren't the only team adept at extending its playoff lives. The Cardinals had won all six of their elimination games over their last two postseasons, and already had prevailed in an intense, winner-take-all Game 5 to get past the Washington Nationals in their NLDS.

The Giants invited Kenny Lofton, their walk-off hero who beat the Cardinals in the 2002 pennant clincher, to throw out the first pitch. For the first time since the deciding game of the 1962 Fall Classic, a Game 7 would be played in San Francisco. It was Cain versus right-hander Kyle Lohse for the right to represent the National League and face the Detroit Tigers in the World Series.

The Giants no longer had to claw back against the Cardinals. They were on equal footing after winning Game 6, and they had reason to feel confident. Several hitters remarked that they let Lohse off the hook in Game 3, when they collected 12 baserunners but just one run in his 5⅔ innings. They vowed that they wouldn't let that happen again.

Lohse did not appear to have much break on his slider as the Giants struck for a run in the first inning. Angel Pagan singled, took third on Scutaro's classic hit-and-run single—a 2-1 slider to right field—and scored on Pablo Sandoval's RBI ground out that Lohse fielded on the first-base side of the mound.

The bottom of the lineup didn't make it easy on Lohse in the second inning, either. With two outs, Cain barreled up a slider for a hard single up the middle that sent Gregor Blanco diving across the plate.

Lohse clearly wobbled, but Cain wasn't at his best, either. His fastball rode up in the zone, he relied on his defense to make plays, and he survived a choppy, 46-pitch sea over the first two innings. First baseman Brandon Belt made one of those plays, smothering Daniel Descalso's short-hop smash and throwing from his knees for a force out at second base. Then shortstop Brandon Crawford made a backpedaling, leaping catch to snare Lohse's line drive and strand two runners.

Cain gained his bearings after that, and began to execute a simple but devastatingly effective game plan. He kept throwing high fastballs, daring the Cardinals to beat him. And the hitters who put together so many smart, hungry, and amazing at-bats against Washington were never able to land a kill shot.

By the end, it was obvious: the Giants had taken a professional, polished opponent and gotten into their domes. They found their weakness—an appetite for high heat—and force fed them like geese.

"There's adjustments all the time," said Posey, "and I just think the pitchers did a great job making those adjustments."

The Giants did not need long to recognize that Lohse had little finish on his slider and wasn't throwing inside. Scutaro started the third inning with a line-drive single. Sandoval, whose timing could not be disrupted in the series, guided an outside pitch down the left-field line for a double. Posey walked on a 3-2 pitch to load the bases, and bring Matheny to the mound.

Lohse was done and a season was on the line, but Matheny did not immediately go to his best reliever, Trevor Rosenthal, and his 99-mph fastball. He summoned Joe Kelly, instead, to face Pence.

The next pitch would do more than make history. It would bend the laws of physics.

Pence, on the day he first set down his red Phillies duffel bag in the Giants clubhouse, introduced himself to reporters with these words: "I've got to be honest. Every now and then, I do things you don't see very often."

Including a triple-double.

Kelly threw a 95-mph fastball that splintered Pence's bat halfway up the handle. That was the first impact. As he continued his swing, the shards of wood traveled through the zone faster than the ball. That was the second impact. On super-slow replay, it was discernible: horsehide and bat fragments kissed one more time, coaxing the ball in a way that would make Isaac Newton furrow his brow.

A pool-hall shark couldn't have created more English on the ball, and Cardinals shortstop Pete Kozma had no chance. He read the swing and broke toward third base, then nearly tripped over his feet in amazement as the ball shot past him up the middle. Two runs scored. When center fielder Jon Jay dropped the ball, third-base coach Tim Flannery waved home Posey, who scored from first base without a play, too.

Pence hit the flukiest bases-clearing double in baseball history, and as he stood on second base, he had to laugh. Earlier in the game, he had been talking with Clark about how good hitters don't get jammed. Pence told him he'd be ready for an inside pitch and try to stay short.

"I've never hit a ball like that," Clark said with a laugh. "I've never *seen* a ball hit like that. That's the beauty of baseball. The baseball gods were shining on the Giants tonight."

The Giants led 5–0 and weren't done. They sent 11 men to the plate in what became a five-run third inning.

Belt chopped a single off Kelly's bare hand, Blanco walked to load the bases, and Crawford hit a grounder to short. Kozma, who couldn't help but feel like he'd stepped in the Twilight Zone after Pence's hit, had lost all sense of timing. Despite playing at normal depth, he tried to throw for the force at home. The unwise attempt had no chance as Pence scored, then descended the dugout steps to a raucous reception.

Cain took advantage of the 7–0 lead in more ways than one. Facing Holliday to start the sixth inning, he threw an 0-2 fastball that rode hard inside and plunked the batter on the arm. The Giants settled the score, and Holliday knew he had it coming. He took his base without incident.

Cain recorded two outs in the sixth before Bochy went to his relievers, and although the crowd gave the right-hander a standing ovation, he still refused to doff his cap. Even with a big lead, Cain left a runner on base, and Game 7 is no time to abandon superstition.

Before the season, no Giant in 130 years had ever pitched a perfect game or won a Game 7. Cain was on the cusp of accomplishing both in a four-month span. He wasn't his sharpest, but his defenders were. Even Scutaro made a pirouette while fielding a short-hop grounder for an out.

The ballpark pulsated with anticipation and Belt, who struggled most of the series, licked some icing when he hit a solo home run to set off the steam cannons in the eighth inning. The only thing left was to count down the final three outs, and this countdown would be as charged as anything Times Square had ever seen on New Year's Eve. Sure, the Giants had just won a World Series two years earlier. But all three of their series-clinching victories in 2010 came on the road. Watching their team win its first Game 7 in franchise history would be a moment to soak in.

And, as it turned out, a moment to be soaked in.

The pregame forecast called for a chance of showers, and with Javier Lopez on the mound in the ninth inning, the storm arrived with no warning and in full force. Small lakes formed between third base and short. Water drained in sheets from both dugouts. Lopez tried somehow to shelter the baseball, at least, so he could throw a pitch.

At second base, Scutaro tipped back his head, closed his eyes, and opened his mouth, in a cinematic pose.

"It never rains here in the Bay Area," he said. "I spent four years in Oakand and I don't think it rained once."

"The best part was how our fans were cheering it," Pence said. "They were cheering the downpour."

Lopez did his best to keep a grip, but walked two of the four batters he faced. Bochy went to his bullpen to get the right-handed matchup, and hoped crew chief Gary Darling wouldn't suspend play during the pitching change. Romo entered, and lo and behold, Holliday stepped to the plate with two outs.

Crawford, at shortstop, with no kayak at his convenience, wondered how he would ever manage to field a ground ball and throw to first base.

"It kind of summed up the whole postseason," Crawford said. "It never rains like that in San Francisco. A little mist, maybe. There was standing water all over the place. I didn't know if I'd have been able to make a play."

In the relative shelter of the dugout, Vogelsong said a prayer: "Please, please, let us get a pop up or a strikeout. Please."

Romo got Holliday to hit one in the air. Scutaro saw a speck of white through a sky of water. He squeezed the Cardinals' last life between his fingers. And then he felt no pain.

"Please, I've got to catch this ball," Scutaro recalled telling himself. "I got kind of lucky. When he hit it, the rain stopped a little bit. A couple minutes earlier, maybe I don't catch it."

He did, and the Giants drenched themselves outdoors, indoors, and everywhere in between. They claimed their fifth NL pennant in 55 seasons since leaving the Polo Grounds, and they frolicked on the field like grade-school kids running through lawn sprinklers.

"No big deal," bench coach Ron Wotus said. "We were all going to get wet after the game, so it didn't matter."

On a night when Pence bent the laws of physics, the Giants celebrated their 20th pennant in franchise history amid a Biblical rainstorm. There was no question that Scutaro, who hit .500 in the series, including three hits in Game 7, would be named Most Valuable Player.

He received his trophy in one of the strangest, shortest, and wettest presentations in memory.

"All those guys in there, I love every single one," Scutaro said. "I think to win a championship, it takes more than 25 guys. It takes the front office all the way to the bat boy, and you have to have that chemistry going. And now here we are in the World Series."

It was time to get good and soaked indoors. Romo scampered about, holding a souvenir newspaper and yelling, "The Giants win the pennant!" Vogelsong got blasted with eye-stinging champagne as a ski visor the size of night-vision goggles sat atop his head. Outside the ballpark, thousands of car horns blared and a city buzzed once again over their focused, passionate team that held onto belief when everyone else let it slip like a curveball in the rain.

There was no dampening this party.

"That just didn't make any sense," said Cain, talking about the rain as much as those six elimination victories over the Reds and Cardinals.

The Giants outscored the Cardinals 20–1 over the final three games. In their six elimination wins, their bullpen allowed a total of two runs.

"We're a little numb right now, to be honest, with our backs against the wall as long as they've been and to do this," said Bochy, after his gang of Gideons blew their horns. "This is a special group. They have that 'never say die' attitude. They didn't want to go home, and they found a way to get it done."

It was the first postseason series the Giants clinched at home since the 2002 NLCS and Lofton's walk-off hit. That time, Matheny was the St. Louis catcher who couldn't reach back to tag David Bell as the Giants walked off with the pennant. This time, Matheny was the team's rookie manager delivering the concession speech in the interview room.

"We got to this point by being the team that's hot," Matheny said. "But we just couldn't make it happen these last two games. We tip our hats to the Giants. They had all aspects of their game going, and capitalized on opportunities."

The Giants played flawless defense all night, but someone in the front office made one major error. Pence's broken bat, the one that held so much magic on that bases-clearing double, was authenticated and taken to one of the souvenir stands, where it sold in a silent auction. Rick Alagna, a software engineer from Pleasanton, was stunned when he was able to walk away with the bat for $400. That night, his son, J.D., served as his father's conscience. Such a venerated piece of Giants history, he told his dad, really should be returned to its rightful owner.

"I'm going to say good-bye to the collectible of all collectibles," said Alagna, who received a full refund and World Series tickets as part of the bargain.

Scutaro was supposed to be broken after that hard slide, too. Instead, he became the first player in LCS history to post six multi-hit games in one series. Of his 14 hits against the Cardinals, 12 of them came after Holliday knocked him to the dirt and sent him hobbling to the X-ray room.

Scutaro was the embodiment for a team knocked down but never out. And the outpouring of emotion that night was unforgettable.

Chapter 15

To the Third Power

"It's not the bat. It's you. It's everything you've got inside you."
—Pablo Sandoval

Wednesday, October 24, 2012
World Series Game 1 vs. Detroit

For Bruce Bochy, the hardest part of being a big league manager wasn't drafting the lineup or engineering double-switches or even soothing superstar egos.

It was delivering bad news.

It was every cut-down day in spring training, every time he had to call a struggling player into his office, every sentence he had to begin with "We've gotta make a change here..."

Bochy made it to the major leagues as a third-string catcher. In the waning days each spring, with opening day right around the corner and the equipment trucks already rolling out of camp, Bochy's own roster spot remained unsecured. One little hamstring tweak to a pitcher or an outfielder could convince the GM to carry added coverage there at his expense. Bochy knew what it sounded like to receive bad news. Maybe that's why, after becoming a major league manager, he tried to deliver it with such compassion.

No matter how carefully he chose his words, though, it was impossible to mask the full truth. When you tell a player he didn't make the club, you're essentially telling him that he wasn't good enough.

In 2010, Barry Zito wasn't good enough.

Zito was four seasons into the whopping seven-year, $126 million contract that Peter Magowan lavished upon him, in the skewed hopes of providing the franchise a fresh star to market who didn't have Barry Bonds' toxic baggage. The way Magowan saw it, Zito was ideal for that role. He charmed fans in Oakland, where he formed a rotation triumvirate with Tim Hudson and Mark Mulder that pushed the A's to one playoff appearance after another.

Zito was a left-hander through and through, complete with a guitar, surfboard, yoga mat, pink silk pillow, and a collection of stuffed animals that he'd take on the road in his rookie season. His first year or two in the big leagues, he changed the color of his hair highlights as often as his uniform. The purple-on-black raven motif was an especially bold look.

He showed the same boldness on the mound from the time he made his major league debut, in July of 2000, against the Anaheim Angels. The 22-year-old walked six batters, hit another, and faced the heart of the Angels lineup with no outs and the bases loaded in the fifth inning. Then he came back to strike out Mo Vaughn on a curveball, Tim Salmon on a high fastball, and Garret Anderson on a slider in the dirt. It was a loud and impressive introduction.

Two seasons later, Zito went 23–5 with a 2.75 ERA to win the AL Cy Young Award, collecting more first-place votes than Pedro Martinez despite an ERA that was a half-run higher.

Zito remained a steady and durable presence through 2006, when he qualified for free agency, but there were signs his stuff was in decline. His walk rate had increased, his strikeout rate had decreased, and his 1.4 baserunners per inning was the highest of his career. He was just 41–34 with a 4.05 ERA over his final three seasons in Oakland. When Magowan recruited him and courted him with the richest contract ever given to a pitcher in major league history, the opinion around baseball was near-unanimous: the Giants made a $126 million mistake the moment they signed the deal.

None of that was Zito's fault, of course. He didn't take the money at knifepoint. He made the decision to sign with the Giants even though the Seattle Mariners had hinted at a willingness to throw even more cash his way. And besides, he was popular and comfortable in the Bay Area.

Although the Bay Bridge is just six miles long, the Giants might as well have played a universe away from Oakland. Zito went from a loose, goofy, frat house environment to a buttoned-up, passive-aggressive, and highly political clubhouse under intense daily media scrutiny in 2007 as Bonds counted down the home runs to Hank Aaron.

That first spring, the distraction that Zito provided the press from Bonds wasn't always a positive one. Coaches watched with their mouths hanging open as Zito walked to the mound for his first throwing session in a Giants uniform, set up a personal video camera, pulled out a tape measure, and marked a spot in front of the rubber. Then he pitched from an exaggerated crouch, nearly sitting in a squat as he took a gigantic step backward to begin his motion. It didn't look anything like his previous delivery. It didn't look anything like *anyone's* delivery.

Zito had spent most of that off-season working with a kinesiology professor at San Diego State, hoping to restore a bit of steam to his fastball. Instead, he received brutal honesty from his new pitching coach. Dave Righetti suggested Zito's changes could work—if he didn't lose his balance and fall off the back of the mound.

"I looked at his tapes from Oakland," Righetti said with a snort. "That was a waste of time."

"We'll see how his groin feels tomorrow," Righetti continued. "It'll wear him down. He's going to over-stride and it's going to be tough for him. He's a good athlete and he got himself in shape for it, so maybe it's all tied in together. I guess he felt he needed to do something."

"But to me, it'll be about making his pitches. If he loses the curveball, which he could because he's throwing from a different angle now...his ball flight is going to be different, no doubt about that."

The way the Giants saw it, they didn't invest in an experiment. The way Zito saw it, there was no harm in trying something new if it can make you better. He was curious and open-minded by nature, and no matter how many millions he was guaranteed, that wasn't going to change.

It can be a rough ride, though, when you are a free-thinking individualist in an environment of such rigid conformity. The same little quirks or opinions or biographic scraps that make a successful player delightfully unique turn him into a punch line when he's struggling. With the A's, Zito was young, unassuming, and the toast of the town. There was no reason to think it'd ever change.

And then it did. Zito struggled to a losing record in his first season with the Giants, then led the league in losses when he went 10–17 with a 5.15 ERA in '08. A productive month here or there aside, Zito was 40–57 with a 4.45 ERA over the first four years of his contract with the Giants.

For Zito, noise-canceling headphones became as important as oxygen whenever he was in public. He didn't handle negativity well, and even though Giants fans carry fewer pitchforks than most, the backlash got way too personal. Zito tried to do normal things. He couldn't.

"I tried Twitter," he said, "and it was a pretty devastating experience for me."

Even when he signed up for Facebook under an alias (Baron Von Zitenhausen, for one), it wasn't long before the trolls found him, throwing boulders.

At the end of his fourth year as a Giant, in the penultimate game of the regular season in 2010, Zito had a chance for a redemptive, signature moment. A victory over the San Diego Padres would clinch the NL West. If Zito could deliver it, there would be so much savory mixed with the sweet.

In the first inning, Zito loaded the bases. Then he walked a batter. Then he walked another. He had his chance to erase so much misery, and instead he added to it.

The Giants managed to clinch the following day, but Zito practically sealed his fate concerning the postseason roster. He was the highest-paid player on the team but its fifth-best starting pitcher, and his 50-minute, long-toss ritual before every outing meant there was no way to carry him as a reliever.

It was the worst bad news that Bochy ever had to give a player.

But Zito continued to say and do all the right things. He continued to throw off a bullpen mound and work on his mechanics, just in case the Giants had an injury or made a roster change in between playoff series. Bochy never forgot how Zito carried himself through what had to be an emasculating experience.

But being a major league manager also afforded Bochy his share of delights: telling the rookie he made the club, informing a journeyman that he made the All-Star team, presenting the lineup card after a historic performance.

And in this case, a day after clinching the 2012 pennant in a heavy downpour, picking up the phone to tell Zito that he would be starting Game 1 of the World Series.

There was just one problem. Zito accidentally left his cell phone in the clubhouse.

"I had to hold off announcing it," Bochy said. "But I think we all knew that Barry was starting, and I think he had a good idea. He was ecstatic. He was proud, honored that we have the trust in him to start Game 1."

That's right. Not only would Zito, for all the slings and arrows directed at him over the years, start Game 1 of the World Series, but that decision had become a foregone conclusion. It was a storyline that nobody could've predicted—especially by anyone who had their eyelids open that spring, when Zito allowed 44 baserunners in 19⅓ innings, struck out only one batter, and couldn't have gotten hit harder if he were a coach with an L screen in front of him.

There are sunk costs. In the spring of 2012, Zito was the RMS *Lusitania*. The *San Francisco Chronicle* cited an unnamed source as saying the Giants were close to the scuttling point, ready to release him with more than $40 million in checks still to be written.

Zito had been experimenting again that spring, using elements of the momentum philosophy espoused by controversial pitching Tom House, trying any number of mechanical changes to give him a shot at being competitive. The Giants respected the effort and gave him as much slack as they could, but at the end of camp, it just wasn't working. They ordered him to stay back and start from scratch with his old delivery. As the rest of the team headed north for the final exhibition games, Zito had one minor league scrimmage and two side sessions to figure it out.

After the team started the year 0–3 in Arizona, the Giants continued to Colorado, Bochy handed the ball to Zito—and resisted a powerful urge to shield his eyes.

Zito threw a shutout. In Coors Field.

He rescued the Giants from what would've been their first 0–4 start since 1950. It was his first shutout in nine years—the first ever by a Giant in 18 seasons at Coors Field—and he did it with his old delivery. He did it by being himself, and trusting that would be enough.

"I always say if you catch me on a good day when stuff's working, things are going to turn out good regardless of the team," Zito said after blanking the Rockies.

Afterward, Righetti wordlessly padded out of the coaches' room in his shower shoes and carefully placed the lineup card in Zito's locker. Sometimes the smallest acts carry the greatest amount of respect.

Zito encountered the invariable rough stretch or two that season, but the Giants were scoring more runs and he always pitched better with a lead. Their outfield of Gregor Blanco, Melky Cabrera, Angel Pagan, and, later, Hunter Pence, was the best defensive group the Giants assembled in years—a boon to a fly-ball pitcher.

All these years, as it turned out, Zito was a hothouse tomato plant. He just needed certain conditions to thrive. And down the stretch in 2012, the Giants made it downright toasty for him. They were 11–0 in his starts to end the regular season, ensuring this time around that there would be no uncomfortable message from the manager.

Bochy made Zito a part of the playoff rotation. Another former Cy Young Award winner, Tim Lincecum, became the odd man out this time after he faltered to a 5.18 ERA—the highest among all 48 qualified starting pitchers in the National League. Lincecum had the kind of bounce-back arm that could work in relief, though, and his stuff played up in shorter bursts. From the day the Giants drafted him, they thought Lincecum could be a wipeout closer if he didn't prove durable enough to start. He would be on the playoff roster, but not in the rotation.

The Giants put the season in Zito's hands for Game 4 of the NLDS at Cincinnati, hoping he wouldn't come unhinged in this shot at redemption as he did in that potential clincher against the Padres two years earlier. The 34-year-old didn't make it out of the third inning against the Reds. He allowed two runs, walked four, and gave up a home run, but the Giants rallied back to win. And although the natural conclusion to draw was that Zito choked again, he looked back at video of his start and realized his stuff wasn't that bad. He worked with a tight strike zone from plate umpire Dan Iassogna, and might have nibbled at the corners a few times too many. But most of the time, his cutter, changeup, and curve had plenty of late movement. He didn't crater into self-doubt. Instead, he hoped for another chance.

The Giants gave him one. They captured all three elimination games in Cincinnati to punch through the first round, but then lost three of the first four games to the St. Louis Cardinals in the NLCS. Once again, they had to win three consecutive elimination games to advance, but the mountain did not appear too slick or steep this time. They still had the prospect of Games 6 and 7 in front of their fervent fans at AT&T Park. If they could win Game 5 at Busch Stadium, they liked their chances.

The Giants had won 12 consecutive times with Zito on the mound. Their playoff lives depended on going 13-for-13.

The Giants were one loss from getting shot down. And they handed the baseball to their easiest target of all.

You would expect the buildup to Zito's start in St. Louis to be doom and gloom. Instead, it was a wondrous wellspring of support. The vitriol and derision that once chased Zito off social media had evaporated, replaced by something odd, organic, and completely original.

The images came across Facebook, Twitter, and every other corner of the Internet, as Giants fans everywhere replaced their avatars to embrace a new identity.

There were avatars of Barry Zito with a 1970s-era mustache. Zito with a blue-steel modeling gaze. Wedding Zito. Smiling Zito. Maniacally smiling Zito. Possessed Zito. Chill Zito. Guitar-strumming Zito. Sprawled-in-the-grass Zito. Shirtless Zito. Bed head Zito. Toy pooch–carrying Zito. And floating Zito heads Photoshopped into one ridiculous context after another. (On the back of a unicorn, for example, riding on a beam of rainbows.)

It was the #RallyZito movement in full flower, and it spoke to more than the Giants' dire set of circumstances. Few ballplayers offered such rich returns on a Google image search, and for so many years, those tremendous images made him an easy mark. They made him the tallest nail in the hammer aisle.

Now those images were being re-appropriated by fans as a show of support, complete with a hashtag.

Zito was more than a trending topic. He was the Giants' last hope.

He was nails, all right.

Against a Cardinals lineup that featured six batters with better than a .300 average against lefties—and one that harassed fellow lefty Madison Bumgarner in Game 1—Zito kept St. Louis completely off balance. He threw just off the plate with his breaking pitches, nudged and bent umpire Ted Barrett's strike zone, and when he knew hitters were hunting for something down in the zone, he fearlessly threw his 84-mph fastball at the letters.

He knew exactly what he wanted to do, often shaking off Buster Posey until he got the signal he wanted. He even surprised the ballpark by going on his own and putting down a perfect bunt single that scored Blanco in the fourth inning.

"Shocked," Giants third-base coach Tim Flannery said. "That's what I was. We work on it. We talk about it. But he did that all on his own. It was beautiful—brilliant."

The squeeze play gave the Giants a 4–0 lead, and almost everyone knew the stat: Zito was 125–7 in his career (and 40–3 as a Giant) when he received four runs of support.

Zito took a shutout into the eighth inning, and after a 5–0 victory, he took the NLCS back to China Basin.

"He was pitching," Cardinals manager Mike Matheny said. "He was raising eye level. He was in the top of the zone, just above, on the edges, just off. He was moving in and out, back and forth. He was taking speeds off his breaking ball and changeup. That's what pitching is. You don't have to have 99 on your fastball if you can locate and keep hitters off balance.

"We never, never did get into a good groove. It looked like we started to guess a little bit, tried to anticipate what he was going to do. He was one step ahead."

After winning Games 6 and 7 in San Francisco, the Giants went from three steps behind to celebrating a pennant. And eventually, Bochy was able to deliver the good news: Zito would start Game 1 of the World Series against the Detroit Tigers.

"I couldn't be happier for him," Bochy said. "It says a lot about his mental toughness, his makeup. For him to keep grinding and trying to get better, I was really proud to tell him, 'I'm glad to hand you the ball on the first game,' with all he's been through and the way he's handled it. It's been off the charts."

The Tigers had Miguel Cabrera, baseball's first Triple Crown winner in nearly five decades. They had Prince Fielder. Above all, they had right-hander Justin Verlander, whose buzzing, 98-mph fastball dominated through the first two rounds.

The Giants countered with Zito, a pitcher who wasn't even on the World Series roster two years earlier. Now he would carry their torch.

"I feel like I've grown up in this game, you know?" Zito said. "When I came up in Oakland, I felt like I was a boy in this game. You have talent and you just keep going to the next level, and all of a sudden people are looking at you and there's fans chanting your name and stuff, and you don't know why. And then, to mature in this game is a big deal.

"That process is a huge part of becoming a free agent, going to a new team, signing a big deal, and dealing with everything that comes with that.

"So I feel like an adult in the game now."

The Giants entered Game 1 of the 2012 World Series in a familiar position: with home-field advantage and underdog status.

The Tigers had just finished making the New York Yankees look like the Columbus Clippers in a four-game sweep, and had the luxury to align their rested rotation from the top down.

Verlander was a no-brainer to start Game 1. He was 3–0 in the post-season, having allowed only two runs in 24⅓ innings. He led the AL with 239 strikeouts. He was the reigning AL Cy Young and MVP, too. And in the ALDS, against a Bernie-leaning A's club that entered October as the hottest team in either league, Verlander dominated them twice—including in a winner-take-all Game 5.

Even Marco Scutaro, who almost never swung through a third strike, had eight whiffs in 23 career at-bats against Verlander.

The Giants already proved they could get under the skin of an ace. The Rangers' Cliff Lee appeared just as untouchable before losing in Game 1 of the 2010 World Series. But with Lee, at least, you could hope to foul off enough put-away strikes and drive up his pitch count. Verlander offered no hope there. He was a physical beast and a throwback who could easily exceeded 120 pitches without a soul unbuttoning a jacket in the bullpen. He possessed that rare ability to throw harder as the game went on.

The Giants were facing a Formula One racecar, and sending an Oldsmobile with a top speed of 84 mph to the mound.

The Tigers lineup inspired fear, too. Cabrera and Fielder combined for 74 home runs in the regular season. The Giants' entire club hit just 103.

But one Giants hitter was brimming with confidence.

Pablo Sandoval endured his own ignominy in 2010. Like Zito, the Kung Fu Panda was more spectator than participant that October. His ongoing weight issues clearly began to affect his play down the stretch that season, especially his defense. At the plate, he was a gifted hitter with supreme hand-eye coordination and a knack for getting the barrel to almost any pitch, in or out of the zone. But when he began to put on pounds, he couldn't clear his hips. He'd begin to over-rotate at the plate and it took very little change of pace to get him completely out of whack.

The Giants included Sandoval on every postseason roster in 2010, but he lost his job as the starting third baseman and rode the bench in all three postseason series clinchers. His World Series experience consisted of three hitless at-bats as the DH in Game 3 at Texas.

When you're pushed aside on a World Series winner, the champagne spray stings the eyes just as much. But maybe it tastes a bit flatter.

It was setting up to be another frustrating year in 2012 for Sandoval, who hit just 12 home runs in the regular season. He missed six weeks with a fractured hamate bone in his left hand—an injury that he sustained one year to the day after surgery to remove a fractured right hamate. Sandoval went back on the DL again after the All-Star break when he strained a hamstring. It was disheartening, but injuries were one thing. A perceived lack of commitment was another.

"In 2010, he didn't play in the four most important games of the year," Giants hitting coach Hensley Meulens said. "When he didn't play in the World Series, he said, that's not going to happen again."

Like Zito, Sandoval was recording his own redemption song in the 2012 postseason. He hit .320 in the first two rounds and was especially productive when the team needed him most, going 10-for-24 (.417) with three doubles, two home runs, and six RBIs in the six elimination victories over the Reds and Cardinals. He even hit a three-run triple off Verlander in the All-Star Game to help the Giants lay claim to home-field advantage in the World Series.

After all the pregame pomp and pageantry, the Giants needed somebody to break the ice against Verlander in Game 1. With two outs, the bases empty, and an 0-2 count in the first inning, Sandoval dug in his axe.

Verlander threw a 95-mph fastball above the top of the strike zone—a place where heaters only tantalize hitters before they pop into the catcher's mitt. Sandoval opened his stance, raised his hands, and found a way to keep from being overpowered. He hit a deep drive that slipped over the center-field fence and into the second row of the bleachers for a home run. The team that spent so much energy catching up in this postseason had struck for the first lead in the World Series.

It was the first home run hit by a Giant in the first inning of a World Series game since Mel Ott in 1933. It was just the fourth home run, and first of the season, Verlander had given up on an 0-2 pitch in his major league career.

Sandoval ran the bases in businesslike fashion as the stadium erupted. These fans cheered so many monumental home runs in the short history of AT&T Park, but you could understand if they were out of practice. The Giants hit just 31 of them in their 81 regular season home games.

Instead, the Giants scored most of their runs in 2012 with tough at-bats and keen baserunning. By the time Sandoval batted again in the third, his teammates had put those skills on display. Pagan and Scutaro started the rally, each working Verlander for eight pitches while reaching base. Pagan fouled off three pitches with two strikes before hitting a

The list of men who have homered three times in a World Series game is a short and prestigious one: Babe Ruth, Reggie Jackson, Albert Pujols...and Pablo Sandoval.

grounder down the third-base line that took a crazy/lucky deflection off the bag for a double. Scutaro fouled off two 98-mph fastballs with two strikes before shooting a slider up the middle for an RBI single.

Detroit pitching coach Jeff Jones walked to the mound to check on Verlander, who laughed as he appeared to ask, "What are you doing out here?"

Verlander had been impossibly good all season. There was no reason to believe the Giants would get to him again.

Except Sandoval did.

Verlander altered his approach, first trying without success to get Sandoval to chase a pair of changeups in the dirt. With a 2-0 count, there was little doubt a fastball would be next. Against Verlander, though, it often didn't make much difference if you knew his hole cards—especially if one of them was an outside fastball at the knees and on the black.

But as Verlander was about to learn, there simply wasn't anyplace safe where you could pitch the Panda. Sandoval tracked a 95-mph heater running off the plate, extended his arms, and kept his balance despite a lunging swing. He stayed through the pitch and drove it to the opposite field, using Verlander's supplied power to generate backspin.

The ball carried into the left-field bleachers for a two-run homer. Verlander wasn't smiling any longer. Instead, he whirled around, watched the ball disappear, and mouthed one word.

"Wow."

"It was extremely impressive," Verlander said later that night. "I wish I hadn't contributed."

Verlander was more Terminator than man that season. Sandoval had just picked him up and flung him into a vat of molten steel.

"He's got an uncanny ability to hit the ball in all nine quadrants of the zone," Meulens said. "The ball down in the zone is the one he hits the hardest, the one we want him to focus on. But when he's locked in, he can hit anything. That was as far down and away as you can go, and Pablo stayed on it."

Sandoval's second home run gave the Giants a 4–0 lead. Once again, Zito had his magic quota of runs, along with something else. For the first time in his six seasons as a Giant, he felt nothing but unconditional love pouring from the stands, and he did not misplace the fans' newfound faith in him. He kept the Tigers swinging over the top of his curveball, stranded two runners in the first inning, and stayed true to his game plan.

No matter what the strike zone looked like (and plate umpire Gerry Davis was known to have a tight one), Zito pledged to stay aggressive against the Tigers. Inning after tidy inning, and with help from two high-light catches from Blanco, he did just that. He even added to his hitting lore by following up his surprise squeeze bunt in St. Louis with an RBI single on a 97-mph Verlander fastball.

Zito always joked that he didn't hit the ball so much as he massaged it. His little shank through the left side in the fourth must have felt like a Dutch rub to Verlander, who hadn't given up a hit to an opposing pitcher in almost six years. He'd have all winter to figure out what happened after throwing 98 pitches and netting just 12 outs.

Verlander was done. But the Panda show wasn't over.

His third trip to the plate came in the fifth inning against right-hander Al Alburquerque, who had seen enough to know that challenging Sandoval with a fastball was a poor notion. Alburquerque tried to get him fishing on a 1-1 slider. The pitch was ankle high. Catcher Alex Avila's glove skimmed the dirt as he moved to receive it.

Sandoval already hit home runs on two pitches that weren't mistakes. He did it once more, digging out Alburquerque's slider and somehow driving it over the center-field wall to send the crowd into pure jubilation.

Sandoval raised a fist as he rounded the bases. Just as the original Mr. October, Reggie Jackson, did 35 years earlier, he thrust his helmet in the air while receiving a curtain call.

He hit 12 homers in the regular season. Suddenly, he had six in a single postseason. And with three home runs in a World Series game, Sandoval joined a list that was as short as it was prestigious: Reggie, Albert Pujols, and Babe Ruth.

Thirteen years after the Dodgers' Kevin Elster hit three home runs in the first game at AT&T Park, Sandoval became the second player to do it. Hard to believe, but even Barry Bonds, at his 73-homer height, never accomplished a three-homer game in the ballpark supposedly built for his swing.

Sandoval, the round third baseman once benched because of his weight, had never been bigger. He whistled a single in his last at-bat to complete a 4-for-4 night, too.

"He just had one of those nights where anything we threw, he hit," Tigers manager Jim Leyland said. "I think you certainly tip your hat to what Sandoval did tonight. You can't sit up here and say what he did tonight was a fluke. I mean, it was unbelievable. The guy had one of those unbelievable World Series nights that they'll be talking about for years. So I tip my hat to him."

The fans did the same for Zito. In the two most important starts of his baseball life, Game 5 at St. Louis and the World Series opener against Detroit, the 34-year-old left-hander had spun 13 consecutive scoreless innings. The Tigers finally scratched him in the sixth when Austin Jackson doubled, Cabrera singled him home, and Delmon Young lined a two-out hit.

Before Bochy took his second step toward the mound, the sellout crowd already stood in unison for Zito and began to rain down applause. For the first time in five seasons, chants of "Barry! Barry!" echoed through AT&T Park. They were meant for someone new, and they were at least as loud as the night the all-time home run record fell.

Bochy took the ball and deployed a scenario that would've sent you to a padded room if you suggested it in the spring: Lincecum rushing in from the bullpen to take over for Zito in Game 1 of the World Series.

As if there wasn't enough emotion already crackling in the ballpark that night, the crowd went from one ear-throbbing ovation to the next as one former Cy Young Award winner replaced another. Lincecum quieted the rally but not the din, retiring all seven hitters he faced while striking out five.

"To have him in the bullpen, it's just ridiculous," Zito said. "It was just really special personally, too, to watch Timmy carve them up and just do what he does."

The Giants had to trust themselves to win six elimination games to reach the World Series. Once there, thanks to a historic contribution from Sandoval and a deeply meaningful one from Zito in an 8–3 victory, they didn't trail again.

Madison Bumgarner, who had been pulled from the rotation in the NLCS after an 11.25 ERA in his first two postseason starts, returned in Game 2 and dominated over seven two-hit innings in a 2–0 victory.

Ryan Vogelsong was just as unyielding in another 2–0 win in Game 3 at Detroit. The Giants swept the series a night later, taking the lead when Scutaro's single scored Ryan Theriot, the player whose job he had taken earlier in the season.

In 2010, the Giants won their first World Series in the San Francisco era with a team of outcasts and misfits. But even then, a subculture existed. There were outcasts among the outcasts, misfits among the misfits.

Two years later, two of those pushed-aside players—Zito and Sandoval—struck the tone that would make the Giants champions once more.

"It just goes to show you that this game…this is a great game," said Posey, a smile of admiration spreading across his face. "If you work hard and persevere, good things will happen. Those two guys never complained in 2010, not that I heard, anyway, and they have a love of the game. That counts for a whole lot."

After his three-homer romp into the history books, Sandoval revealed that his bat, the one he used to homer twice off Verlander, cracked when he fouled off the first pitch in the fifth inning. He used a new bat to make four left turns on Alburquerque.

The Hall of Fame gladly took possession of the broken one, which Sandoval had used all postseason.

"I don't get too much superstition," Sandoval said. "There's more bats in there to swing. It's not the bat. It's you.

"It's everything you've got inside you."

Chapter 16

Electric Again

"It didn't feel like a 'stuff' day. It felt more like a 'location' day."
—Tim Lincecum

Wednesday, June 25, 2014
Tim Lincecum no-hits San Diego

Tim Lincecum always had a lot going on.

His unique delivery involved so many hinges, so many timing mechanisms, and required so much athleticism, that the untrained eye seldom noticed when he'd make a subtle tweak.

But cut his hair? Now that'll lead to a flood of Instagrams.

When the players showed up for the Giants' annual FanFest prior to the spring of 2013, nobody's arrival garnered more head turns than Lincecum's. Gone were his shoulder-length locks, which flowed in the bay breeze while he won his second Cy Young Award in '09 and pitched the Giants to a World Series title in 2010.

The hair was the most visible part of Lincecum's counter-culture image that resonated with Giants fans. He let everything hang out on the mound. His talent was so immense and his pitches so caffeinated, he didn't have to put much thought into his craft beyond, "It's cool, I've got this."

But even in 2010, there were signs that Lincecum's stuff was in decline. His 3.43 ERA was nearly a full run higher than the previous season, when he won his second Cy Young. During one particularly rough stretch in May, catcher Bengie Molina confided in a quiet moment that Lincecum's fastball wasn't as consistent from start to start as it used to be.

"Some nights, he is getting them out with his name," Molina said.

By 2012, reputation and illusion were doing no favors for Lincecum. His fastball, which topped out at 99 mph and averaged 94 when he burst into the big leagues, was barely cracking 90. If he had to labor in the first inning, as he often did, he didn't possess the stamina to reach back for something extra later in the game. He still threw his lethal changeup, which allowed him to continue striking out a batter per inning. But he seldom put himself in counts to get a defensive swing. Baserunners abused him because he couldn't make efficient pitches from a slide step.

By season's end, Lincecum's 5.18 ERA was the highest among all NL pitchers who threw enough innings to qualify.

His dominance out of the bullpen that October saved an otherwise lost season. Sometimes entering the game with as few as two warmups on the bullpen mound, Lincecum made five relief appearances and gave up just one run on three hits over 13 innings. He walked two and struck out 17. Over 4⅔ innings in the World Series, the Detroit Tigers were hitless against him.

He became a powerful weapon, and a difference maker. But Lincecum had no wish to transition to a relief role in 2013. For one, he'd be a free agent after the year, and he'd be worth millions more if he could reestablish himself as a reliable presence in the rotation. More than that, though, he felt a deeper motivation.

"I need to take care of my job and not embarrass myself out there, and that's pretty much my mind-set," Lincecum said. "It's not just the jersey, but it's the name on my back, which is reflective of my family and work ethic."

His goal was nothing less than to "re-stake my claim as a starting pitcher and a good one.... Right now, my perspective isn't to be in the bullpen. My perspective is, I want to be a starter and I want to get back to that elite status that I was at."

So Lincecum walked into a barber shop and asked for a makeover. If he was going to try to reinvent himself, he had to snip away his past and start over. It was the story of Samson in reverse: he lost his strength, so he cut his hair.

When he arrived at the FanFest, a media member remarked that Lincecum, neatly groomed and with dark-rimmed glasses, looked like a poet.

"I feel like I could write a pretty good poem or two," he said.

Lincecum always would be a lyrical name for Giants fans, no matter where he stood in the ERA rankings. He represented the first flash of brightness in the post-Bonds era. He was a full-fledged phenomenon on the mound and likable off it, never binding himself to baseball's conventional ways. Amid celebratory clubhouse scenes, and with a mischievous smile, he'd drop F-bombs in live interviews.

He was as much a paradox as a phenomenon, though—an irreverent introvert who wore a big league uniform before he had a chance to grow up. He was the kid who partied so hard he missed an All-Star Game in New York, who took his father's secret recipe to throw a baseball and became a star, who achieved so much fame in such a short time.

When those waters receded, he had to retreat to a quieter, more serious place. He was learning to hear the sound of his own voice. Fame wasn't what motivated him, even in the best of times. He already knew that. But he needed to figure out what did.

He came up with an answer.

"I feel like as an introverted person myself, I reflect more on things, how they affect me and what I think I should do differently," he said. "A lot of those answers came from myself and what I didn't want to go through. And I didn't want to go through last year again.... I just tried to take a fresh slate and approach this year as if I'm just another guy on the team, trying to do my job and do what I can."

It would be a critical year for Lincecum. GM Brian Sabean confirmed he had no plans to engage in talks about a new contract during the season.

That hardly came as a surprising stance, given the way the right-hander struggled in 2012.

One other question kept coming up again and again. Lincecum seldom worked with Buster Posey in 2012. Bruce Bochy often put his starting catcher at first base or gave him the day off when it was Lincecum's turn to pitch. Bochy kept insisting there was no underlying issue. Lincecum just happened to be starting day games after night games, or other opportune times to rest Posey. Plus, it made sense for the sake of continuity to have backup Hector Sanchez catch the same starting pitcher. And catching Lincecum, with all those pitches in the dirt, often meant catching a beating. Bochy said he wanted to save Posey some of that wear and tear.

But this was Posey and Lincecum—the former and current faces of the franchise. Their names carried too much weight. The question wasn't going away, and Lincecum acknowledged that he hoped to get on the same page with Posey during the 2013 season.

There was truth in each of Bochy's explanations, but perhaps not the full measure. In fact, it had become easy for Lincecum and Posey to find themselves on different pages. Posey was the Dean's list student who studied the scouting reports, knew hitters' tendencies, and wanted to pitch to their weaknesses. Lincecum was the jazz musician who figured out what sounded good in the bullpen, then threw the pitches he trusted the most.

Posey put down signs and designed pitch sequences based on the hitter. Lincecum wanted to throw what felt best for him. And because Lincecum internalized everything on the mound, if he had to shake off to a pitch, he was more likely to question it as he released it. He was more attuned to a rah-rah catcher like Molina, and rah-rah was not Posey's personality.

They liked each other. They just didn't have much of a rapport.

The jazz approach worked for Lincecum when he was younger, his fastball was firmer, and there was more differential between his hard stuff and split-change. He won two Cy Young Awards as a devastating, two-pitch guy. As he got older, though, he had to work harder and think deeper to get hitters off balance. Part of that was doing something he always skipped in his career.

His homework.

He finally acknowledged to himself that competition wasn't a one-way street. It wasn't merely in between his own ears. The competition he needed to embrace was between himself and the batter, and that batter had weaknesses to exploit. Lincecum began spending more time with the scouting reports. The introvert began to think externally.

He grew fond of listening to one song as he entered the 2013 season: "You Get What You Give" by the New Radicals. It served as a reminder that he needed to put in the work to get the results that came so much easier to him in the past.

"I've got to open eyes again," he said.

Lincecum's first 18 starts that season weren't unwatchable, but they were a disappointment. He pitched a bit better than his 4.61 ERA would indicate, but the Giants were 7–11 in those outings and he twice matched a career high with 10 hits allowed in a start. He had trouble bottling up big innings, and although he was able to get more outs with his slider, he paid for the ones he hung. Lincecum gave up a home run to Brandon Phillips on July 2 in Cincinnati, when the Reds' Homer Bailey threw a no-hitter.

Even ardent Lincecum fans began to murmur that management should act before the trade deadline and pawn perhaps the most beloved, accomplished, decorated pitcher in franchise history. Even if he stayed, how long could he sublet his place in the rotation?

Two starts after the Giants got no-hit in Cincinnati, Lincecum took the mound July 13 at San Diego's Petco Park hoping for a quality start and a positive mind-set heading into the All-Star break.

There was a time in Lincecum's career when he would jog to the mound and Bochy would ponder a no-hitter before the first pitch. This was not one of those nights. Not by the longest shot.

But anyone who watched Lincecum's last handful of starts could notice a pitcher who was using his curveball more, changing eye levels, and doing more mixing than a blender in Cancun. He was coming off a start in which he struck out 11 Mets. And he always matched up well against the Padres.

Lincecum had good stuff again, and a plan to use it. He had gone over the scouting reports with Posey, and by the time he passed through the Padres lineup a second time, every hitter except Carlos Quentin had struck out at least once. Lincecum matched a career best when he struck out six consecutive batters from the second inning to the fourth.

By the end of the night, Lincecum generated 26 swings and misses. Even at the height of his powers, he'd never gotten so many in a regular season game before. Nine of the whiffs came on sliders, six on fastballs, six on changeups, and five on curves. There wasn't a pitch the Padres could key on, or eliminate—or square up.

He finished with 13 strikeouts, his most in a start in four years.

Lincecum had taken a no-hit bid into the seventh inning two other times in his career, including the day before Jonathan Sanchez no-hit the Padres at AT&T Park in 2010. Back then, everyone expected Lincecum to be the one. Three years later, so much had changed. A no-hitter from Lincecum would be just as unforeseen as Sanchez's feat.

Lincecum hadn't won on the road in three months and hadn't thrown a complete game in two years. Yet there he stood in the eighth, with no hits allowed—and Bochy was a wreck.

Lincecum had walked four, hit a batter, and all those strikeouts drove up his pitch count. He threw his 100th pitch in the sixth inning. It didn't matter. Any no-hitter carried significance. This one, for obvious reasons, meant even more.

Hunter Pence stood on the balls of his feet in right field. He once joked that if the Phillies had traded him to the Giants a couple months earlier in 2012, Matt Cain wouldn't have thrown his perfect game. There's no way he would have gotten near that ball in deep right-center field, the one that Gregor Blanco donned cape and cowl to catch.

Pence might have been selling himself short. Just as Blanco did for Cain and Aaron Rowand did for Sanchez, Pence came to the rescue for

Lincecum. With two outs in the eighth, he charged and made a sliding catch of Alexi Amarista's sinking line drive as Lincecum raised a fist.

Pence hit a bases-clearing triple and a home run, too. The Giants led 9–0 but there was so much still in doubt entering the bottom of the ninth. Lincecum struck out Chase Headley, got Quentin to fly out, and then Yonder Alonso lofted a fly ball that Blanco squeezed in left field to set off a celebration.

Lincecum's reaction was beyond understated. It's almost as if he didn't understand the game had ended. He watched the ball return to earth with his eyes wide, and gave the gentlest pump of the fist. He never saw Posey coming. He only felt the sudden bear hug from behind, as the catcher scooped him up like a forklift.

It's hard to say that catching Lincecum's no-hitter was more meaningful than winning a World Series for Posey. But the euphoria was on a different level. Without a doubt, the Buster Hug provided the enduring image from the night—two of the Giants' icons, still in their twenties and yet already ensconced in franchise lore, coming together in a moment of pure joy.

"Oh, it doesn't get old," Posey said. "I don't think it ever will. It's just as fun every time. It's history. It's a great accomplishment. You don't know if you'll be a part of it again."

Lincecum didn't see any of it coming. Not the no-hitter, and not Posey.

"No, I definitely did not," he said with a laugh. "I felt it, though. Yeah, he got me pretty good in the back, but when I went up the air, my mind-set was that this game is still going on and this is not the end of the no-hitter. I was on adrenaline and my mind was to keep pitching, I guess."

Lincecum became the third Giant in three seasons to throw a no-hitter, and if it had come as a 23-year-old rookie, or amid one of his two Cy Young seasons, it would've ranked as another electric night in a meteorological phenomenon of a young career.

But it didn't happen when he was splashed across magazine covers and video game boxes. It happened when all of that quieted down, and his own voice was the only sound that mattered.

"I don't think right now I really have a whole idea of what just happened," Lincecum said. "I'm just kind of pinching myself.... I'm just kind of coming down and I don't really know where to be emotionally."

Bochy let Lincecum throw 148 pitches, the most by a Giant in a start since Vida Blue in 1979.

"I don't think they were able to pattern him at all," Posey said. "He was pretty aggressive in the zone and he let his pitches work, but he also knew when to expand at the right times. That was a big part of it. Just thinking back, I blocked a lot of the two-strike pitches. It's not like he was leaving much in the zone.

"It's a concentration and a focus that he's really committed to."

Lincecum laughed when asked if the "why doesn't Posey catch him" questions would finally stop.

"I guess it looked like we were so angry at each other when he picked me up off the mound," he said, smiling.

Ryan Vogelsong dumped an ice bucket on Lincecum and the team opened a few bottles of champagne in the visiting clubhouse.

This was not a night for laments. But if Lincecum had one, it's that he didn't accomplish the no-hitter at home. He could only imagine how loud it would've been.

The no-hitter did wonders for Lincecum's morale, and his improved second half in 2013 compelled the Giants to take no chances with the open market. They had to overpay to wrap him up before the free-agency period began and they did, agreeing to a two-year, $35 million contract.

The Giants took their share of criticism, but they've always operated that way. They bid against themselves the last two times they extended Barry Bonds. They always pay their stars.

Lincecum usually disappeared to Seattle in the off-season and wouldn't touch a baseball for months. Prior to the 2014 season, though, he rented out a warehouse and started throwing off a mound. He used to be able to roll into spring training, spend a month fighting his mechanics, and figure it out in the nick of time before opening day. He wasn't going to pull an all-nighter again. He wanted to focus on opposing hitters, not on his own mechanics.

"I think you have to buy into the right changes and not be resistant to them and be accepting of what that means," Lincecum said. "It doesn't necessarily mean getting results you need right away. It's studying the hitters better and going over my mechanics to the point where I'm not trying to overthrow. It's more about working on placement."

Lincecum never was a command pitcher, but he knew that's what he had to become. His effectively wild years weren't coming back. His goal was to keep the ball down and get quicker outs.

"Crappy contact," he said. "That's kind of what I'm going for."

Did he have to be dragged into embracing some of those changes?

"It's...a fair assumption to say that," he said.

Although Lincecum had the best spring of his career, his first 15 starts in 2014 offered more of the same maddening inconsistency. He'd strike out 11 one start and give up eight runs in another. Even though he wasn't throwing 95 mph anymore, he still had plus movement with three off-speed pitches.

In a May 28 start against the Cubs, he was lifted with a no-hitter after five innings because he'd already thrown close to 100 pitches. He was a flickering candle, but whenever the flags in his mind happened to be still, he had a chance to shine.

There wasn't anything unusual about June 25, 2014, when Lincecum took the mound at AT&T Park. The Padres were back in town, but even that wasn't much of a storyline. Sure, he no-hit them a year earlier. But he had faced them twice since then, coughing up eight runs in 11⅔ innings.

The Giants, who blazed to baseball's best record at 43–21 at one point in early June, suddenly hit a 3–11 skid. They merely hoped for a competitive start from Lincecum so they could avoid being swept in a three-game series.

From the first inning, Bochy knew Lincecum would give them much more than that.

"I'm not just saying this, but early in the game, I said he's got a chance to get a no-hitter," Bochy said. "It was just the way he was locked in.... He looked more compact, putting less effort in it, and hitting his spots. Sometimes he makes it a little too hard out there.

"That's what I liked today. It looked like he was putting very, very little effort in his delivery."

Lincecum didn't snap violently across his body as if trying to force pitches to tumble and fade. He loosened his grip and let it happen on its own. He had finish on his changeup, slider, and curveball and put himself in counts to use them.

He operated out of the stretch just once, in the second inning after walking Chase Headley with one out. But Tommy Medica struck out and Amarista grounded to second base.

From there, it was loads upon loads of crappy contact. Three fly outs in the third. Two ground outs and a fly out in the fourth. A strikeout of Headley and another ground out in the fifth. Amarista sprayed a ball to right field, but it didn't require anywhere near the same effort from Pence as his catch did a year earlier at Petco Park.

This no-hit bid didn't sneak up on anybody in the stands. The fans began giving Lincecum standing ovations in the sixth inning, after Will Venable grounded out, and again in the seventh, when Quentin bounced to short.

In Lincecum's no-hitter at San Diego, Bochy had the bullpen busy in the sixth inning. This time, nobody unbuttoned a jacket.

Everything about Lincecum was relaxed, from his delivery to his demeanor. The seventh-inning stretch had come and gone, he still had

Thrown almost one year after his first career no-hitter, Tim Lincecum's second, against the Padres in 2014, was just as improbable.

a no-hitter intact, and there he stood in the dugout, talking with fellow pitcher Tim Hudson and laughing out loud.

To hell with superstition.

The Padres went down in order in the eighth, with Amarista again making the loudest contact. Gregor Blanco gloved a fly ball just short of the warning track to end the inning.

Pinch hitter Chris Denorfia, a difficult out for the Giants over his career, struck out on a slider in the dirt to start the ninth inning, throwing his bat in desperation at the pitch. Pinch hitter Yasmani Grandal was next, worked the count full on a couple close pitches, then hit a tapper that Lincecum raced off the mound to field and underhand to first base.

The surging crowd kept getting louder and louder with every out. With one more to go, it reached a crescendo.

Venable hit a grounder to second base and Joe Panik, making his fourth major league start, fielded it without incident and made the most important 40-foot throw of his life to end it.

Nineteen days short of the one-year anniversary of his no-hitter against the San Diego Padres at Petco Park, Lincecum did it again. He turned an ordinary, Wednesday afternoon get-away game into a banner headline achievement in his pantheon of greatness.

Lincecum wasn't lost in the fog this time as he watched Posey catch the 27th out at first base. He pumped his fist, fully aware of what he'd just accomplished, as his teammates mobbed him. Hector Sanchez, who had just caught his first no-hitter, was the first to embrace him.

Lincecum held the Padres to just a walk and struck out six while throwing the 16th no-hitter in Giants history in a 4–0 victory. He joined Christy Mathewson (in 1901 and '05) as the only pitchers in Giants history to throw two no-hitters.

"It really was an artist out there, I thought," Bochy said.

Other than the pitcher and opponent, though, there was little in common between the two no-hitters. Lincecum pitched on a different mound this time, threw to a different catcher, and the bullpen was a much quieter place.

In his no-hitter at San Diego, Lincecum was Jackson Pollock: all drips and splatters and scattered tosses. In front of his home fans, Lincecum was Piet Mondrian: tidy, sparse, structured, and restrained. This time, he didn't throw his 100th pitch until the ninth inning. He finished with a final count of 113 (73 strikes), and the no-hitter didn't even require any strenuous defensive intercession.

Lincecum only had 12 swinging strikes this time. But all the contact was good and crappy.

He mixed his slider 40 times and threw just 39 fastballs among his 113 pitches. His 36 percent fastball rate was his lowest percentage in any start in three seasons, and his third-lowest in his 236 career starts. The Padres kept rolling over his slider, putting it into play 13 times without a hit. His 12 ground-ball outs also were the most he'd induced in the past three seasons.

"To be honest, I didn't think my stuff was great," Lincecum said. "It didn't feel like a stuff day. It felt more like a location day."

Every no-hitter is a confluence of events. For a sellout crowd, this one tasted especially clean and refreshing. And at the very end, as the fans stood in anticipation and teammates perched hopefully near the dugout rail, Panik was certain the action would be on him.

"I was expecting it to come to me, just because of the pitch selection," the rookie said. "I was pretty well waiting for it to come to me, actually."

That's how predictable, how easy, how safe it felt. Even the rookie with four big league games under his belt understood how it would end.

"The more the pitches were down, the more movement I thought I had," said Lincecum, who shook to his slider for the final two outs in the ninth. "I've always been that guy who goes for the strikeout. Today I just tried to be more efficient, take what they gave me. They were giving me a lot of ground balls and fly balls. I just tried to get the first out [each inning] and go from there."

Giants fans had to understand by now: no matter what he did on a given day, there was no such thing as a "he's back" moment for Lincecum, no retouching the Tesla coil that made him a two-time Cy Young Award winner.

The next time Lincecum took the mound, you couldn't know what you were going to get. As it turned out, the Giants were forced to remove him from the rotation in August of 2014 and didn't display the same confidence to use him out of the bullpen down the stretch or into the postseason.

But for that afternoon in June, 10 days after his 30th birthday, Lincecum stood atop the baseball world for one more day. He joined Sandy Koufax as the only pitchers in major league history to accomplish two no-hitters, two World Series championships, and two Cy Young Awards.

Lincecum and Giants fans celebrated one more grand revival, and soaked up one more unforgettable moment at the ballpark by the bay.

Posey, who caught Panik's throw at first base and leapt off the bag in celebration, couldn't sneak up on Lincecum this time. That was all right. He was locked in an embrace with 40,000 of his best friends.

"Gosh, I mean, they're just fun," said Posey, stopping to scan the faces of reporters. "Are no-hitters as fun for you as they are for us?"

Chapter 17

Champion's Blood

*"I told them earlier, there's nobody's will that's
stronger than theirs or a desire that's deeper."*
—Bruce Bochy

Tuesday, October 7, 2014
NLDS Game 4 vs. Washington

It is the most heartbreaking part of a clubhouse manager's job. Mike
Murphy and his kids had to do it more than once.

For all the superstition in baseball, a clubhouse celebration required
a few advance preparations. You couldn't stage a champagne-spraying
party in the clubhouse without the champagne. You needed plastic sheeting to protect the lockers. You didn't wait until the final out to fill the
ice tubs.

And when the worst scenario came to life, when you lost Game 7 of
the World Series or failed to clinch the division or otherwise postponed
the celebration for another day or another season, you had to roll up the
plastic, hide the suds, and do it all as quickly and discreetly as possible.

So in a sense, Murphy and his crew had it easy on September 25,
2014. The Giants had no shot of catching the Los Angeles Dodgers and
their unassailable ace, Clayton Kershaw, in the NL West. But by virtue
of Milwaukee's loss earlier in the day, the Giants had clinched one of two
NL wild-card spots.

The Giants didn't have to beat the San Diego Padres that day. They knew they were backing into the playoffs, having played wretched baseball in most of June and July while blowing their 10-game lead. They didn't care. No matter the outcome that afternoon at AT&T Park—win, loss, or forfeit due to a rabid seagull attack—the Giants knew they were guaranteed at least one postseason game. And they were going to celebrate.

In 2010, they were a fourth-place team at the All-Star break and won the World Series. So what did it matter that they were one of baseball's worst teams for one-third of the '14 season? Who cared that they went 21–36 over more than two months, or that they couldn't even beat the 96-loss Colorado Rockies in their season series?

They didn't have Angel Pagan, their difference-making leadoff hitter, who underwent back surgery at the end of September. They didn't have Michael Morse, who strained his oblique at the beginning of the month. They barely saw Marco Scutaro, whose chronic back injury limited him to a five-game cameo. They weren't sure what to expect from the recently returned Brandon Belt, whose season got chopped up by a broken thumb and then by recurring concussion symptoms following a freaky batting-practice injury in July. Most critically, they didn't have Matt Cain, the pitcher who started all three of their playoff-clinching victories in 2012. Those thorny bone chips in his elbow finally became too much to ignore. He underwent surgery shortly after the All-Star break.

No sane analyst or commentator would pick the Giants to win their third World Series in five years, or even survive an opening round. But after a summer's labor, they had banked enough early victories to make it in. Two-thirds of the league did not. And Hunter Pence insisted that the Giants celebrate.

He walked into Bruce Bochy's office a week earlier and asked his manager's permission to make merry. His manager replied: "I hoped you guys would."

To an outsider, it might have been an awkward time to pop corks. It would've been odder still if the Giants had lost to the Padres that day—

and they nearly did, blowing a six-run lead only to have Pablo Sandoval heat up with three hits and four RBIs, Belt splash his first homer in almost two months, and Pence score the winning run on rookie Matt Duffy's safety squeeze.

After Gregor Blanco slid in the grass while catching the 27th out, the Giants swapped jerseys for wild-card T-shirts in the handshake line and celebrated with fans. Their clubhouse party? It was as wild as any of their other clinching celebrations in recent years. The champagne was sprayed, not sipped.

Pence, the playoff orator of 2012, was keen to drag his pulpit out of storage—and anyone who viewed the live television broadcast learned that the Reverend is not always fit for a churchgoing audience.

Pence didn't let the cameras deter him while delivering an impassioned speech that had more expletives than a George Carlin routine. This wasn't the Giants' first rinse-your-mouth-out moment on live TV, of course. Will Clark famously shrieked in a postgame celebration that he had been "waiting since the [bleeping] amateurs." Tim Lincecum's succinct on-air contribution in 2010 was, "[Bleep] yeah!"

Pence kept the treasured tradition alive, and then he [bleeping] expounded on it.

"We earned this mother [bleeping] burn," yelled a stomping and pacing Pence, spiking a pair of ski goggles onto the carpet. "Our goal is to play in the [bleeping] World Series, and guess what boys, we're going to the [bleeping] dance! We had mother [bleepers] out all the time, all year long. We've had [bleeping] big injuries, we've had [bleeping] all sorts of [stuff], ups, downs, but...

"We've got the mother [bleeping] champion blood."

The final tally as it was broadcast on Comcast SportsNet Bay Area: eight F-bombs into living rooms everywhere. Or was it nine? It all happened so fast, it was hard to tell. CSNBA issued an apology to Pence, and another to its audience—not that anyone cared. The station didn't receive a single call of complaint.

And what about the champion blood? Pence borrowed that phrase from Bochy, who used the term in a team meeting as the club continued to founder in early August. The manager looked around the room, began counting World Series rings in his head, and encouraged his players to do the same. They had it in their blood. They had beaten the odds before. They just needed to find a way into October baseball.

The postseason is all about managing tension, turning it from a negative to a positive. If the Giants could make it back to the postseason, Bochy knew those old instincts could kick in. His roster, although incomplete and imperfect and hit hard by injuries, was mostly the same group that won six elimination games in 2012.

So what if this season would come down to one wild-card game. It was just another elimination game, right?

"You know what? Last year was a rough year and I think we had some extra motivation when we went into spring training," Buster Posey said. "I couldn't be happier with the guys we have to have a shot to win one game and move on."

The Giants did move on past the Pittsburgh Pirates, stepping into as fervent a road playoff atmosphere as they had ever experienced only for Madison Bumgarner to turn the black-shirted grandstands into church pews at a funeral. He threw a four-hit shutout, Brandon Crawford's grand slam was the first by a shortstop in postseason history, and the Giants took an 8–0 victory at PNC Park.

"We just know when Bum takes the mound, he'll rise to the occasion and he did that," said Belt, who drove in three insurance runs and worked a pair of critical walks in his first two plate appearances. "It was amazing how loud it was, consistently loud, and it didn't bother him at all. It didn't bother any of us at all."

The Giants eliminated a Pirates team that had best home record in the NL and went on a 17–6 hot streak to end the regular season.

Their next challenge was far greater: the Washington Nationals, who finished with the league's best record at 96–66, trounced the Giants in five of seven regular season games, boasted one pitcher, Jordan

Zimmermann, coming off a no-hitter, and had another, Stephen Strasburg, with unmatched potential.

The Giants pitched their way to their World Series titles in 2010 and '12, but it was difficult to envision that happening again. Their rotation ERA ranked just 10th out of 15 NL teams in 2014. The Nationals had the league's best starting staff. And the Giants, by design as the wild-card entrant, were paying a stiff fine after spending Bumgarner to get past the Pirates. They would be able to start their best pitcher just once in the best-of-five series.

The Giants were underdogs, but that meant nothing to them. They were typecast by now. Maybe Jack Nicholson didn't set out to play crazy, but he was darn good at it. The Giants played the underdog role as easily as an axe can split a door.

There was something poetic about the Giants and Nationals meeting in an NL Division Series, too. Two years earlier, the Giants sat aboard their charter jet on the tarmac in Cincinnati, unsure whether they would fly to Washington or go home to face the St. Louis Cardinals in the NLCS. The Nats were one strike away. The Cards came back to win. It was a painful ending in more ways than one for the Nationals, who faced endless second-guessing for capping Strasburg's innings limit and refusing to let him pitch in the postseason.

Against the Giants, though, Strasburg would be lined up to pitch Game 1 and make the long-awaited first postseason start of his career. The kid from San Diego would draw Jake Peavy, the pitcher he grew up admiring.

"I don't think anybody is picking us, at this point in time, to do much of anything," said Peavy, who came over from the Boston Red Sox just prior to the July 31 trade deadline and had a 1.35 ERA as the Giants won eight of his final nine starts.

"You know, this bunch, we believe in ourselves. You have to respect who [the Nationals] are and what they've done. But you've got to see yourself going in there and winning.

"If you don't believe, you got nothing."

Right-hander Tim Hudson, a few beers deep into the celebration in Pittsburgh, put it in more graphic terms.

"Obviously they have a talented group over there, there's no question," Hudson said. "They have some great pitching. Come playoff time, talent can take you a long ways, but what do you have between your legs? That's going to take you real far. And I think we've got a group in here that really has some of that."

All factors considered, the Giants hadn't been bigger playoff underdogs since they toppled the Phillies in the 2010 NLCS. Zimmermann was coming off a no-hitter. So was Roy Halladay when the Giants beat him in Game 1 of that series.

"You know, they have such a balanced club, starting pitching, bullpen, their lineup," Bochy said of the Nationals. "They have been tough on us. Their record is what it is. They are a good, solid club and you have to play your best ball to beat them. They really don't have a weakness. I just think that when you have the best record in the league, you have to be considered the best in the National League. They should feel like that."

The trip to Washington held emotional significance for Bochy, who spent several of his formative years in northern Virginia while his father was stationed at the Pentagon. Bochy played little league at Bailey's Crossroads, lived in Falls Church, went through a basketball phase, had a paper route.

"I was an Evening Star guy," he said. "I couldn't get up early in the morning."

His family eventually moved to Melbourne, Florida, but not before Bochy formed a baseball bond with the Washington Senators—"I was a Frank Howard guy"—and spent his paper route earnings on 15-cent bus fares to see them play at RFK Stadium.

"It was great to wake up this morning knowing we are still playing baseball," Bochy said. "I've always liked Washington in October."

He wasn't alone. The Giants won both games at Nationals Park, shocking the home crowd by pecking eight singles off Strasburg for a 3–2 victory in Game 1 and then surviving one of the greatest postseason sieges of all time by beating the Nats 2–1 on Belt's home run in the 18th inning of Game 2.

The series hinged on one very controversial decision by a rookie manager with two outs in the ninth inning of Game 2.

Zimmermann was one out away from a three-hit shutout and a 1–0 victory when he issued a five-pitch walk to rookie second baseman Joe Panik. He had thrown just 100 pitches. Yet Matt Williams, the former Giants All-Star, walked to the mound and took the baseball.

Drew Storen entered. Three pitches later, Posey had singled, Sandoval had dumped a double to left field, and the Giants had shocked a sellout crowd by tying the game. If not for a crisp relay to the plate to throw out Posey, along with an inconclusive replay, the Giants would've taken the lead, too.

"I know I was pretty happy," said Hudson, who pitched brilliantly into the eighth but was on the hook for a 1–0 loss before Sandoval's double. "They have some good arms down there as well, but Zimmermann was just so tough on us tonight.

"They probably could've brought in Sandy Koufax and we would've had a smile on our face."

The Giants did not have Koufax in their bullpen. But they had Yusmeiro Petit, the strike-throwing savant who made headlines earlier in the season when he retired 46 consecutive batters to break Mark Buehrle's major league record. Making Petit's record-setting streak all the more impressive, it didn't come over the span of two starts. It happened over eight appearances, six of them in long relief, sometimes with eight or nine days off in between. Petit crept up on the record so quietly, nobody in the Giants organization even noticed until he was just a handful of batters away.

The Giants had grown to have faith in Petit's deceptive if not over-powering stuff, along with his complete fearlessness on the mound. He didn't have a blazing fastball, but he also did not nibble at the fringes of the zone. He matched precision with a "here it is" mentality.

The record-setting streak was just desserts for Petit after he came tantalizingly close to throwing a perfect game in a September 6 start the previous season. He faced the Arizona Diamondbacks that day at AT&T Park and retired 26 batters before Eric Chavez barely held his swing on a two-strike curveball. Petit followed up with a fastball that Chavez lashed for a single, and a ballpark groaned with disappointment. Instead of becoming the 24th pitcher to throw a perfect game, Petit joined an even more select club: he became the 12th pitcher to know the heartache of getting within an out of one, only to come up short.

Yet when Petit retired the next Arizona batter, he did not react the way you might expect. He thrust an arm in the air and gave thanks to the heavens for his first complete game in the major leagues.

"Best day in my career," Petit said the following spring. "I couldn't sleep at all. I was so happy."

What would you do if you hit all six Powerball numbers, only to have the wind snatch away your ticket? That's what made Petit's night so remarkable. It wasn't that he became just the 12th person in baseball history to experience the agony of getting within one out of a perfect game. It's that he didn't feel any agony at all.

"God gave me that for a reason," Petit said. "He knows the reason he didn't give me the perfect game. I believe in Him. I believe He will give me another chance."

Sure enough, a year later, Petit accomplished something even grander when he broke Buehrle's record. Maybe that's what God had in mind for him. Maybe it was something even more important.

The Giants had stunned the Nationals by tying the score in the ninth inning of Game 2. But they were still the away team, and the bottom half of any inning on the road is a potential poison pill. Any mistake could result in a walk-off. Even on a windy and chilly night with drives dying on the track, the Nationals had a lineup studded with power threats.

Petit took the ball in the 12th inning and Bochy became immediately alarmed when he walked the first batter.

There was a perfectly good explanation for that. It's hard to throw strikes when you can't feel your fingers.

It got cold in extra innings. Space heaters burned through propane tanks in both dugouts. More than three hours after Sandoval's double tied it, there they were: the Giants and Nationals marching through the deepening drifts of a postseason game that felt more like a Russian winter.

Petit got them to the 13th. Then he got them to the 14th. And on, and on, and on. He pitched six shutout innings, yielding just one hit. And when Belt lofted his home run over the right-field fence off Tanner Roark in the 18th inning, Petit became the first pitcher to throw at least six shutout innings in relief and earn a victory in a postseason game since Pedro Martinez in 1999.

"He stands out to me for a couple reasons," said Posey, who caught all 18 innings. "He had to go through that lineup a couple times, and to keep them off-balance like he did, in a postseason game, on the road, for me, it's one of the best performances I've ever seen.

"That has to be one of the greatest pitching performances in postseason history."

Between Hudson and Petit, the Giants received two quality starts in one night.

"I feel like I started the game," Petit said. "I feel like I started the biggest game of my life."

It was the longest game of his life, for sure. It ended three minutes after midnight at Nationals Park, exactly six hours and 23 minutes after it began—besting the previous postseason record of five hours, 50 minutes, set when the Astros needed 18 innings to beat the Braves in Game 4 of an NLDS in 2005.

Hudson remembered that game well. He started that one, too, and his side lost.

The Nationals matched a postseason record by using nine pitchers in the game—on a night when their starter, Zimmermann, was a batter away from tossing a shutout. You had to wonder what Williams was thinking. Belt had more of a one-track mind.

"I'm thinking that I'm going to take a nap," he said.

The Giants were going home with a 2–0 series lead, but Hudson knew better than to take anything for granted. The 39-year-old was the major leagues' active leader in career victories, but in six trips to the postseason, his team had never won a division series. He played for an A's squad that lost three consecutive to the Yankees after holding a 2–0 edge.

Sure enough, the Nationals fought back in Game 3, beating the Giants' ace when Bumgarner made a wild throw to third base. The Giants sent Ryan Vogelsong to the mound in Game 4 against left-hander Gio Gonzalez, hoping to avoid a return trip to Washington.

Anyone who remembered that 2010 NLCS in Philadelphia understood: Bochy would be prepared to use anyone at any time. He used three-fourths of his playoff rotation in a non-elimination game to beat the Phillies in Game 6 of that series.

He wasn't interested in packing a bag, returning to Washington, and retracing his old paper route—or seeing a fully rested Zimmermann one more time.

It kept happening again and again, to the point where all Ryan Vogelsong could do was laugh.

He fought through so much adversity over his two-decade baseball life, going as far as Venezuela and Japan to keep his career on a respirator, enduring so many demotions while always clinging to the belief that he was capable of something more.

He was right. His return to the Giants as a minor league free agent in 2011 provided one of the most heartwarming stories in franchise history. He went from being 32 years old and released from two Triple-A affiliates in one year to a spot on the NL All-Star team the next and to a World Series champion the season after that—a parade the Giants never would have enjoyed without winning all four of his postseason starts in 2012, when he posted a 1.09 ERA.

But Vogelsong endured a difficult season in 2013, struggling to maintain his stuff even before he fractured his throwing hand while swinging at a pitch that hit him. His average fastball velocity dipped for the third consecutive season. He was put in the position of proving himself once again, and this time the doubters included some in the Giants front office after the club declined his $6.5 million option. They later signed him to a lesser guarantee with incentives.

"Let's just say the chip is firmly placed on my shoulder," said Vogelsong, "and they know that."

"When the option got declined, I was upset and more hurt than anything else," he said. "But after taking a couple days and gathering myself and reading between the lines a bit personally, I felt San Francisco and this family here was the best place for me. I was just hoping at the end of the day we were able to make things work and I'm glad it did."

The 37-year-old gave the Giants what they wanted in 2014, making every one of his turns in the rotation and usually giving them a chance to win. His numbers at the end appeared rather ordinary—8–13 with a 4.00 ERA—but they didn't tell the whole story. Quite simply, Vogelsong caught every bad break imaginable.

The Giants scored one run of support or fewer in 17 of his 32 starts, and didn't score at all in six of his last eight home assignments. When the tarp malfunctioned in an August downpour at Wrigley Field, resulting in the league's first upheld protest in 26 years, it was in a Vogelsong start. When the bullpen couldn't hold a lead, it often was Vogelsong's decision that disappeared.

And in his final regular season start, one he understood could be his last as a Giant, the last batter he faced, Padres backup catcher Rene Rivera, hit a broken-bat water balloon of a two-run single. Those last two runs notched up Vogelsong's season ERA to 3.996—to be rounded up to 4.00 on the back of his baseball card.

Rivera held nothing but the bat handle as he ran to first base. It was emblematic for Vogelsong, who drew the short stick over and over.

"That's what makes this game even tougher to take, because you never know," Vogelsong said after that last start against the Padres. "I wanted to end it with a good note with the possibility this is my last home game, depending on what happens in the playoffs. I just really wanted to have a good one to finish up.

"And I just blew it."

That was a classic Vogelsong description, to take a two-run, broken-bat single and make it sound as if he had sold state secrets. There was validation, though, in the 184⅔ innings he threw—something that scouts who watched him in the spring doubted he could provide.

Anyone who spent any time around the intense right-hander—the one who gained Puritanical therapy out of shoveling snow all winter at his Pennsylvania home, who was such a slave to pregame rituals that he ate chicken enchiladas the night before every start, who was so focused in the hours before he took the mound that teammates considered eye contact a dangerous proposition—knew better than to bet against him.

"I don't play this game for money," he said. "I play this game for the love. A couple dollars here or there won't make me happy or mad. I'm just gratified I took the ball every fifth day and I gave us a chance to win in a pretty good amount of them."

After losing Game 3 of the NLDS to Washington, the Giants put their chips behind Vogelsong again.

As he began to warm up for Game 4, Posey took notice of Vogelsong's fastball. It was popping the glove a little harder than usual. When the game began, the right-hander had 10 days of rest and held nothing back.

He hit 95 miles per hour in the first inning—the hardest he'd thrown since October of 2012—and established his presence right away with a called strikeout of Denard Span. He threw turbocharged stuff while holding the Nationals to just one walk the first time through the order.

The Giants even gave him a bit of run support. They applied pressure to Gonzalez with four hits the first time through the order. But they did not seize opportunities to score so much as they fell backward into them.

They took a 2–0 lead in the second inning on a rally set up by Crawford's one-out single and an error. Outfielder Juan Perez, getting his first career postseason start, followed with a topspin dribbler that took a pinball bounce off Gonzalez's glove.

Vogelsong followed with a perfect bunt up the third-base line, and for some reason, Anthony Rendon wasn't crashing home on the play. In a fit of miscommunication, both Rendon and Gonzalez expected the other to take charge, Vogelsong had himself a single, and the bases were loaded.

Blanco drew a walk to force in a run and Panik, who stayed so calm all October even when batting with two strikes, coaxed an 0-2 pitch into play for an RBI ground out to first base.

A single, an error, a bunt, a walk, and a ground ball.

For Vogelsong, a banquet. Not that he felt sated at any point.

"I was hoping it wasn't going to get to me, to be honest," he said. "But I just had the crazy feeling it was going to come down to me for Game 4, and I just had to get the job done."

Vogelsong knew Bochy stood ready to throw his entire staff, if necessary, at the Nationals. This was no time to hold back. He began to mix his changeup and curve the second time through the order, and when he needed to spit fire in the fourth, he threw a running, 3-2 fastball that crackled up and away to strike out Rendon, the Nationals' hottest hitter.

"He pitches off feel and he knows what he wants to do, and I could tell in the bullpen," Posey said. "The fastball was coming in with a lot of life. I wouldn't have guessed 95 [miles per hour]. But it's funny what adrenaline can do for you."

Vogelsong was not like Peavy, who let his emotion spill out onto the field. Peavy barked at himself whenever he missed a pitch location, even when it resulted in an out. He screamed when a double play wasn't turned behind him, yet his infielders understood that he wasn't showing them up.

Vogelsong's intensity was different.

"Like he's boiling under the skin," Panik said.

The Nationals didn't have a hit until Ian Desmond singled to start the fifth, but once they put Vogelsong in the stretch, they made him battle. Bryce Harper stayed on an outside slider long enough to thread an RBI double down the third-base line.

The Giants were clinging to a 2–1 lead, and Bochy had Petit warmed up in the bullpen. When Vogelsong walked pinch hitter Nate Schierholtz after a 1-2 count, missing with a fastball, curve, and changeup, it wouldn't have surprised anyone if Bochy walked out to make a pitching change. Pitching coach Dave Righetti went to the mound instead. He didn't need to deliver a message of faith to Vogelsong. Bochy, by continuing to stand in the dugout, had sent it.

Vogelsong remained in the game, and no, he did not blow it. He got Span to roll over a 2-2 curveball and escape the inning.

Few managers in history had a quicker hook in October than Bochy had shown in his tenure with the Giants. As well as his bullpen pitched over the years, his sense of urgency was understandable. So it spoke strongly to his belief in Vogelsong that he let the right-hander begin the sixth inning, despite the fact his fastball wasn't humming as it did the first two times through the order.

Vogelsong poured out whatever he had left, but it wasn't much. Rendon lined out to start the inning and then Jayson Werth crushed a ball to the right-field wall.

Pence raced back, timed his jump, and his back crashed into the chain-link fence in the No. 4 archway. He raised his glove just before the ball struck the outfield padding, and held on to it through the impact.

The moment Pence made the catch, his tongue wagged, and his splayed arms and legs resembled a perfect Air Jordan silhouette. He saved the one-run lead with one of the best defensive plays in Giants postseason history, and their fans never would look at the No. 4 archway again without conjuring memories of that moment.

The crowd erupted. Vogelsong raised a fist. Two years earlier in Cincinnati, when the Giants won the first of six elimination games to survive to a World Series parade, it was Pence's sliding catch that helped

Vogelsong settle into a solid start. Now Pence did it again to end the right-hander's hard-fought night.

"What did I say?" said Vogelsong, smiling. "Well, I can't tell you what I said because you'd have to bleep out half of it, but that's what he's supposed to do. He makes a great catch every time I'm pitching in the postseason. I knew it had to show up at some point, and it did. And thank goodness it did, because that's probably a triple if he doesn't catch that ball."

Ryan Vogelsong rewarded the Giants' belief in him and, thanks to a great catch by Hunter Pence, pitched the team into the 2014 NLCS.

Vogelsong held the Nationals to a run on two hits and two walks while striking out four in 5⅓ innings. He threw 49 of 81 pitches for strikes. His career postseason ERA actually went up, to 1.19.

He became the first pitcher in major league history to allow one run or fewer in each of his first five postseason starts.

And he made one more contribution—one that stunned anyone who was watching in the home dugout. It happened in the bottom of the fifth inning, after Sandoval popped up with the bases loaded and wasted a chance to put the game away.

Sandoval trudged down the dugout stairs and was shocked at who met him. It was Vogelsong, and his mouth was moving. He never talks to his teammates while he's still in the game. Blanco blinked, did a double-take, and blinked again.

"I couldn't believe it," Blanco said.

"I leave him alone, always," Sandoval said. "I don't talk to him when he pitches. But he came to me and he told me one thing: 'You'll get an opportunity to win this game.' I believed him."

"I just told him, 'You'll get another chance,'" Vogelsong said. "He's a big, big piece of this team. I just had this weird feeling he'd get another opportunity. I felt like he needed to hear it. I know he was disappointed, popping up in that spot. I honestly just had to tell him, 'Hey, I have a vision here.'"

Nobody had more clairvoyance in the postseason than Bochy, who pressed so many of the right buttons during the two title runs over the previous four seasons. But he did not have his best night in Game 4. He probably got away with leaving Vogelsong in the game too long, and his faith in rookie Hunter Strickland proved to be misplaced.

Strickland, a September call-up, had a blistering fastball but not enough experience to use it. When Bochy brought Strickland into the game in the seventh inning, it took one mistake down the middle for the Nationals to tie the score.

Harper turned on a 3-1 fastball and watched its flight as he stood in the batter's box. Pence would've needed a Neoprene suit and a 10-minute head start to catch this one. The ball splashed between two watercraft in McCovey Cove as Harper and Strickland exchanged hard looks around the bases.

Bochy loved Strickland's moxie and his upper-90s fastball, but this was the second time Harper connected off him in the series. Maybe Strickland wasn't emotionally ready for this kind of stage yet. But at least after surrendering the lead, he pitched around a single and preserved the tie when pinch hitter Ryan Zimmerman popped out.

Harper hit three home runs in the series. The Giants hit just one: Belt's shot in the 18th to win Game 2.

The rest of their runs were an amalgamation of opportunity, hustle, base hits…and charity.

As it turned out, Vogelsong's vision was correct—in a sense, anyway. The Giants scored the tiebreaking run in the seventh with Sandoval at the plate, although not exactly how Vogelsong had pictured it.

Panik and Posey started the rally with consecutive one-out singles off Matt Thornton. Aaron Barrett replaced him and Pence battled him for a seven-pitch walk. Sandoval had another chance with the bases loaded, and Barrett knew he was facing a hitter who could hurt him anywhere near the strike zone.

Barrett's 1-1 pitch was nowhere close to the zone. The ball splashed in the dirt, catcher Wilson Ramos missed with a backhand stab, and the wild pitch scored Panik with the go-ahead run. The inning almost got a lot weirder when Barrett tried to intentionally walk Sandoval, and floated the 3-1 pitch over Ramos' head. It required a hard bounce off the backstop and Barrett dropping his knee in front of the plate to prevent Posey from scoring.

It wasn't pretty, but the Giants had the run they needed. They had the lead. They just needed six more outs, and the Nationals had the top of their order coming up in the eighth.

Sergio Romo, who lost his closer role in midsummer, rediscovered the bite on his signature slider to reestablish himself as a fearless performer in the postseason. He made quick work of Span, Rendon, and Werth on three shallow fly balls to the outfield.

Then Santiago Casilla, as underappreciated as any Giant who owned two World Series rings, survived a deep fly off Adam LaRoche's bat before issuing a careful two-out walk to Harper in the ninth.

When Ramos grounded out to Panik at second base, the Giants had done it. They dispatched the NL's top seed in a 3–2 victory, and in keeping with their tradition, they did it with three one-run victories.

For all the cracks in their rotation during the season, the Giants toppled the team with the NL's most feared staff by outpitching them. Their rotation combined for a 1.04 ERA over the four games, not including Petit's absolutely critical, life-extending six innings that allowed them to prevail in Game 2.

They won Game 4 on a bases-loaded walk, an RBI ground out, and a wild pitch.

"It definitely fit the kind of game we were able to play today, where we're tested and pushed and kind of see who wants it a little bit more," Romo said. "No knock on them, but maybe we wanted it just a little bit more tonight."

It was far from a glittering show, but it was enough to advance to St. Louis. The Giants would play for the pennant for the third time in five years. The Cardinals were in their fourth consecutive NLCS.

The Nationals might have led the league in victories and the archrival Dodgers led in dollars, but the Giants had something deeper. They had Bochy's acumen, Posey putting down the signs, and some of the best advance scouting in the business.

They had one more thing, too. Even though there's no diagnostic test for champion's blood, no telltale genetic markers or cell counts, the Giants had it. Their veins ran thick with it.

"They know how to win," said GM Brian Sabean, his black shirt sticking to his skin as the clubhouse celebration began to dry out and the locker room turned into a mellow, Merengue dance floor. "I can't articulate it. The will to win and the ability to compete overrides everything.

Having said that, you also have to stay in the moment, and whether it's a tough Game 1, or 18 innings, or Game 2, or putting aside the ugliness of [losing Game 3], they did that."

The Giants lost on Bumgarner's day. They won on the other three.

"A lot of things aren't supposed to happen," said Vogelsong, who was part of a victory for the fifth time out of his five postseason starts. "That's all I can say on that."

The Nationals had more talent, but Williams didn't deploy his weapons as aggressively as he could have. In theory, anyway, Strasburg was available to pitch in Game 4. There were times when he could have entered with that diving, 90-mph changeup of his and served as a rally tourniquet. But he never even got warm. Strasburg was more cashmere scarf than all-purpose gauze, anyway.

The Giants? They did not have players who came with special instructions.

"I told them earlier, there's nobody's will that's stronger than theirs or a desire that's deeper," Bochy said. "They were determined not to get back on the plane and go to Washington. They couldn't quite put the game away, but they kept fighting. And when [Washington] tied the game, we put the pressure right back on them.

"It's all about them. It's fun to see a group of guys that come together and are so unselfish and play with so much grit."

Nobody soaked up the clubhouse celebration with more glee than Hudson, the old veteran, who was moving past the best-of-five round for the first time in his career.

"Huddy said it best," yelled Vogelsong, amid a raucous scene as teammates gathered around. "Are we a team with some big balls?"

"Yes! Yes! Yes!" the rest shouted back, shaking and spilling their success.

Chapter 18

Shot Heard, Part 2

"It looks like me. It just doesn't seem like me."
—Travis Ishikawa

Thursday, October 16, 2014
NLCS Game 5 vs. St. Louis

It was the most important pitch ever thrown to him, and Travis Ishikawa couldn't remember seeing it.

He only remembered standing in the batter's box one moment—and then writhing in the dirt the next, the pain blinding him like a white blur, holding both hands to his jaw out of fear it would fall off his face if he let go.

It was 2004 and Ishikawa had just joined Single-A San Jose after a promotion from the club's Low-A affiliate in Hagerstown, Maryland, walking straight off a cross-country flight with no luggage and into a new lineup. He earned the promotion in part because of a hitting adjustment he had worked to make against inside pitches. When he kept his front shoulder closed, he kept from getting jammed. He knew that Giants officials would be watching him carefully to see how he adjusted to a higher level of competition. He wanted to make certain he didn't fall into any bad habits on the first day.

He stayed on the inside fastball too long. The pitch hit Ishikawa flush on the right cheek.

"It was the best hit-by-pitch of my life," Ishikawa said years later. "It changed my life. It went from the worst thing in the world to the best thing in the world."

Without getting hit that night in San Jose, Ishikawa wouldn't have gone to the dentist to get his teeth checked. Without going to the dentist, Ishikawa wouldn't have met the young office assistant, the one who was so attractive that he couldn't muster up the courage to say hello. (The fact he was still waiting for his luggage, and wearing the same clothes for a third straight day, didn't help.)

Without that follow-up visit to the dentist's chair two weeks later, he might never have introduced himself to the future Rochelle Ishikawa. And, for certain, he wouldn't have his youngest two children, Faith and Jordan, in his life.

Ishikawa understood better than most: a moment of failure or frustration will knock you off your path, but the new trajectory might lead you to a place of joy and fulfillment. Some would call it fate. For Ishikawa, it was all part of God's plan.

Ishikawa was a star athlete in suburban Seattle long before he became a devout Christian. He signed for a bonus of nearly $1 million, he made it to the big leagues, and he won a World Series with the Giants in 2010, drawing a key walk and scoring the tying run in the ninth inning of a critical NLDS victory at Atlanta. But he did not grow into the everyday first baseman the team once envisioned. When the Giants received their rings at the beginning of the 2011 season, wearing special uniforms adorned with gold thread, Ishikawa humbly stood among his former teammates in a plaid shirt and jeans. The club had demoted him to start the year in Triple-A Fresno.

After that season, the Giants took Ishikawa off the 40-man roster. He bounced from Milwaukee to brief stints in Baltimore (six games) and an even briefer stop with the Yankees (one game), mostly serving as a Triple-A insurance policy.

In 2014, he made the Pirates' opening-day roster and started at first base. Three weeks later, Pittsburgh traded for Ike Davis and designated Ishikawa for assignment. Not only was he headed back to the minors, but he wasn't even guaranteed a place in the lineup at Triple-A Charlotte.

He began to count how many days he saw his family the previous year: 14. Two weeks between February and September.

He had the right to refuse the assignment and become a free agent. He knew he'd exercise that right. He didn't relish the idea of starting someplace else, inhabiting another series of hotel rooms. He was a 30-year-old strongly considering retirement.

"But I didn't just want to up and quit during the season," he said. "I was going to finish the season out. The off-season was going to be about reflection and prayer and what's best for my family. It wouldn't have left a very good example for my kids if I left during the season."

So Ishikawa jotted down a short list of clubs that might come calling. He never stopped for one second to consider the Giants. They had an everyday first baseman in Brandon Belt, and no need for a player they'd already taken off the roster once.

When Giants vice president Bobby Evans called, Ishikawa couldn't believe it. And he couldn't agree to return fast enough.

The Giants did not have much depth behind Belt in the upper minors, and their left-handed bat off the bench, Tyler Colvin, had a history of back issues. Ishikawa was a depth signing, nothing more. The team didn't even announce it to the media. It was a line of small type at the end of the reporters' notebooks.

Even when Belt broke his thumb in May, the club shifted left fielder Michael Morse to first base. There wasn't any indication that Ishikawa would get another shot in the big leagues, and worse yet, as much as he appreciated being closer to his family in Fresno, he wasn't playing every day for the Grizzlies.

He asked coaches to give him some work in the outfield, hoping it might open another avenue to at-bats. If this would be his last experience as a professional baseball player, he wanted to spend it on the field, at least.

Then circumstances changed again—with another baseball to the cheek. This time Belt was the poor recipient, struck by a ball in a freak accident during batting practice prior to a July 19 game at Miami. Second baseman Marco Scutaro, who was making a last-ditch effort to play through his chronic back pain, had thrown the ball to first base when Belt wasn't looking.

Belt played that night, but felt waves of nausea after scoring from second base. He was diagnosed with a concussion, and went on the seven-day disabled list.

Not long after that, Ishikawa was back in the big leagues. And coaches noticed an immediate difference in his demeanor. He wasn't the twenty-something kid with the ticking clock in his head, fretting over losing the opportunity to be an everyday player. He was looser and laughing more, content just to wear a familiar uniform and be among friends again. He learned that he didn't need to squeeze the bat so hard, and it was making a difference at the plate.

In his second at-bat as a Giant in almost four years, Ishikawa laced a two-run pinch single. He ended up hitting .280 with a home run and six RBIs in 25 at-bats off the bench. He found a niche.

Ishikawa, like many young players, spent years fretting over an opportunity to play every day. It came when he wasn't even looking for it.

When Morse strained his oblique in batting practice on September 1 at Coors Field, Ishikawa was glad for the time he had spent in left field at Fresno. Manager Bruce Bochy tried Juan Perez and rookie Chris Dominguez in left field over the final week of the season, but neither hit enough to hide in the lineup.

This wasn't the first time Bochy had to invent a left fielder during a season. There was Pat Burrell in 2010, and Gregor Blanco in 2012. He couldn't use Blanco there this time. He already was replacing Angel Pagan in center field.

So Bochy turned to Ishikawa. In the third-to-last game of the regular season, Ishikawa made his first career start as an outfielder. When he didn't fall on his face in those three games against the Padres, it was enough to convince Bochy: he had his left fielder for the playoffs.

Coincidentally, the Giants were going to play the wild-card game at Pittsburgh—the same place where Ishikawa opened the season.

Just imagine telling Ishikawa on opening day, when he was starting at first base for the Pirates, that he'd be back here at PNC Park, wearing a Giants uniform again for the first time in four years, playing against his current teammates in an NL wild-card elimination game.

"Yeah," said Ishikawa, "all that, and I'd probably be an outfielder, too. If you told me that, I'd have called you crazy."

Bochy didn't stop to ponder the cosmic craziness of it all. For him, it was this simple: Ishikawa was his best option, he looked comfortable at the plate, and the only way to win in October was to put your best players out there.

Although Bochy hoped to have Morse back in the lineup, all the cortisone in the world couldn't turn a six-week injury into a four-week one. As hard as the training staff worked, and as much as Morse insisted that he could find a way to compete with the oblique strain, it became clear September 19 that he was in no condition to help. Morse came off the bench that day and got two at-bats to test his side. He struck out both times.

Bochy hardly ever looked deterred, but the Morse situation bothered him. He knew the kind of impact Morse could make on the lineup. He was the rare power hitter who could shrink any park, even the wide expanses in San Francisco. With his hulking shoulders and shaggy hair, he wouldn't have looked out of place dragging a club to home plate. The Giants weren't much of a home run–hitting team, but there was nothing Bochy liked better than a three-run dinger. In the winter before the 2014 season, Bochy knew exactly how he wanted to address the team's vacancy in left field. He remembered the 31 home runs that Morse hit for Washington in 2011, many of them drives that carried over the opposite-field fence.

In his eight years with the Giants, Bochy never lobbied harder for a free agent.

"He's got big, big thunder," said a beaming Bochy, on the day at the winter meetings when Morse agreed to a one-year deal.

Sure enough, Morse was a key part of the Giants' hot start. He owned 13 home runs by the first week of June when the team's 42–21 record stood as the best in the major leagues. He fit perfectly into their goofy clubhouse dynamic, too, becoming best pals with Hunter Pence and bringing a new tradition to the locker stalls.

Morse bought himself a black Spartan helmet complete with a huge black plume, and before long, the Giants clubhouse began to resemble an armory from antiquity. Pence ordered a shiny Maximus helmet identical to the one Russell Crowe wore in *Gladiator*. Sergio Romo had one with a skull mask fit for a feudal Dia de los Muertos. There were Viking horns and bucket-shaped great helms. Jeremy Affeldt's version, with an eye slit, was called The Crusader. It looked just like the one worn by the "flesh wound" knight who loses his limbs in *Monty Python and the Holy Grail*— appropriate enough for the accident-prone left-hander who once stabbed himself while trying to separate frozen hamburger patties.

Some teams crank up the music after victories at home. The Giants did that, and they donned their medieval helmets. After Tim Lincecum threw his no-hitter in June, he greeted his cheering teammates as a sartorial non sequitur, wearing a Team USA soccer jersey and the masked, lion-head helmet worn by Tigris of Gaul in *Gladiator*.

The players didn't get Bochy involved into the tradition, though. It would've taken a tub of butter to pry one of those helmets off his 8⅛-inch dome.

As the Giants slumped badly in midsummer, the medieval war dances became less and less frequent. Although Pagan's back injury was cited as a major factor, Morse's power outage was a part of the freefall, too. He hit two homers in June, two in July, and one in August. With his big,

big thunder showing up so infrequently, it became harder and harder to justify his defensive deficiencies in left field.

But he still cast a long shadow in the dugout. Sometimes, in the play-offs, a threat could be enough to influence an opposing manager's moves. As the regular season ended, Bochy hoped simply to have Morse available as a bat off the bench.

Bochy couldn't forget how Morse won a game for them back on July 5, when he led off the ninth inning at San Diego with a tying home run off Padres closer Huston Street. Morse's reaction was the most memorable part, as he took a spastic, arm-raising, helmet-thumping scamper around the bases. It resembled Joe Carter at the Skydome in the World Series, and why not? Street had been 23 for 23 in save chances. Morse hadn't homered in a month. The noise in the Giants dugout went from manufactured to mayhem. It was exactly what a foundering team needed, and although it didn't spark them for more than that one day, it was a reminder that Morse could take an otherwise uncomfortable, late-inning matchup and make an impact.

"It's so easy to be negative and down," Morse said after that win in San Diego. "It takes a true warrior to stay positive at all times, and this is a team of 25 warriors. We believe in each other."

Belief is one thing. Health is another.

Morse wasn't cleared to make the roster for the wild-card game in Pittsburgh. He was crestfallen when he couldn't get healthy in time to play against his former team, the Nationals, in the NLDS.

Finally, after the Giants advanced to play the St. Louis Cardinals in the NLCS, Morse's side had loosened up enough to pass muster as a pinch hitter only. Bochy would have his big, big thunder—or at least the threat of it—on the bench.

In the meantime, Ishikawa's move to left field was working out. He hit an RBI single off Cardinals ace Adam Wainwright to drive in the first run in Game 1 of the NLCS at Busch Stadium. What's more, Ishikawa even left his feet to catch Yadier Molina's sinking line drive in the fourth inning—a surprising contribution that Madison Bumgarner gratefully accepted in a 3–0 victory.

Ishikawa joked that he was able to cover ground because he was wearing a new pair of space age–looking, Mike Trout–model Nike cleats—even though most of his teammates thought they weren't his style.

"I went up to a couple guys today and said, 'Hey, can I pull these off?'" Ishikawa said.

"If you look fast, you feel fast," Bumgarner told him.

Ishikawa stepped into another NLCS spotlight moment in the first inning of Game 3 at AT&T Park, hitting a bases-clearing double off John Lackey that gave the Giants a 4–0 lead. Bochy had nudged Ishikawa up one spot in the order that afternoon, to seventh. The maneuver put Ishikawa in the right place at the right time.

"That's as good as I can hit a ball," said Ishikawa, who posed in the box before realizing his presumed grand slam would more closely resemble a three-run double, or something less than that if he didn't hurry. "I guess I forgot how much the wind can push it to the biggest part of the field."

The wind that day was straight out of the mid-1970s. A few more hot dog wrappers, a little less mercury, and a lot more orange seats and it could've been Candlestick Park. Outfielders did not camp under fly balls. They stumbled after them, changing directions from one moment to the next.

The Giants' lead did not last. Kolten Wong hit a two-run triple off Tim Hudson in the fourth. Randall Grichuk connected for a tying, solo home run in the seventh. The game went to extra innings, and the Cardinals would've taken the lead if not for Pablo Sandoval's diving stop of Matt Holliday's grounder over third base, followed by a nimble recovery and accurate throw.

The Giants had been outhomered in the series 5–0. But when Blanco saw Sandoval make that play in the top of the 10th, he knew it: they were going to win in the bottom of the inning.

They did, and it wasn't with a home run—or even an RBI. It was another statistical acronym: the run thrown in, or "RTI," as third-base coach Tim Flannery called it.

Brandon Crawford began the winning rally by working an eight-pitch leadoff walk against left-hander Randy Choate. The Giants caught a break when Perez fouled off two bunt attempts only to line a single to left field. And then Blanco, sent up to advance the runners, perfectly deadened the ball on his second bunt attempt.

Choate fielded the bunt, spun toward first base, and threw the ball halfway to Livermore as Crawford raced home with the winning run.

A run thrown in. A walk-off, 5–4 victory. And a 3–1 series edge, with one chance to clinch at home behind Bumgarner in Game 5.

"I'm a little delirious, I guess," Bochy said. "Man, these are hard-fought games. But it's something you're used to. It's our way."

Could it get more exciting than that?

Why, yes. Yes it could.

Left field wasn't the only position that Bochy had to patch during the season.

For most of the year, the Giants' most glaring vacancy was at second base, after Scutaro's ailing back failed to make it out of spring training. He was limited to five games all season, and even that stint amounted to a Hail Mary after countless treatments failed to allow for any rotation in his swing.

The Giants were forced to begin the season at second base with non-roster invitee Brandon Hicks, who hit a bunch of home runs in April and May—even taking Clayton Kershaw deep—before the league adjusted to the truck-sized holes in his swing. When Hicks went a solid month without a single hit, the Giants acted out of desperation and picked up a discarded Dan Uggla. That experiment lasted for 72 hours and two errors.

Finally, having exhausted all other options, they turned to rookie Joe Panik—a player who GM Brian Sabean acknowledged wasn't ready to face big league pitching.

Except he was.

The 23-year-old kid from a place in New York called Hopewell Junction might as well have dropped out of the sky. He hit .305 in 73 games, then he appeared as calm as a seasoned veteran through the first two rounds of the playoffs.

"Well, he's shown that from Day One, since he was called up," Bochy said. "I said it from the get-go: he really looked comfortable and that he belonged up here. And then as the season went along and the games became more meaningful, he was the guy, I think, that was probably as consistent as any hitter we had."

Panik had so many of Scutaro's attributes. He seldom struck out or chased pitches. He had tremendous bat control. He looked as comfortable hitting with two strikes as he did on the first pitch. Bochy could feel confident putting runners in motion when Panik was at the plate.

The only time he caused anyone to, well, panic was when he received word that the Giants were calling him up from Triple-A Fresno in June. He immediately called his parents on the East Coast.

"Dad answers the phone in a groggy voice and Mom gets on the speakerphone and asks what's wrong," Panik said. "I said, 'This is the first good call you'll get at 3:00 AM.'"

Paul and Natalie Panik went into *The Amazing Race* mode. They immediately booked flights to Arizona, went straight to the airport, and landed at Sky Harbor Airport before Joe did. Everyone got to Phoenix before Panik's bags, which got waylaid in a connecting city. So wearing Romo's pants and using Sandoval's glove, Panik took pregame infield practice and made his debut that night. He drew a five-pitch walk in his first plate appearance.

There was even something borrowed about his new jersey. Clubhouse manager Mike Murphy issued him No. 12. When Panik saw it hanging in his locker, he immediately thought of his favorite Yankees player as a kid: Wade Boggs, a fitting idol for a contact hitter.

The next day, Panik received his first start and went 2-for-4 with an impressive left-on-left hit off sidewinder Joe Thatcher.

Like any rookie, Panik had adjustments to make. But even when he hit .200 through his first 25 games, he didn't lose hope. And after he finished the regular season above .300, hitting coach Hensley Meulens quietly offered him the lineup card and his congratulations.

Panik was appreciative, but far from overwhelmed.

Did he really believe he could have instant success against major league pitching?

"Honestly, yeah," he said, managing to sounding more self-aware than haughty. "Wherever I've gone, I've always believed I can be a good hitter and nothing has changed since I got here. I got off to a slow start but I've always believed in myself."

When the Giants advanced to play the Cardinals in the NLCS, it set up a rematch of two grinding, contact-oriented clubs. Although Panik had ably filled the Giants' void at second base and in the No. 2 spot, nobody in their right mind could expect him to replicate what Scutaro did against St. Louis in 2012, when he blistered 14 hits in 28 at-bats and survived Matt Holliday's takeout slide to win series MVP honors.

It was a testament to Panik's calm and confidence that the Giants didn't expect much of a dropoff.

"I expect him to come up in some big spots for us," said Posey, who enjoyed his view of Panik's at-bats from the on-deck circle. "I mean, I haven't seen a situation he seems intimidated by."

Posey understood what it was like to walk out of Triple-A and into a pennant race. He was the NL Rookie of the Year when he led the Giants to a World Series in 2010. He never felt compelled to share any advice with Panik, though. The kid just didn't seem to need it.

"He's a guy you like near the top of the order," Posey said. "He's very quiet. He doesn't jump at the ball, and I know as a catcher, those kinds of at-bats are tough because there aren't a lot of holes to exploit."

Panik had spent the previous two springs in major league camp watching Scutaro, and taking notes.

"I did a lot more watching than talking," he said. "I try to pattern myself as a typical 2-hole hitter. I'm not hitting too many home runs, but I'm going to try to get on base and go the other way and see the ball deep. If you can get on base for the middle-of-the-order guys, all it takes is one big hit."

The Giants were finding ways to win in the postseason without that big hit. When they took the field for Game 5 of the NLCS against the Cardinals, they hadn't launched a home run since Brandon Belt's shot in the 18th inning of Game 2 in the NLDS at Washington.

Yet they were one victory over St. Louis from joining the 1990 A's as the only teams since 1919 to win a postseason playoff series with zero home runs—and they were confident in their ability to close out the series at home in Game 5.

They knew the Cardinals did not have a fully charged battery, with catcher Yadier Molina unable to start because of an oblique he strained in Game 2 and Adam Wainwright's elbow feeling the strain after four consecutive seasons of heavy lifting into October.

Wainwright spent most of the week insisting that there was nothing wrong with his arm. Privately, Cardinals players acknowledged their ace was far from 100 percent. But they'd seen him cut and sink his way through lineups on fumes before. They hoped he would have enough to match Bumgarner.

Instead, it was Bumgarner, the hottest and best pitcher on anyone's postseason roster, who lacked his best command and stuff.

He allowed hits to two of the first three batters of the game, and it took a tremendous defensive play at third base from Sandoval to keep the Cardinals from putting up a crooked number in the first inning. The third baseman needed every bit of extension to make a leaping catch on Jhonny Peralta, then his accurate throw to second base doubled off Jon Jay to end the inning.

Bumgarner needed more help, though, after issuing two walks in the third inning. This time, the Cardinals found a weakness. The Giants did have a first baseman playing in left field, after all.

Jay sent a line drive toward Ishikawa, who for the first time all post-season, looked like an infielder moonlighting in the outfield. Ishikawa took a bad route as the otherwise catchable ball went over his head for an RBI double. The Giants trailed 1–0, and Ishikawa knew he was at fault.

"I was playing a little shallow because he kind of dunked one earlier," Ishikawa said. "The wind was blowing, but I didn't take a good route. That was on me, nobody else. I was feeling as low as I can feel in that moment. You give the Cardinals a run, as tight as it's been in this series, it's so detrimental."

Ishikawa felt a weight on his chest the rest of that inning, but then two things happened. Bumgarner got a pair of non-threatening fly outs to strand two runners in scoring position, and then Blanco offered another kind of support.

"Hey, I'm really proud of you," Blanco told Ishikawa as they jogged together back to the dugout. "You've been doing so, so good out there and I'm so proud of how you've played out there. Whatever you do, it's going to be okay."

Blanco wasn't the only one. Coaches, trainers, and teammates came up one at a time to lend words of encouragement. The night was far from over. Who knew what events were yet to be set in motion?

Wainwright, though, was pitching as if he had all the run support he'd need. He compensated for a lack of velocity by using every trick he knew to disrupt the Giants' timing. He'd follow a slow leg lift with a quick pitch. He'd pause in the middle of his delivery. The first time through the lineup, Blanco managed the only hit. When he batted again with two outs in the third, he coaxed another single to right field.

Panik stepped to the plate. Wainwright didn't have much of a book on him, but he tried to throw a cutter on the rookie's hands. Panik was hoping to slap something through the right side, maybe allow Blanco to get to third base. He did much more than that.

He lofted a deep fly ball that landed in the right-field arcade for a two-run home run that gave the Giants a 2–1 lead, sent the sellout crowd into a mania, and ended the team's six-game, two-inning power drought.

The Giants went 242 plate appearances without a home run. The kid who broke the streak had hit one homer in his 287 regular season plate appearances. Now Panik had one home run, to go with just one strikeout, in 44 at-bats in the postseason.

But the euphoria wore off quickly, and the Giants' lead lasted just four pitches into the fourth inning.

Cardinals first baseman Matt Adams, who had wrecked the Dodgers' Clayton Kershaw in the NLDS, clocked a 1-2 curveball from Bumgarner into the arcade—the first home run Bumgarner had allowed to a left-handed hitter since April 11, when the Rockies' Carlos Gonzalez connected against him.

The Cardinals took the lead three batters later when Tony Cruz barreled up a slider. Bumgarner watched the ball disappear over the left-field fence and did a full-body bend at the waist. When the Giants went ahead on Panik's homer, nobody expected the Cardinals to answer back. They sent two loud messages to the contrary, and led 3–2.

The Giants were poised to respond in the bottom of the fourth after Sandoval sliced a leadoff double, extending his franchise record to 23 consecutive postseason games reaching base. Pence walked and Belt followed by smoking a line drive, but second baseman Kolten Wong snagged it to start a double play.

Sandoval reacted as quickly as he could, but there was no way to prevent getting doubled off.

It was fair to wonder if this just wouldn't be the Giants' night, especially when Wainwright found his bearings. He kept varying his times to the plate, and just when the Giants started taking better swings against his cutter, he began doubling down on his overhand curve.

Wainwright sent a ski field of those mogul-shaped curveballs to the plate while retiring the last 10 batters he faced, striking out Posey, Sandoval, and Pence in the sixth. He walked off the mound in the seventh to applause from every corner of the Cardinals dugout. It was the gutsiest performance by a St. Louis pitcher at AT&T Park since Matt Morris left everything on the mound to try to send the series back to Busch Stadium in Game 5 of the 2002 NLCS. The Cardinals were six outs away from accomplishing what they could not do a dozen years earlier.

For the first time all series, Cardinals manager Mike Matheny had his bullpen set up precisely how he wanted it: right-hander Pat Neshek and his jumping-jack delivery in the eighth, followed by closer Trevor Rosenthal and his 99-mph fastball in the ninth.

Neshek held right-handers to a .176 average during the regular season, throwing a sweeping slider from a deceptive motion that looked like it was invented in a binary star system six parsecs away. No matter whom Bochy sent to the plate, it was going to be an uncomfortable at-bat.

The pitcher's spot was due to lead off for the Giants, and Bochy knew he wouldn't ask Bumgarner to go any further. His ace did enough by retiring his last 13 batters to keep it a one-run deficit. Besides, Bochy already had signaled his intentions in the bottom of the seventh, when he had sent Morse to the on-deck circle with two outs. Wainwright retired Crawford to end the inning, leaving Morse to practice his cobra-like warmup swings and wait for another chance. As the Cardinals cleared off the field, though, Morse did not turn a heel back toward the dugout. He continued to stand on deck for a few moments longer, coiling and gripping his bat and guiding it to an imaginary pitch.

"I just wanted to stay up there and feel the atmosphere, and sort of knock all the nerves out of my body," Morse said. "I was ready to hit. Right from that moment, I was ready to go."

"I know, I saw," Bumgarner said. "I was walking out there to pitch and he was still standing there swinging. As I was pitching in that eighth inning, I was thinking, *I've got to get through this without giving up any runs....* I mean, it don't make no sense. But I just had a feeling he was going to tie the game."

Bochy was resolved: Morse would pinch-hit to begin the eighth. Neshek was not the pitcher anyone wanted to face, let alone a rusty hitter like Morse who was limited by injury to 13 at-bats over the previous six weeks—half of them coming in rehab games against low-level prospects on a back field in Arizona.

But when Neshek hung a 1-1 slider, Morse attacked it.

After 15 seasons at AT&T Park, you could ask a dozen fans for the loudest moment in the ballpark's history and get a dozen different answers. There was J.T. Snow off Armando Benitez, or any of the Barry Bonds milestones, or the hoarse-voiced glee the moment that Blanco saved Matt Cain's perfect game.

Not anymore. The debate simply didn't exist. As Morse's drive screamed over the left-field fence and he raised gorilla arms and flailed and bounced around the bases, barely touching each one, the crowd was loud enough to melt eardrums. And the loudest spot in the ballpark was the home dugout.

"It was absolutely pure elation," Pence said. "I literally lost 30 seconds of my life. I blacked out. It was chaos."

Bochy had legitimate concerns that hands might be broken as Morse galloped down the steps and began issuing high-fives. Meulens received one of the first while still trying to make sense of it all. Then he realized there was no point in it.

"It's why we put him on the roster," Meulens said. "We don't want him to hit a single. That was the moment we needed someone to pop one, he's got the power to do it, and we've got to give him a lot of credit for that. That's one of the toughest right-handed pitchers in the game. He's only given up two home runs to right-handed batters all year.

"I was thinking, *How is he going to get this done?* And he hung a slider, and he's all in."

Morse had lost his home run swing three months earlier. But Bonds gave him a tip before Game 5, telling him to be sure to get his front foot down. Morse did, and the results were seismic.

"For Bruce Bochy in that situation to have the faith in me to take out his ace and pinch-hit me, I just told myself I couldn't waste that at-bat," Morse said.

Ishikawa watched Morse's mad scamper in wonderment. The Giants hadn't homered all series, but Panik had contributed one improbable swing. Morse followed with an unbelievable one. The game was tied again. What would happen next?

"On this team, any guy in any moment can do that," Ishikawa said. "To be able to do that against a tough righty, you can't even describe how huge that scene was. It gave us the realization that we've gotta do this right now."

The Giants needed to do more than hit home runs, though. Their infield defense already bailed out Bumgarner once in the first inning. Crawford came through with another incredible play to preserve the tie behind Santiago Casilla in the ninth.

After a one-out walk and a single, Wong hit a hard grounder that Sandoval deflected with a diving attempt. Crawford, showing his elite blend of instincts and athleticism, somehow changed direction at the last instant, grabbed the ball, spun around, and threw accurately for the force at second base. It was a play that required more than skills and smarts. It required the kind of jazz-like improvisational genius that only truly gifted shortstops possess.

The Giants hadn't escaped the ninth yet. After Cruz walked to load the bases, Bochy summoned Jeremy Affeldt. He knew he was asking a lot of his left-hander. Affeldt was appearing for his third consecutive day, and the seventh time in the club's last nine postseason games. But Affeldt had gone 17 playoff appearances in a row without giving up a run. In a situation with no margin for error, there was nobody that Bochy trusted more.

Tension gripped the stands, but curiously, it wasn't gripping the playoff-tested Giants. During the pitching change, as Affeldt took his warmup tosses, Crawford played a prank on Belt and hid his glove behind his back.

"He was lost for a split second, and that's all I was going for, really," said Crawford, smiling.

With Affeldt ready, the Cardinals sent up the best pinch hitter remaining on their bench: rookie Oscar Taveras, who hit a home run in Game 2. Affeldt enticed him to reach for an outside pitch and hit a tapper near the mound. Bulky leg brace and all, Affeldt scooped it up and sprinted all the way to first base. As he joked later, the brace didn't come with any brake pads.

The Giants escaped the top of the ninth and there was no way for anyone to know it at the time: tragically, that at-bat would be the last of Taveras' young life. Just 10 days later, the 22-year-old rookie would lose control of his speeding Camaro in the Dominican Republic. Both he and his girlfriend lost their lives in the solo-vehicle crash. It's a numbing thought: if the Cardinals had won the pennant instead of the Giants, Taveras would've been playing in Kansas City instead of back home.

The game headed to the bottom of the ninth, and Matheny still had plenty of options in his bullpen. He could have begun with Rosenthal and worked his way backward. Instead, he reserved his closer for a save situation. Matheny failed to see the reality: when it's a tie game on the road in the ninth, and a loss sends you home, isn't that the ultimate save situation?

Instead, Matheny went with Michael Wacha, the MVP of the previous year's NLCS, who had missed chunks of the season because of injuries and hadn't thrown a competitive pitch in 20 days. Wacha came out throwing gas, but it was straight as a string.

Sandoval, who hit .400 in the series, started the rally with a single. Pence lined out, and Belt drew a four-pitch walk to push pinch runner Joaquin Arias into scoring position.

Ishikawa was next. Wacha missed with the first pitch. Then he threw ball two. He had thrown six in a row outside the strike zone. In the dugout, Meulens contemplated putting on the take sign. He assumed it wouldn't be necessary.

"How do you swing there, 2-0?" Meulens said. "I mean, how about that?"

"No," Ishikawa would say later, looking a reporter straight in the eye. "I was looking to swing from the first pitch on."

Wacha threw a 96-mph fastball and Ishikawa reacted. He kept his front shoulder closed, whistled his bat through the zone, and felt the connection. There was no need to hope as he watched the ball shrink up into the stars, only the need to run. He knew he'd gotten enough of it, that at least the ball would hit the brick arcade and the winning run would score.

When Ishikawa saw the ball clank off the green metal roof atop the right-field arcade, he let out a yell that nobody could hear but him. Morse's decibel record in China Basin lasted all of one inning. The Giants won the pennant, and Ishikawa's three-run home run clinched it in a 6–3 victory.

Ishikawa buzzed around first base, his arms stiff and palms out like wing flaps on takeoff. The stands thundered, bodies flew everywhere, and the Giants engulfed home plate to await their hero's arrival. In the GM suite, cameras captured Sabean, as stoic a presence in baseball, sobbing into his hands.

Ishikawa joined Chris Chambliss (1976 Yankees), Aaron Boone (2003 Yankees), and Magglio Ordonez (2006 Tigers) as the only players in major league history to hit a walk-off home run in the LCS to send their team to the World Series.

Back before the LCS existed, of course, there was Bobby Thomson, with his Shot Heard 'Round the World in 1951 at the Polo Grounds, which inspired the greatest pennant-clinching radio call of all time.

Now 63 years after Russ Hodges shouted "The Giants win the pennant!" over and over into his microphone, the franchise had witnessed a Shot Heard for a new generation of Giants fans.

"Swing and there's a drive! Deep into right field! Way back there! Good-bye!" came Hall of Famer Jon Miller's clear voice on KNBR. "A home run for the game! And for the pennant! The Giants have won the pennant!"

It would have counted the same no matter who touched a baseball up into the firmament, through immortality and on to a World Series. The fact it was Ishikawa, a 31-year-old part-time player who came home when he least expected it, who gave serious thought to retirement just a few months earlier, and who truly inspired sentences that began with "It

An iconic moment in Giants history: Travis Ishikawa heads for home after his three-run, walk-off homer against the Cardinals in the 2014 NLCS.

couldn't have happened to a nicer guy" made the moment at Third and King all the more monumental.

It was unbelievable. Unless you already believed.

"I could, yeah, because I feel any guy on this roster can get it done," Posey said. "I mean, you can't dream up a moment much better than that."

The Giants did more than win a baseball game. They did more, even, than claim an NL-record 20th pennant. They gave the city a moment it could wrap its arms around. They inspired a 43,000-strong group hug. Hours after Ishikawa tore around the bases and into everlasting franchise lore, car horns continued to blare outside the ballpark. It was the greatest closing crescendo ever seen or heard on the shores of McCovey Cove.

The most amazing part: the night would be remembered for more than a single belief-suspending home run. Morse did the same an inning earlier. There was the brilliance of Crawford and Sandoval in the field and Panik's shot off Wainwright. There was the bitterness of Ishikawa's misplay in left field, a prologue to the sweetest of all redemptive acts. All things considered, it was the greatest of so many great games that Giants fans had witnessed at AT&T Park.

Ishikawa went to bed at 2:30 AM that night. That was not when he went to sleep. Even after a long time spent staring at the ceiling, he couldn't process what he'd done.

"A blur. It feels surreal," he said. "I've seen the replay a bunch of times. It looks like me. It just doesn't seem like me."

As he streaked around the bases, and most of his teammates joyfully skipped to home plate to await him, Jake Peavy burst out of the dugout and tried to greet Ishikawa between second and third base. Ishikawa gave him a forearm shiver and shed him like an open-field tackler.

Peavy wasn't wearing his eyeglasses. He assumed Ishikawa had hit a game-winning double.

"Y'all, I feel terrible," Peavy said. "I couldn't see a sign 60 feet in front of me, so I sure as heck can't see a rubbed-up baseball 400 feet away. If I knew, I would've done it differently. I just knew we won. I was so excited for the team and for Ish, and what he's been through in his career."

Ishikawa had no idea who was getting in his way. He had lost all semblance of reality.

"I don't remember touching third," he said. "And I don't remember touching home."

It was the second-most-important pitch of his life. He couldn't remember seeing this one, either.

Chapter 19

Fire on the Mountain

"Took my fam'ly away from my Carolina home/Had dreams about the West and started to roam/Six long months on a dust covered trail/They say heaven's at the end but so far it's been hell/And there's fire on the mountain, lightnin' in the air/Gold in them hills and it's waitin' for me there."
—Marshall Tucker Band

Sunday, October 26, 2014
World Series Game 5 vs. Kansas City

It's a true story, if embellished a tad. But don't ask Madison Bumgarner to narrate.

He's too embarrassed to tell it.

It happened in Colorado, not too long after Bumgarner got called up to the big leagues. The Giants' bus broke down along the lonely stretch of road between the airport and the club's hotel in Denver.

"Hey, Bussie!" yelled Bumgarner from somewhere in back, his voice flavored with North Carolina vinegar. "Let me off. I got this."

The kid lefty with the broad back and doleful eyes ambled outside, popped the hood, and the next thing anyone knew, the bus was purring away. He hopped back aboard to hoots and shouts and applause and uncontrollable laughter.

He's reticent to tell that story because, well, he took occasion to have a few beverages on the flight that night—something he rarely did—and his teammates took great pleasure in seeing a buzzed Bumgarner come out of his silent shell.

"Oh, you don't…nah, you don't want to hear about that," he'd say, when pressed for details on the bus story. "That was nothin'."

Somewhere down the line, though, Bumgarner's inhibitions loosened a bit. How else to explain that three-can cascade of light beer that he dumped down his gullet, cameras capturing it all, when the Giants clinched a playoff berth in 2014? Or the four-bottle cataract that gushed after he personally hog-tied the Pittsburgh Pirates in the NL wild-card game?

"Well, you know, you're not actually *drinking* much of it…" he said.

Sipped or sprayed or glug-glug-glugged from high above, Bumgarner became the toast of baseball in 2014 while dominating the postseason like no pitcher in the sport's celebrated history had done before. While other elite arms like Clayton Kershaw and Adam Wainwright sputtered or sagged under the weight of 200-plus innings, the left-hander from the North Carolina hills had the sass and finishing kick of a Blue Mountains mule. He strong-armed and subdued hitters as if they never had a chance. Maybe they didn't.

And then it was five. And then a six-pack.

And finally, a World Series performance beyond the achievements of even the game's greatest ghosts: two dominant starts, and then, on two days of rest, an unthinkable five-inning save at Kansas City's Kauffman Stadium in Game 7 as the Giants won their third title in five seasons.

In the hours before Bumgarner put forth one of the greatest Game 7 pitching performances of all time, he stood in the outfield with Jake Peavy, curious to get his teammate's prediction at how the night would play out. He told Peavy that if Tim Hudson could get the ball to him, he could deliver it to Sergio Romo in the eighth.

"Madison," Peavy told him, "when you get the ball, you're not coming out of the game, pal. You're the best guy we've got."

Bumgarner smiled. "Man," he said. "That's exactly what I hoped you would say."

"That's exactly what he wanted," Peavy would later say. "He just needed some confirmation and someone to believe in him as well. I told him, 'You fight, big man. I think America would want to see you fight.' What he did, it's going to go down as the best ever."

The Giants did something that no team had accomplished in the World Series since 1979: they won a Game 7 on the road.

What Bumgarner did was unmatched, period.

Nobody ever had recorded two wins and a save in one World Series before Bumgarner, who struck out 17 and walked one while yielding just one run to the Royals over 21 innings. Nobody ever had thrown as many as 52⅔ innings in a single postseason, a span over which Bumgarner posted a 1.03 ERA. And no pitcher ever came close to recording a five-inning save in a World Series game. Heck, it hadn't been done in a regular season game in 12 years.

Bumgarner didn't just fix the bus. He commandeered it.

In Game 7, Bumgarner entered a 3–2 game to begin the fifth inning. That's where the score stood with two outs in ninth and the tying run on third base following a hit and an error in center field. Bumgarner faced Salvador Perez, whose home run in Game 1 accounted for Kansas City's only run against him.

An entire season winnowed down to one confrontation. A home run would give the Royals a championship. One more out would have the Giants celebrating on foreign ground yet again.

With a runner on third, no matter how much faith Bumgarner had in catcher Buster Posey, he knew a breaking ball in the dirt came with a risk. The decision was made: high fastballs, one after the other.

When you call in the herd, it is no time to be subtle or tricky.

"We talked about it and Buster kept calling it and I had faith," Bumgarner said.

The sixth and last of those high fastballs jammed Perez, and third baseman Pablo Sandoval raced under the foul pop. Posey threw off his mask, revealing an expression of pure awe and delight. Posey stole a glance at Bumgarner on the mound, then looked back to make sure the final out really and truly would land in Sandoval's glove.

It did, and Sandoval splashed flat on his back in foul ground, giving in to both gravity and ecstasy. The Giants were champions for the third time in five years, and Posey prepared to tackle an onrushing steer.

"I was thinking maybe if he could get through the eighth, that would be amazing," Posey said. "But he got stronger. He got locked in. I asked him during that first inning, he wasn't too crisp, so it's, 'Hey, are you okay?' And he goes '[Grunt] Yeah, man, I just gotta get loose.'"

Said manager Bruce Bochy: "In fact, I was staying away from him every inning because I was hoping he wouldn't go, 'I'm starting to get a little tired.' Because there's no way I would have taken him out unless he would have told me that. We just got on his horse and rode it."

Bochy dressed that saddle from the very beginning of the season.

It was a mild surprise in spring training when Bochy announced that Bumgarner would be his opening-day starter, even though right-hander Matt Cain, who had the honor the previous year, hadn't really done a whole lot to lose it.

By the length and breadth of a horse barn, though, Bumgarner was the Giants' best starting pitcher in 2013. He was a first-time All-Star, fifth in the NL with a 2.77 ERA, and he finished one strikeout away from 200. Among NL pitchers, only Clayton Kershaw and Jose Fernandez held batters to a lower average (.203).

Bumgarner wouldn't turn 25 until August, but he already owned two World Series victories (at Texas in a Halloween night Game 4 in 2010, and against Detroit in a Game 2 smothering in 2012 after he'd been pulled from the rotation earlier in that postseason). And every year, he kept getting better. Some pitchers learn to adjust and compete out of necessity after their stuff deteriorates. Bumgarner was reaching that rarest of career intersections: still at the height of his powers, and possessing the wisdom to use them.

As a rookie in 2010, Bumgarner lived for a time in reliever Jeremy Affeldt's rental house. Affeldt awoke one morning to a scraping sound coming from the backyard. It was Bumgarner, practicing his roping technique on the patio furniture.

With his lariat-like delivery on the mound, Bumgarner came to understand how best to ensnare opponents at the ankles and make them fall under their own weight. In the minor leagues, he was a homesick yet headstrong kid who sliced through lineups with nothing but a fastball. When the Giants tried to tinker with his syrupy motion, he relented and got hit around for a couple starts. Even then, he trusted himself enough to tell coaches: "Look, I have to go back to throwing like I throw."

Bochy said he knew Bumgarner was something special when he read the reports from a game in Triple-A Fresno when the big left-hander boiled over at an umpire, drew an ejection, and angrily threw a baseball from the dugout to, maybe, someone's windshield. Nobody can say for sure. Nobody saw the ball land.

Cain realized it the first time he saw Bumgarner pitch, when the teenage prospect reported to Scottsdale Stadium to fill out a spring-training exhibition roster. Manny Ramirez was in the lineup for the Dodgers. Bumgarner, all of 19 years old, asked Cain how he should pitch him.

"I said 'Hey, try to bust him in,'" Cain said. "I mean, why not? He goes out there, three pitches, and busts him in, strikes him out, and he's 19 years old. When you see that, when you see him able to keep calm in any situation, you know that's the guy you want out there."

For all his competitive fire, Bumgarner wasn't a red ass away from the field. He arrived in the big leagues before his 21st birthday but made no assumptions and had no sense of entitlement. That's just the way he was. He married Ali Saunders, his high school sweetheart, while wearing jeans with a knife in his pocket. He never really left his home in the North Carolina hills. He never considered himself a big deal, and perhaps that's what helped him become one on the mound.

Bumgarner fashioned a cutter during his rookie year and had enough brass to use it over and over in Game 4 of the World Series at Texas. He came to rely on his slider and changeup. And when he needed to rear back and fire, he came to understand the value of changing eye levels. So many pitchers beat themselves by internalizing the competition. Bumgarner kept the battlefield between the rubber and the plate, not between his ears. He focused on taming hitters, not his own nerves.

So Bochy set aside seniority and privilege. He gave the ball to Bumgarner on opening day.

"I think he was in shock and a little bit in awe," said Cain, smiling. "He'll enjoy it, I think. He'll be a good guy to lead the rotation."

Cain, as it turned out, wasn't in position to lead the Giants rotation anyway. He pitched for years with bone spurs in his elbow, and when they became too painful to press on, he underwent season-ending surgery just after the All-Star break. It was almost impossible to imagine the Giants making the playoffs without Cain, to say nothing of managing a deep run. Cain started all three of the Giants' series-clinching victories on their way to the title in 2012. He was the pressure-treated lumber that held everything up.

The Giants struggled to overcome the loss of Cain while enduring several other key injuries and gave back the entirety of a 10-game lead they held over the Los Angeles Dodgers in early June. Over an eight-week stretch, they had the worst record in the National League. The Giants finished the season staring up at the NL West champion Dodgers and Clayton Kershaw, who turned in a year for the ages while going 21–3 with a 1.77 ERA to win both the Cy Young Award (unanimously) and MVP—an award that no NL starting pitcher had won since Bob Gibson in 1968.

But the Giants banked enough wins early in the season (42–21 at one point) to clinch one of two NL wild-card spots. The addition of Peavy from the Boston Red Sox helped to soften the blow of losing Cain. The Giants and Pirates finished with identical 88–74 records, but the season-series tiebreaker meant that the one-game playoff would be held in Pittsburgh.

Although Bumgarner had another fine season (18–10, 2.98 ERA), Peavy was the Giants' hottest pitcher down the stretch. The club won eight of his last nine starts, in which he posted a 1.35 ERA. And given his past relationship with Bochy in San Diego, you had to wonder if Bochy would consider pushing his chips behind Peavy in a winner-take-all knockout. Besides, Bumgarner had never pitched in an elimination game; Cain, Barry Zito, and Ryan Vogelsong started those six win-or-go-home games against the Reds and Cardinals in 2012.

Bochy never wavered. He gave the ball to Bumgarner in Pittsburgh.

"I don't think there's any question who was going to pitch that game," Bochy said.

Bumgarner faced a Pirates lineup that included reigning NL MVP Andrew McCutchen and a team that finished the season on a 16–4 blitz. No NL team won more home games than the Pirates during the regular season. The thirsty, black-shirted atmosphere at PNC Park might have exceeded anything the Giants had seen in their recent postseason travels.

Bumgarner turned the atmosphere into a funeral dirge.

He threw a four-hit shutout. He struck out 10. He didn't allow a runner to reach third base until the eighth inning, and that was after a pair of errors.

"Honestly, I don't say it much, but in the bullpen you just had that feeling," Posey said. "He was throwing the ball wherever he wanted. The moment just didn't seem too big for him."

Brandon Crawford hit a grand slam—something no shortstop, not even Derek Jeter, had ever done in a postseason game—that silenced the ballpark in the fourth inning. Bumgarner upped the ante to four beer cans in the celebration following the 8–0 victory, and some people wanted to get it flowing earlier.

"When that ball went over the fence, I mean…game over," right-hander Tim Hudson said. "Give Bum a 4–nothing lead, I don't give a damn. It's, 'Let's go spray some champagne.'"

Posey marveled at Bumgarner's command, how he pounded left-handers inside and worked right-handers away to generate all those pop-ups and strikeouts—the best percentage plays a pitcher can get.

Back in 2010, Posey and Bumgarner formed the first all-rookie World Series battery since the Yankees' Spec Shea and Yogi Berra in 1947. They went through that fire together. After the next four seasons together, they understood each other. They respected each other.

And after beating the Pirates, in the NLDS against the Washington Nationals, they sought to protect one another when Bumgarner made his only big mistake of the postseason.

It was a scoreless tie in the seventh inning of Game 3 at AT&T Park when Washington catcher Wilson Ramos rolled a two-strike bunt toward the mound. Bumgarner had no shot to force Ian Desmond at third base but whirled and tried anyway. He threw a baseball. A wet bar of soap came out of his hand. The throw was so wild that Bryce Harper scored all the way from first base, and the Nationals took a 4–1 victory.

"He tried to do a little too much there. He tried to rush it," Bochy said. "He threw it away. He threw it away *well*, too."

After the game, wave after wave of microphones and notepads crashed in front of Bumgarner's locker, each one attempting to pull him in with the same question: What was Posey yelling? Where was he telling you to throw?

"I'll, I mean…well," Bumgarner started. "Buster, you'll have to talk to him. I thought we had a shot there."

Next wave. What, if anything, were you hearing from Posey? And again. Doesn't the catcher direct you there…

"You'll have to talk to him," Bumgarner said. "That's the fourth time someone's asked me that."

Bumgarner could not tell a lie. But he also could not chop down a tree and allow a teammate to stand under it. He answered the question without answering the question. On his way out the door, though, he shook his head in self disapproval.

"Doesn't matter," he said. "He didn't tell me to throw it into left field."

Posey, of course, acknowledged the rest.

"Yeah, I told him to throw to third," Posey said. "I just thought the way it came off the bat, we had a shot. It happens. I made a mistake telling him to throw to third. It just happens."

Afterward, Posey learned how Bumgarner, while answering wave after wave of the same question, refused to let his catcher get sucked in the undertow.

"Is that so?" said Posey, his face lighting up.

This was a group that protected one another, and the Giants protected their house to clinch the NLDS in Game 4. They knocked off the club that had the league's best record and was considered a heavy favorite to win the pennant, and they did it despite paying the wild-card penalty of not being able to start Bumgarner in Game 1. They ended up losing on his day. No matter. They won the other three.

Now they could line up their left-handed ace in Game 1 of the NLCS against the St. Louis Cardinals—the team that advanced past the Dodgers after twice stunning Kershaw with a pair of damaging, seventh-inning rallies.

In every postseason series, aces were getting ambushed. But Bumgarner continually held the high ground. He pitched into the eighth inning of a 3–0 victory in Game 1 at St. Louis, and by night's end, his streak of 26⅔ scoreless innings on the road was the longest in postseason history.

Bumgarner pays no heed to history or context in the middle of a game. In the seventh inning, however, after the Cardinals collected a pair of one-out singles to enliven the crowd at Busch Stadium, he acknowledged that the thought crossed his mind: this was the time and place when they wrecked Kershaw.

"I knew the seventh inning would be big-time," Bumgarner said. "I knew that was a big inning to get through. Regardless of whether I gave them anything to hit or any momentum, I kind of figured they'd feel they had some going into that inning."

So he left nothing to chance when Kolten Wong hit a grounder to first base. Brandon Belt fed a shovel pass to Bumgarner, and it was all gridiron from there. The pitcher was blind to the runner and could have reached across his body with a wing and a prayer, hoping he didn't tag air.

Instead, Bumgarner lowered his right shoulder, veered into the base-line like a stock car driving an opponent into the wall, and applied the tag as Wong bounced off him like a scowling racquetball.

Bumgarner set the tone for a series that would last five games and end with Travis Ishikawa becoming a modern-day Bobby Thomson, winning the pennant with a walk-off home run. The clubhouse celebration was wilder than ever, and one song kept playing on a loop over the clubhouse speakers: "Fire on the Mountain," the campy 1970s tune by the Marshall Tucker Band, with Charlie Daniels on fiddle, a prominently slacked steel guitar, and a flute riff straight out of a Ron Burgundy solo:

"Took my fam'ly away from my Carolina home/Had dreams about the West and started to roam/Six long months on a dust covered trail/They say heaven's at the end but so far it's been hell/And there's fire on the mountain, lightnin' in the air/Gold in them hills and it's waitin' for me there."

Michael Morse cranked it louder and hillbilly-stomped his way around the room. This was more than one pitcher's walk-out song. It was becoming the Giants' anthem, even if they only knew a couple words in the chorus by heart.

It was on to the World Series, where the Giants opened at Kansas City—the first time in the Bochy era when they didn't have home-field advantage in the Fall Classic. The fans at Kauffman Stadium waited nearly 30 years for the World Series to return to the town where Hallmark makes its corporate home.

The Giants cared enough to send their very best.

Just as he did in Pittsburgh, Bumgarner stepped into a frenzied environment, threw noise-cancelling stuff, and single-handedly stopped the momentum of a team that entered on a steep-grade squeal. The Giants won 7–1 to hand the Royals their first loss of the postseason.

The Royals never were able to adjust. They were 0-for-8 with five strikeouts the *second* time through the lineup, in part because Bumgarner planted an unsettling seed by floating a couple of 67-mph curveballs—a super slo-mo variety he hadn't shown more than a handful of times during the season.

The Royals and Giants split the first four games of the series, and prior to Game 4, there was an unsubstantiated report that Bumgarner had demanded the ball on short rest.

It wasn't true. Bumgarner did not demand the ball in Game 4 of the World Series. He merely refused to give it up in Game 5.

It had become a postseason tradition: the Giants invited a different celebrity for every home game to cry "Play ball!" and fire up the crowd. As Game 5 of the World Series was about to begin, though, there was no microphone stand set up on the field.

The guest appeared on the video board, and everyone who watched caught their breath. The Bay Area remained in shock over the untimely death of Robin Williams, and there he was, shouting "Yes indeed!" while waving an orange towel. The Giants were replaying footage from his appearance in Game 1 of the 2010 NLDS. It was as if they brought him back to life.

Giants fans had witnessed so many incredible performances in 15 seasons at AT&T Park. They marveled at Barry Bonds' otherworldly power and hitting intelligence, cheered two surprise-party no-hitters, experienced the reverent joy of a perfect game, and watched Tim Lincecum strike out 14 in a two-hitter to win that 1–0 game against the Atlanta Braves. It was impossible to imagine a more dominant, more impressive playoff pitching performance than that.

Bumgarner, then, did the unimaginable.

The Giants' World Series championship in 2014 will be remembered, and rightly so, for the flame-retardant blanket that Bumgarner threw over the Royals in the final five innings of Game 7 at Kauffman Stadium.

Game 7s have a way of being reductive like that. And besides, those 68 pitches that Bumgarner threw on two days of rest spoke to more than just his talent, durability, and physical brawn. In an era of micromanaged pitch counts, bullpen specialization, and biometric data, it spoke to a partnership of trust: a manager unafraid to win by abandoning convention, and a pitcher who kept donating more and more and more of that champion's blood without ever appearing faint.

It would be a pity, though, if two other performances did not persist in memory. One belonged to Affeldt, Bumgarner's onetime housemate, who took over after Hudson recorded just five outs in Game 7. Somehow, in baseball's ultimate winner-take-all game, a "Johnny Wholestaff" situation turned into an advantage for the Giants. Affeldt's 2⅓ innings was the longest postseason outing of his career and extended his streak to 22 consecutive scoreless playoff appearances over a five-year span—one appearance behind the Yankees' great Mariano Rivera for the all-time record.

The other performance? That belonged to Bumgarner in Game 5 at AT&T Park. Because quite simply, it ranked as one of the greatest World Series games ever pitched.

Regardless of the outcome, it would be the final game of the year on the shores of McCovey Cove. When the Giants' five-decade title braeakthrough finally came in 2010, their fans had to accept the minor inconvenience that the celebration happened in Texas. They savored every bit of the Giants' punishing, four-game sweep over the Tigers in 2012 even though it meant watching the players cavort in the chill of Detroit's Comerica Park.

They arrived for Game 5 against the Royals already aware that if the Giants were to win their third title in five years, it'd happen in road grays again. It's a small price to pay, given the century's worth of franchise high notes they've witnessed in just 15 seasons at the most picturesque ballpark in the country.

They came through the turnstiles for the final home game of the season ready to give their team one hell of a sendoff.

Madison Bumgarner was dominant during the 2014 postseason. He blanked the Royals in Game 5 of the Fall Classic, becoming the first pitcher to win his first four World Series starts since Lew Burdette in 1957–58.

Bumgarner had his own message to impart. In Game 1, he used his fastball to overwhelm the Royals the first time through the order. He knew they would be looking to swing at heaters, especially in the first inning, before he had a chance to get on solid footing.

But Bumgarner stood on bedrock from the moment he left the bullpen mound. Even in fastball counts, he threw his liquid slider again and again. He threw two sliders and then a curve to strike out Eric Hosmer in the first inning.

He struck out the side in the second inning, first spinning four sliders to Mike Moustakas and then setting down Omar Infante and Jarrod Dyson on three pitches. The sequence to Infante—86-mph slider, 91-mph fastball, and 76-mph curve—was almost against the spirit of fair competition.

Third inning: 12 pitches. Alex Gordon waved helplessly through a curve in the dirt to end it.

The fourth inning brought a challenge. If one Royals batter saw Bumgarner well, it was Lorenzo Cain. In Game 1, the gifted center fielder worked him for 14 pitches while reaching base in two plate appearances (walk, hit by pitch). He singled in his first at-bat of Game 5. Bumgarner knew he had to do a little more to disrupt Cain's timing. It was time to break out that Highway Patrol–compliant curveball. He threw pitches that ranged from 86 to 75 to 65 to 92 to 76, never doubling up any one offering, and Cain bounced out to shortstop.

Bumgarner shaped his slider and cutter at will the first time through the lineup, letting out more slack when necessary. It was not the traveling exhibit on fastball pointillism he showed the Royals in Game 1. He adjusted to them before they could adjust to him. And he could afford to do that early because of a curveball that acted like a snag in a rug runner the next time through the order.

"He just...he did what he wanted with the baseball," Posey said. "That's the simplest way I can describe it.... Fastball to both sides of the plate, breaking ball to both sides of the plate, expanded with fastballs, expanded with breaking balls—it was everything, all night."

Even Bumgarner's threat as a hitter—he crushed two grand slams in the regular season, a near-mythic feat that no pitcher had done since 1966—had a gravitational pull on the Giants' scoring rallies.

They threatened against James Shields in the second inning when Hunter Pence hit a ground single and Brandon Belt attacked an extreme infield shift by putting down a bunt hit to the vacant left side. The play surprised the Giants coaching staff, along with everyone else. This wasn't a page out of Belt's playbook. He had never bunted for a hit in his career. He only had one sacrifice bunt, back in 2013.

"I wanted to open the field back up for myself," Belt said. "They kept shifting on me. So I figured that was a good opportunity."

The Giants made the most of their opportunity against Shields in part because they ran the bases so well. Pence and Belt both tagged up on Ishikawa's deep fly ball, leaving first base open with one out for Crawford in the No. 8 spot. Not only did Yost pitch to Crawford but he played his infielders back, conceding a run on a ground out—perhaps too conservative a strategy in a Bumgarner start.

Because Belt made a good read on the bases and was able to tag up on Ishikawa's fly ball, Crawford didn't have to worry about bouncing into a double play. He took what Shields gave him, hitting a ground out to second base that scored Pence for a 1–0 lead.

Crawford stepped to the plate again in the fourth after Pablo Sandoval singled and Ishikawa extended the inning with a two-out hit. It wasn't a pure pitch-around situation with Bumgarner on deck, but there was no chance Shields would give in and throw Crawford something straight over the plate. He snapped off a curveball that had plenty of late movement, but Crawford stuck out his bat and blooped it to center field. Sandoval tapped the brakes as he rounded third base but Tim Flannery furiously waved him home as soon as he saw the short hop clank off Dyson's glove in center field.

The Giants did what they needed to do. They scratched a 2–0 lead off Shields, removing the impetus to score against the Royals' almost untouchable frontline relievers. Since Kelvin Herrera, Wade Davis, and

Greg Holland didn't pitch in Game 4, the Giants knew almost certainly they would make appearances in Game 5.

The Giants battered them anyway. Herrera gave up singles to Sandoval and Pence in the eighth, then Davis, who hadn't allowed a home run all year, faced defensive replacement Juan Perez and served up a double off the top of the wall. Pence tailgated Sandoval down the third-base line as both scored, and then Crawford followed with another single to left field that capped the three-run inning and gave the Giants a 5–0 lead.

Perez stood on second base after his double with tears in his eyes, and not just because he fashioned a World Series moment for himself after struggling all season with the bat. During the game, word had spread that St. Louis Cardinals outfielder Oscar Taveras, whom the Giants had just opposed in the NLCS, died in a car crash in the Dominican Republic. Perez played winter ball with Taveras and they were close. He was shaken the rest of the night, yet somehow cleared his mind of the grief long enough to turn around a fastball.

Royals manager Ned Yost went to his best pinch hitter, Billy Butler, in the eighth and had pinch runner Terrance Gore ready to wreak havoc on the bases. But Bumgarner still had 100-proof stuff. He threw two more syrupy strikes, then backdoored one more of those super-slow curves. It was a burst of Freon to Butler, who stood there helplessly as strike three tumbled into Posey's mitt.

Bumgarner hit for himself in the eighth inning, and as he took his usual full-tilt, county fair hacks, the sellout crowd began to serenade him: "MVP! MVP!"

He had thrown 107 pitches. There was zero discussion about taking him out.

Yost joked earlier in the week that his three-closer bullpen allowed him to turn his brain off in the late innings. On Bumgarner's day to pitch, Bochy could spend all game in a hammock. In an era of accelerating bullpen specialization, and in a series between two teams that were masterful at shortening a game, Bumgarner kicked it old school.

"I mean, you have to say, 'Is there anybody I have to put in this game better than what I've got out there?'" Hudson said. "And there ain't. He's the best player on the field any time he's on the mound."

Said Bumgarner: "You want to finish the game. That is the ultimate goal, to go out and give them innings. I feel like if you throw a lot of innings, all the other stuff will take care of itself."

Bumgarner took care of the Royals in the ninth. He went through the heart of Kansas City's order on just 10 pitches and Eric Hosmer grounded out to end the Giants' 5–0 victory.

The simplest way to describe Bumgarner's four-hit, no-walk, eight-strikeout blanking of the Royals is to say no pitcher had ever before met those criteria in a World Series game.

It was the first World Series shutout since Josh Beckett for the Marlins at Yankee Stadium in 2003 and the first by a Giant since Jack Sanford tossed a three-hitter to beat the Yankees in Game 2 of the 1962 Fall Classic. It also was the first no-walk shutout in the World Series since 1985, when Bret Saberhagen did it in Game 7 for the Royals.

There's more. Combined with his 10-strikeout command performance in the wild-card game at Pittsburgh, Bumgarner joined Beckett, Orel Hershiser, and Randy Johnson as the only pitchers in the division-play era to throw two shutouts in one postseason.

He became the first pitcher to win his first four World Series starts since Lew Burdette in 1957–58, and it would be hard to lose based on what he'd done: 31 innings, one run, 12 hits, five walks, and 27 strikeouts.

"In the history of the game there have been some great efforts, guys that have [thrown] three games and things like that," Bochy said. "But I haven't seen a better pitcher over the course of this postseason and it's been a pretty long one. To do what he's done is pretty historic, I think."

A historic figure was among Bumgarner's many admirers in the Giants clubhouse.

"When I watch him, I know we're going to win," said Giants Hall of Famer Juan Marichal, shaking two electrified fists. "I know we have a chance to win with that man on the mound. He's so good, he has so much power. I told my son he'd go nine today."

When did he make that prediction?

"Before the game," said Marichal, "and during the game. And when [Santiago] Casilla came to the bullpen. I told my son, 'Don't worry. Casilla won't be pitching in this game.'"

There's a statue of Marichal near the Lefty O'Doul bridge that shows him forever frozen in time just as he should be, kicking high into his famous delivery.

It's only a matter of time before the Giants find a suitable place to honor Bumgarner with his own likeness. And when they sculpt him, his statue will be a big, bronzed torso and those divergent arms, the glove hand pointed straight out in front of him, the left loaded so far behind his body, as unnerving to a hitter as seeing the recoil in a pistol duel.

Of course, a statue probably wasn't what Hudson had in mind when he said Bumgarner had "a set of brass balls that are bigger than anybody I've played with."

After Hosmer grounded out to end it, Belt flipped the baseball to Bumgarner, who stuck it in his back pocket. From the first pitch of Game 5 to the Buster Hug, he wasn't going to give it up.

"Nope," Bumgarner said. "I felt great. I felt great all night. Really, this time of year, it's not too hard to go out there and feel good. That's usually not the problem."

Every postseason ace must carry two groaning weights: the leaden pileup of innings and the burden of high expectations. In the 2014 postseason, Bumgarner was the only ace strong enough to load up everything on his pallet.

It's the way Bumgarner dealt with the expectations that most impressed Posey.

"All the attention he's received this postseason, everybody talking about what a weapon he is, he's still just going out and doing it," Posey said. "I mean, we're listening to all of it [in the clubhouse]. It's on in here. For him to go out and throw a shutout, it just speaks to his character. I don't know if all [the attention] adds to the fire or if he just blocks it out. I really don't know which one it is."

Neither did Bumgarner.

"I don't really feel like I know," he said. "It's nice to hear all the good stuff, but you know, as soon as you're not pitching good, it'll be the opposite. So as soon as I get ready to get ready, I forget about all that. You never want to add extra pressure to yourself, even if you have to trick yourself.

"There was a time I'd be saying, 'Shoot, this is the World Series.' But when I get out there, all I want to be thinking about is making pitches."

After Game 5, Yost happened to be walking down an exit corridor when he saw Bumgarner.

"I'm glad we don't have to worry about you anymore," said Yost, oblivious to the faulty assumption he was making.

Bumgarner nodded politely, walked away, and felt a smile spread across his face. Oh, the Royals would see Bumgarner again. They'd see him with a championship on the line in Game 7. They wouldn't play "Fire on the Mountain," of course, when he jogged from the bullpen in the fifth inning in Kansas City. Bumgarner would set it ablaze anyway. For the Giants, all October, that fire on high was a beacon through the wilderness.

With their Game 7 victory over Kansas City, the Giants dispatched their 10th consecutive postseason opponent since 2010, and for emphasis, here is the litany: Braves, Phillies, Rangers, Reds, Cardinals, Tigers, Pirates, Nationals, Cardinals again, and the Royals.

Bochy matched John McGraw for the most World Series titles in franchise history, and became the 10th manager in major league annals to win a third championship. The other nine are in the Hall of Fame.

"You know, I'm numb, really, all through this," Bochy said. "I mean, I'm amazed with what these guys did and the fact we've won three times in five years. It's not that easy. But when you have a group of warriors like we have, I mean, they continue to just amaze you. They were relentless."

The Giants won in 2010 with a band of misfits and a gold-standard pitching staff. They snuck up on another title in 2012 by dancing in the rain, scoffing at elimination, and once more outperforming three opponents on the mound. The even-year phenomenon held against the Royals, and although the Giants were more than a one-man team that October, Bumgarner fixed so many of their flaws.

To a hero's ovation, he got the bus running again—all the way down Market Street onto the steps of City Hall.

It made no sense only if you underestimated the brawn, bravado, and burning heart of a 25-year-old left-hander with a back wide and strong enough to carry an entire team to the summit.

It is one thing to collect rings. It is another to forge a legend. And sometimes, when it's all said and done, even legends have something to confess.

"You know what? I can't lie to you anymore," Bumgarner said. "I'm a little tired now."

Chapter 20

A Most Amazing Run

"This is the beauty of this game. You'll see something in the course of a season that you've never seen before."
—Bruce Bochy

The Best of the Rest

Travis Ishikawa couldn't remember touching the plate after his home run clinched a pennant. Barry Bonds stomped on the dish with both feet when he hit his 500th career homer. J.T. Snow somehow scored and reached back to grab a little boy's jacket at the same time.

The Giants came home in so many memorable ways over their first 15 seasons at AT&T Park. But the weirdest one of all came the night of September 26, 2008.

It was the night when Bengie Molina did something that no major league player has done before or since.

He received credit for hitting a home run, but didn't score a run.

"This is the beauty of this game," Giants manager Bruce Bochy said. "You'll see something in the course of a season that you've never seen before."

Fans arrived at the ballpark braced to see something unforgettable when Bonds sat on 755 home runs or the Giants were a victory away from clinching or there was an October chill in the air.

But some of the rarest and greatest moments came when there was no buzz or buildup. On any given day, Matt Cain could throw a perfect game or Jonathan Sanchez could fire a no-hitter or Jason Schmidt could strike out 16 or Omar Vizquel could pull off the first straight steal of home by a Giant in 25 years.

Or Molina could hit a home run that breaks a box score.

It didn't require a degree in astrophysics to understand how it happened. But it definitely required a sense of humor. The Giants went 10 innings to take a 6–5 victory over the Los Angeles Dodgers, but the play that flummoxed everyone happened in the sixth when Molina hit a deep drive that smacked the top of the right-field arcade and fell back into play.

Molina, one of the slowest runners in baseball history, only advanced as far as first base and Bochy sent Emmanuel Burriss to pinch-run for him.

Then Vizquel came running up to Bochy in the dugout. He was sure he heard the sharp sound of the baseball striking metal, not the dull thud of horsehide against brick. According to the ground rules, the green metal roof atop the arcade was beyond the boundary. Molina's ball should've been ruled a home run.

Just a month earlier, Major League Baseball had adopted the use of instant replay on disputed home run calls. Bochy immediately walked up to crew chief Bill Welke and requested one.

"Omar and his bionic ears," Bochy said.

Umpires emerged from the tunnel after a brief delay, Welke signaled a two-run home run, and Burriss let out a laugh as he stood on first base. What was supposed to happen next? Nobody knew. First-base coach Roberto Kelly gave Burriss a push, so he jogged the rest of the way home, giving a few comical fist pumps as if he had just gone deep.

"It was hilarious," Burriss said. "I asked Roberto, 'Do I run? Does Bengie come back out?' I was like, 'All right, all right, I'll take it.' I'm not a home run hitter, so I'll take the slowest trot in history."

"Good swing," said a smiling Molina, once Burriss returned to the dugout

Bochy argued that the overturned call should nullify the move to bring Burriss in the game, but Welke was adamant.

"He doesn't get another bite at that," Welke said. "We know the rules. Once a pinch runner touches a base, he's in the game whether he's put in or not…. All we have are the rules, and this was a learning experience."

Bochy played the game under protest, and although Giants didn't need to file it with the league after coming away with the victory, there was other fallout to manage. Statisticians in the press box didn't know what to do. Their computer programs wouldn't allow them to enter a pinch runner for a player who hit a home run. And what to do about the RBIs? It was a two-run homer, but how could Molina knock in a player who replaced him?

Sure, there were instances in major league history when a player hit a ball over the fence without scoring. Robin Ventura hit a walk-off grand slam to win a playoff game for the Mets in 1999, but only advanced as far as first base as his teammates mobbed him. He was credited with a single in the box score.

Molina became the first player in history to be credited with a home run, but not a run scored—a bizarre and obscure bit of baseball history that nobody in the crowd of 33,920 expected to see upon settling in to watch the game.

On the night of May 27, 2003, the fans witnessed something almost as confusing on the basepaths. With the Giants and Arizona Diamondbacks tied 2–2 in the ninth inning, Marquis Grissom hit a drive to the deepest reaches of right-center field. The runner on first base should've walked home with the winning run.

But that runner was none other than Ruben Rivera, and…well, let's defer to Hall of Fame announcer Jon Miller's description:

"Swing and there's a shot! Deep to right-center, racing back is Dellucci, still going back into Death Valley, and it goes right over his glove! He missed it! But Ruben Rivera missed second base! Now he's headed for third and they're going to throw him out by plenty, but the throw to third is botched! Now he's heading home! The loose ball is on the infield…and he's out by five feet at the plate! And that was the worst baserunning in the history of the game! The game should be over, and Ruben Rivera just did the worst baserunning you will ever see. Unbelievable!"

Miller has made so many historic calls over his Hall of Fame career. But when fans see him around town, they mention the Rivera call more often than any other. It's not every night you bear witness to the worst baserunning in the history of the game, after all.

"Ruben Rivera had gone around second base, and then for some reason, seemed to assume that the ball was caught in the outfield," continued Miller, further trying to explain while watching the replay as the crowd continued to stir in disbelief. "He got totally lost and confused out there, and started to go back to second base as Grissom was pulling in at second. Ruben Rivera was the only man in the ballpark, apparently, who did not know what just happened."

Manager Felipe Alou buried his head into his folded arms. At one point, Rivera, already on his way to third and thinking he had to retreat to first base, nearly cut across the infield.

The game went to extra innings and Grissom came through again in the 13th, hitting a triple that scored Rich Aurilia and Jose Cruz Jr. in a 4–3 victory. So no harm done—to the Giants, anyway.

It was another story for Rivera. He played an inning in center field the next night, and then the Giants released him. He never made it back to the big leagues, and his nine-year career would be remembered mostly for "the worst baserunning in the history of the game." Perhaps that wasn't such a bad fate, though. Prior to that, he was known as the player who stole Derek Jeter's glove from his locker.

Thievery is part of baseball, of course, and although many claim the triple is the most exciting play in baseball, that's probably because they've never witnessed the rare straight steal of home. Giants fans were treated to one of those on June 13, 2008, when Vizquel's daring accounted for their only run in a 5–1 loss to the Oakland A's.

The Giants had the bases loaded in the second inning, two outs, and Jose Castillo at the plate against A's left-hander Greg Smith. There wasn't any reason to expect a daring act from Vizquel as he stood on third base—unless you had spent any time watching Castillo try to hit that season, anyway.

Smith led the majors in pickoffs, believe it or not, but he was pitching from the stretch instead of the windup—a curious move with the bases loaded—and Vizquel took advantage of the left-hander's blind side by getting a huge lead. Smith had his head down as he began to come set.

Catcher Kurt Suzuki leapt from his crouch and waved his hands. Third baseman Eric Chavez shouted as loud as he could. It was too late.

Vizquel dashed home and slid feet first across the plate before the ball arrived, then popped up and smiled all the way to the dugout. At the age of 41, he became the first Giant to pull off a straight steal of home since Max Venable did it 25 years earlier.

There were just 15 straight steals of home in the major leagues over the decade that began in 2000. Vizquel accounted for three of those.

"I did it in a playoff game against Boston. It was great. It really fired everybody up," said Vizquel, who was trying to give the Giants a spark amid a losing season.

It was a shock to everyone in the ballpark—even the batter at the plate.

"Castillo said he didn't see anything until I went by him," Vizquel said. "He said, 'What the hell was that?'"

Vizquel had several memorable moments in 2008. In a game at Florida that season, he broke Luis Aparicio's all-time record for games played at shortstop; it stood at 2,709 games when Vizquel retired in 2012 at the age of 45. Although the Giants posted a losing record in all four of

Vizquel's seasons with them, he won the final two of his 11 Gold Gloves while wearing orange and black, and treated fans in San Francisco to so many of his graceful plays in the field.

Vizquel's spark only did so much for the Giants in 2008, though. They ended the year with a 72–90 record. But in addition to Molina's rare replay-confused home run, there were two other notable events in that final weekend series with the Dodgers.

On September 27, the Giants paid the ultimate compliment to one of the most popular players in franchise history. Snow, who played his last game when the Boston Red Sox released him in 2006, received the unprecedented opportunity to retire as a Giant.

The club signed him to a one-day contract, put him on the roster, and wrote his name on the lineup card. Snow ran onto the field by himself, took his position at first base, soaked up a standing ovation, and then Travis Ishikawa replaced him before the first pitch was thrown.

As the ovation ended, Snow looked more confused than overwhelmed. He had a ball in his glove, ready to roll grounders to his infielders, but they all played a joke on him. They waited an extra long time before taking the field. Then when Snow tossed a grounder to Eugenio Velez, the second baseman threw it back on a short hop. When Vizquel and Aurilia did the same thing with their ankle-nipping throws, Snow had to laugh.

"When Velez threw the first one, I didn't know," he said. "Was he not loose? Then Omar threw the second one and I knew they'd gotten together."

The next afternoon, the regular season finale, was memorable because it marked a beginning instead of an end. Tim Lincecum struck out 13 over seven innings of a 3–1 victory over the Dodgers, giving a final push to his Cy Young candidacy. He would become the first Giant to win the award since Mike McCormick in 1967. And Lincecum became the first Giant in the modern era to lead the major leagues in strikeouts, with 265. The ovation he received after the eighth inning was among his loudest and most memorable.

Not every milestone moment happened for the home team at AT&T Park. It ended up being a rather anticlimactic event, but it still counted as history on August 7, 2004, when Greg Maddux pitched into the sixth inning and the Chicago Cubs bullpen barely held onto the lead to protect his decision in an 8–4 victory.

It was Maddux's 300th career win. He became the first NL pitcher to reach the milestone since Steve Carlton did it 21 years earlier. But in typical fashion for Maddux, he made as little fuss over it as possible. He didn't even join in the postgame handshake line, instead watching the end of the game from a TV in the visiting clubhouse. Still, it was a ticket stub worth saving and an important day in baseball history.

"I like to look ahead," Maddux said after the game. "I've never really looked back. When I'm done playing I'll look back. I'm sure I'll pat myself on the back then."

Looking back has its rewards, though. There have been so many more thrilling moments and improbable rallies at AT&T Park, although oddly enough, the Giants' biggest comeback didn't result in a victory.

It happened on a warm, 86-degree afternoon on August 25, 2010. The wind was blowing out for a change. The Cincinnati Reds pounded their way to a 10–1 lead in the fifth inning.

And the Giants came back.

"It happened so fast," Aubrey Huff said. "It's 10–5, then 10–8, then the next thing I know, I'm in the batter's box and it's 10–10. I didn't even know what happened."

Here's what happened: Juan Uribe hit a three-run home run in the eighth inning. Then the crowd went into berserk, stranger-embracing bedlam when Andres Torres hit a tying, two-run double. The Giants took an 11–10 lead on Huff's sacrifice fly. It was the largest deficit the Giants had overcome in franchise history.

Their joy did not last, though, as third baseman Pablo Sandoval's throwing error led to a blown save for Brian Wilson in the ninth. The game went to extra innings, and when Barry Zito made his second career relief appearance to begin the 12th, the Reds' Joey Votto hit a run-scoring single. Torres grounded out with runners at the corners to end it, and the Giants lost one of the wildest games in franchise history by a score of 12–11.

"We have to feel inspired, because we didn't throw in the towel," Zito said. "When there's no momentum in your favor and you muster it back up, that says a lot about the heart of this team."

You couldn't talk about heartbreaking, extra-inning losses at AT&T Park without mentioning May 29, 2001, when the Giants battled the Diamondbacks for 18 innings in an eventual 1–0 loss. A not-so-magnificent seven of Armando Reynoso, Geraldo Guzman, Erik Sabel, Troy Brohawn, Byung-Hyun Kim, Miguel Batista, and Greg Swindell combined to keep the Giants off the board despite allowing nine hits and issuing 10 walks. Shawn Estes pitched the first seven shutout innings for the Giants, followed by Aaron Fultz, Felix Rodriguez, Robb Nen, Chad Zerbe, and Tim Worrell.

The Giants' final pitcher was a fresh-faced 23-year-old rookie with four games of big league experience who had just been recalled and was making his season debut. It was Ryan Vogelsong, who would go on to achieve the greatest second-act career in Giants history. On this night, though, he was just a kid hoping to make an impression and keep from dropping the baton.

Vogelsong pitched two shutout innings before the Diamondbacks tallied a run against him in the 18th when Erubiel Durazo hit an RBI double.

The Giants didn't have any position players left on the bench, so Vogelsong had to lead off the bottom of the 18th, and he surprised the ballpark when he lined a double to left-center field. The Giants managed to load the bases with one out after an intentional walk to Jeff Kent, but Swindell got Armando Rios to hit a shallow fly out to center field. Then Benito Santiago flied out to seal a painful 1–0 loss in a game that took five hours, 53 minutes.

Vogelsong took the loss—his first major league decision. He wouldn't get his first victory for two more years, and it would come in a Pirates uniform after he and Rios were shipped to Pittsburgh for Jason Schmidt. Many years, miles, and even two continents later, when he was a 33-year-old veteran, Vogelsong would return to the team that drafted him on a minor league contract, and finally earn his first victory as a Giant. He'd earn two World Series rings after that, too.

The Schmidt trade ended up being one of GM Brian Sabean's best maneuvers, and that was never more obvious than on June 6, 2006, when the tall right-hander recorded 16 strikeouts in a 2–1 victory over the Florida Marlins. Schmidt broke the San Francisco–era franchise record for strikeouts in a game previously held by one Hall of Famer, Gaylord Perry, and matched the all-time franchise record set by another Hall of Famer, Christy Mathewson, in 1904.

The strikeouts were exciting enough, but the manner in which Schmidt recorded the final three had fans at AT&T Park on the edge of their seats. Felipe Alou was determined to let Schmidt finish what he started in the ninth, even after Dan Uggla beat out a bunt single and Mike Jacobs lined another to center. A wild pitch added to the tension, moving the tying and go-ahead runs into scoring position with no outs.

No less than Miguel Cabrera stood at the plate.

"The last guy I wanted to see," Schmidt said. "I thought if I could get this guy out, we might, just might, have a shot."

Schmidt was thinking strikeout all the way, but not for the glory or the record. It was simply his best hope to escape.

Schmidt got Cabrera to lunge at a 1-2 pitch. Josh Willingham, who homered earlier in the game, went down swinging on a 3-2 pitch. And then Jeremy Hermida did, too. Schmidt stuck out the final three batters, he finished with 124 pitches, and he needed every last one of them to protect the victory and send the Giants spilling onto the field.

"And you guys thought you had to hit the ball out of the park for excitement," Alou said.

Truer words were never spoken. There are few plays in baseball more electrifying than an inside-the-park home run, and the Giants knew from the day they first set foot in Pacific Bell Park that they would witness their share of them. The dimensions almost guaranteed it.

Fernando Viña of the Cardinals collected the first one in the ballpark's history, on May 9, 2000. Dustan Mohr became the first Giant to race around the bases on August 4, 2004, when his drive hit the top of the Chevron car advertisement and rolled all the way into the bullpen. Nate Schierholtz, Conor Gillaspie, and even Huff, as impossible as it might sound, accomplished an inside-the-parker. Ichiro Suzuki did it on the biggest stage on the way to earning MVP honors in the 2007 All-Star Game.

But Angel Pagan accomplished something that none of those others could match. On May 25, 2013, he hit an inside-the-park home run to end a game.

His shot in the 10th inning off the Rockies' Rafael Betancourt sailed over the head of right fielder Michael Cuddyer, hit the base of the arcade, and took a sharp bounce toward center.

"It is off the bottom of the wall, and it kicks away from everybody!" said Duane Kuiper on the telecast. "Pagan…is being waved in! Here's the throw to the plate! It is not in time! And…that…is…the…ball…game!"

The Giants mobbed Pagan and mussed his hair after the two-run home run in the 10th inning sent them to a 6–5 victory. It was as thrilling a finish to a baseball game as you could imagine, and it came after the Giants had erased a 4–0 deficit to force extra innings, too. There hadn't been a walk-off, inside-the-park home run in the major leagues in nine years, since Rey Sanchez of the Tampa Bay Devil Rays did it to beat the Rockies in 2004.

The Rockies did their best to scramble after the ball as it bounced along the warning track in center field. Dexter Fowler picked it up and shortstop Troy Tulowitzki made the relay to the plate. But third-base coach Tim Flannery never hesitated to send Pagan, whose headfirst slide came well ahead of the ball.

In fact, the closest race to the plate was between Pagan and Flannery, who scampered all the way down the line, too.

Later on, Pagan revealed that he felt a pop in his hamstring earlier in the game while breaking to make a catch in center field. He didn't play another game for more than three months because of surgery to repair a torn hamstring tendon.

"If I had to score another run to win another ballgame like that, I'd do it," Pagan said. "Because that's what we're here for."

From around the bases to around the horn, Giants fans witnessed their team turn a rare triple play in a May 30, 2008, game against the Padres. Lefty Alex Hinshaw issued a walk and gave up a single before Keiichi Yabu relieved him. Kevin Kouzmanoff grounded sharply to third base. It went 5-4-3 in the scorebook—Castillo to Ray Durham to John Bowker—although it was a momentary high as the Giants went on to lose 7–3 in 13 innings.

There was much less traffic on the bases on September 6, 2013, when Yusmeiro Petit came within one strike of throwing a perfect game against the Diamondbacks. And there weren't many baserunners for Livan Hernandez when he threw consecutive shutouts August 18–23, 2000, to beat the Braves and Marlins.

Over the years, Giants fans would see a player homer from both sides of the plate (Sandoval, on September 20, 2012, against Colorado) and a pitcher strike out four in an inning (the Dodgers' Zack Greinke, on July 25, 2014). They'd even cheer for the road team on July 23, 2013, when the Giants and Reds played a doubleheader while rescheduling a rainout from earlier in the month at Cincinnati; after the Reds pantsed them in the first game, the Giants changed into road grays and batted first while playing the part of the road team in Game 2. They won 5–3. So fans could say they watched a doubleheader that the Reds and Giants split, but the road team swept.

So many times, Giants fans got loudest with Robb Nen pitching in the ninth. On August 6, 2002, they cheered his 300th career save when he escaped a bases-loaded situation in a wild and memorable 11–10 victory over the Cubs. Nen was the 16th player to join the 300-save club and at 32, the youngest to gain entry. But he sacrificed his arm to try to pitch the Giants to the World Series title that season, shortening an otherwise brilliant toe-tapping career.

Sendoffs and debuts always create memories. A 20-year-old Matt Cain introduced himself to Giants fans in 2005 by battling Todd Helton for 14 pitches and Buster Posey left no doubt that he belonged with three RBI hits in his season debut in 2010.

Posey and Madison Bumgarner entered the record books together on July 13, 2014, when they became the first battery in major league history to each collect a grand slam in a game. Posey and Bumgarner tagged bases-loaded shots off the Colorado Rockies in consecutive innings of an 8–4 victory. (It was also Bumgarner's second slam of the season, something no pitcher had done since the Braves' Tony Cloninger hit two in a game in 1966 at Candlestick Park.)

But of course, one Giant hit more milestone home runs than anyone else.

The Giants' ballpark at Third and King was built by and for Barry Bonds. He considered himself as much an entertainer as an athlete. It's little wonder, then, that he treated his own paying customers so well.

Bonds almost always hit his significant home runs in San Francisco, where they would be most treasured and savored.

He hit his 500th home run on April 17, 2001, off the Dodgers' Terry Adams. His 600th came on August 9, 2002, against the Pirates' Kip Wells. On April 12–13, 2004, he went deep for Nos. 660 and 661 off Milwaukee's Matt Kinney and Ben Ford to tie and pass his godfather, Willie Mays, for third place on the all-time list. At the end of that 2004 season, on September 17, No. 700 came off Jake Peavy. He tied Babe Ruth with his 714th homer, connecting against Byung-Hyun Kim on May 28, 2006. And, of course, there was the night he hit 756.

Like any good showman, he left them wanting more. Bonds hadn't played in 11 days because of a sprained toe when he took the field on September 26, 2007, for what would be his last major league game. His final swing came against Peavy, on a 2-0 fastball that he lifted deep to right-center field. The crowd gasped, but Bonds instantly knew he

Farewell to the king: AT&T Park said good-bye to Barry Bonds on September 26, 2007.

didn't get enough of it. He slapped his bat as he watched the ball die at the warning track. Then he gave Peavy a hug, waved to the crowd, and descended into a church-silent dugout.

Bonds didn't say a word, but teammate Ryan Klesko saw the emotion on his face as he shook his hand.

"This was brought on pretty quick," said Klesko, "and it hit him hard."

A minute later, with the crowd chanting his name, Bonds trotted out for one final curtain call. Then it was over. He grabbed his bats and headed down the tunnel for the last time.

It was the Giants' last regular season home game, and after it was over, the club played a video montage of Bonds highlights set to Frank Sinatra's "My Way." Players emerged from the dugout to toss autographed balls into the stands. But Bonds did not reappear.

Giants fans had gotten their last glimpse.

"There's nothing like it—nothing in the world," Bonds said a few weeks earlier. "It's your home.... I lived a perfect childhood dream starting with Willie and my dad, having an opportunity to play here."

Peter Magowan's eyes welled with emotion after seeing Bonds in an active uniform for the last time.

"We were able to revitalize interest and make this a baseball town again," Magowan said. "Say what you want about Barry, but he was part of winning baseball teams. He made the people around him better. He helped us win. That's what we're in the game to do, and we did win.

"I feel great that we were able to do that."

Eventually, the Giants had to turn the page on the Bonds era. There were so many other fantastic screenplays to be written with new characters.

But the stage had been set. It was the most wondrous stage in baseball.

Acknowledgments

Most of the facts, accounts, and quotes contained in this book were gathered over years of original reporting and interviews, although many other sources provided supplemental information as well and are listed. Verification of facts and records wouldn't have been possible without daily devotion from members of the Giants media relations staff both past and present, including Blake Rhodes, Staci Slaughter, Jim Moorehead, Matt Chisholm, Matt Hodson, Liam Connolly, Eric Smith, and Megan Nelson. A special thanks to them, and to all the dedicated baseball beat reporters who travel in coach, endure mediocre press box food, and spend so many nights away from home for the privilege to tell the story of a season—and maybe, on a given night, write the first draft of history. I'm honored to have lived this life with you.

References

Associated Press (2003, August 31). Bonds Returns, Leads Giants to 2–1 victory.

Associated Press (2002, June 26). Kent Dismisses Scuffle with Bonds as 'no big deal.'

Curry, Jack (2008, July 2). Barry Bonds goes to the Hall, asterisk and all. *New York Times.*

Egelko, Bob (2003, July 9). Fan not having a ball. *San Francisco Chronicle.*

Encina, Eduardo A. (2013, February 25). Orioles baseball: Travis Ishikawa hopes he's in the right place at the right time. *Baltimore Sun.*

Fainaru-Wada, Mark, & Williams, Lance (2006). *Game of Shadows: Barry Bonds, BALCO, and the Steroids Scandal that Rocked Professional Sports.* Gotham Books

Jenkins, Lee (2007, July 11). All-Star Game Is a Dress Rehearsal for Bonds. *New York Times.*

Kepner, Tyler (2012, July 26). Next act for superstar: Conquering New York. *New York Times.*

Knapp, Gwen (2009, July 12). Sanchez's Dad, Righetti savor no-hitter. *San Francisco Chronicle.*

Kroichick, Ron (2002, October 26). Home plate dash thrusts him into limelight. *San Francisco Chronicle.*

Nevius, C.W. (1997, December 7). Sunday Interview – PETER MAGOWAN: San Francisco's Field of Dreams. *San Francisco Chronicle.*

Passan, Jeff (2008, July 15). Ichiro's speech to All-Stars revealed. *Yahoo! Sports.* Retrieved from http://sports.yahoo.com/mlb/news?slug=jp-ichirospeech071508.

Pearlman, Jeff (2007). *Love Me, Hate Me: Barry Bonds and the Making of an Antihero.* HarperCollins.

Reid, Jason (2000, April 12). Three of a Kind Beats Full House. *Los Angeles Times.*

Schmuck, Peter (1992, December 9). Bonds signs deal with Giants-to-be; Lurie protected in $43 million pack. *Baltimore Sun.*

Schulman, Henry (2001, September 18). Bonds' Ecko: 'Stupid.' *San Francisco Chronicle.*

Schulman, Henry (2002, March 19). Giants probing Kent's injury claim. *San Francisco Chronicle.*

Schulman, Henry (2002, October 15). Headfirst into Series / Giants win first pennant since '89. *San Francisco Chronicle.*

Schulman, Henry (2002, October 16). Giants notebook: Lofton draws Cardinals' ire again after game-winner. *San Francisco Chronicle.*

Springer, Steve (2002, October 12). Giants' Baker Tries to Play It Cool. *Los Angeles Times.*

Stark, Jayson (2002, October 14). Call the Giants pennant winners once again. *ESPN.com.* Retrieved from http://a.espncdn.com/mlb/columns/stark_jayson/1446135.html.

Stone, Larry (2010, July 13). Ichiro hitless, but not speechless. *Seattle Times.*

Suchon, Josh (2002). *This Gracious Season.* Winter Publications.